THE
GOLDEN TREASURY
OF
NATURAL
HISTORY

BY

BERTHA MORRIS PARKER

LABORATORY SCHOOL, UNIVERSITY OF CHICAGO
RESEARCH ASSOCIATE, CHICAGO NATURAL HISTORY MUSEUM

PUBLICITY PRODUCTS · LONDON

PUBLISHED BY ARRANGEMENT WITH SIMON AND SCHUSTER NEW YORK
AND WESTERN PRINTING AND LITHOGRAPHING COMPANY LIMITED RACINE WISCONSIN USA
COPYRIGHT 1952 BY SIMON AND SCHUSTER INC. AND ARTISTS AND WRITERS GUILD INC.
DESIGNED AND PRODUCED BY ARTISTS AND WRITERS GUILD INC.
MADE AND PRINTED IN GREAT BRITAIN
BY PURNELL AND SONS LIMITED PAULTON (SOMERSET) AND LONDON

CONTENTS

The following artists have painted the pictures in this book:

PAULINE BATCHELDER ADAMS

DOROTHEA AND SY BARLOWE

JUANITA BENNETT

VIRGINIA BRADENICK

MATILDA BREUER

LOUISE FULTON BUSH

OLIVE EARLE

RUDOLF FREUND

BYRON GERE

JAMES GORDON IRVING

NORMAN JONSSON

ROBERT KISSNER

OLGA KUCERA

ELIZABETH NEWHALL

MARY ROYT

ARNOLD W. RYAN

FREDERICK E. SEYFARTH

The photographs on pages 194 and 197 are reproduced by courtesy of
the Yerkes Observatory and the University of Chicago Press; the one
on page 198 by courtesy of the American Museum of Natural History,
New York.

Many of the illustrations were painted or photographed with the kind
co-operation of the Milwaukee Museum of Natural History.

FOREWORD

THE sky, the stuff the earth is made of, the plants and animals about us, and the life of past ages – these are subjects in which young people have a natural interest. To take advantage of that interest and build up a genuine understanding of the world of nature is the aim of THE GOLDEN TREASURY OF NATURAL HISTORY.

Young people ask many questions about their environment: Can people live on the other planets? How do we know that there were once dinosaurs? How can one tell a butterfly from a moth? Is a tomato a fruit or a vegetable? And so on and on. The author has used such questions as a help in selecting from the vast amount of nature knowledge the topics to be included in this book.

The numerous pictures will help the reader to recognize many of the rocks, plants, animals, heavenly bodies, and fossils he sees. The book is not designed as a nature guide; no section is sufficiently complete to serve that purpose. But the pictures will nevertheless help in identification and, more importantly, will illustrate many basic facts and ideas about the world of nature.

The book makes the reader's experiences with nature much more full of meaning. A shiny pebble is no longer just something pretty to add to one's collection; it is a piece of one of the rock pages on which the earth has written its diary. A garden is not just a source of vegetables to eat and flowers to cut; it is also a collection of plant immigrants from many foreign lands, and of the results of experiments in plant breeding. A star is not simply a twinkling point of light; it is a great sun, perhaps with planets much like our own earth travelling around it. In the same way, an ant is not merely a bothersome little insect; it is one of the few kinds of animals besides man that work together in an organized way.

In science, "truth changes," because better scientific instruments and methods are constantly revealing more of nature's secrets. But one can foresee little or no change during the coming years in the basic ideas presented in this book – that the story of the earth is indeed one of great changes, animals and plants are fitted in wondrous different ways for living as they do, and our little earth is part of a universe so vast that it passes our understanding.

BERTHA MORRIS PARKER

Long ages ago, all animals lived under water.
Some looked more like plants than animals.

NATURAL HISTORY

A Parade of Ancient Animals

FIVE HUNDRED million years ago there were already a great many kinds of animals on the earth. But a parade of them, if there could be one, would not be exciting. For one thing, it would have to be under water, for all the animals of that time – at least all that we know about – lived in the sea. All the animals, moreover, were small.

The centre of the stage 500 million years ago was held by the trilobites. Though few were more than four inches long, they were the largest animals of the time, and there were enormous numbers of them.

The name "trilobite" was given to these animals of long ago millions of years after the last one died. They had no name at all while they were alive; the last one disappeared long, long before there were any people on the earth to name them. Scientists gave them the name trilobite because the hard covering that protected them was divided lengthwise into three lobes.

The trilobites were ancient relatives of our crayfishes and crabs and lobsters. They lived in the shallow water of the seashores. They walked on jointed legs over the floor of the sea just as their relatives do now. Feathery gills helped them swim as well as breathe. Trilobites ate other animals, probably both living and dead ones. They also ate plants. Long feelers and big compound eyes helped them to find food.

The trilobites were simple compared with the higher animals of today. But they were far ahead of the first animals. Five hundred million years ago by no means marked the beginning of life on the earth. Perhaps there had been animals for a thousand million years before the first trilobites appeared. The first animals must have been one-celled and very tiny. The trilobites, scientists think, belong somewhere near the halfway mark between the first animals and man.

For at least a hundred million years the trilobites were the "ruling class." But they had many neighbours. Early in their "reign" there were sponges and corals and worms. There were ancient snails and starfish. There were brachiopods, too, that had shells much like clam-shells, but had very different bodies inside their shells. The sponges of those early times anchored themselves to rocks just as sponges do today. The corals walled themselves up with lime and left their "houses" of limestone behind when they died just as modern corals do. The starfish, worms, and snails were enough like those now living to be easy to recognize.

Later during the reign of the trilobites sea lilies appeared and became common. So did "head-footed" animals called "cephalopods."

"Crinoids" is another name for sea lilies. The sea lilies that lived in the days of the trilobites were not very different from the present-day crinoids. They looked more like plants than like animals, with rootlike hooks that anchored them to rocks, long stems, and arms that spread out like the petals of a flower.

The cephalopods were relatives of the squids of today. They had shells. Some of them were coiled much like giant snail shells. Some were long and straight. Out from the end of the shell the animal's head and arms protruded.

The picture on the opposite page shows a trilobite with a cephalopod, three sea lilies, and a mass of coral. The coral animals that built the coral do not show. A scene like this was common 400 million years ago.

The ancient trilobites were not all exactly like the one shown on the floor of the sea. The hard coverings of some were much less simple. Some had long, and what would seem to be useless, projections.

Life in an Ancient Sea

For a tremendously long time the trilobites had no real rivals. Then, although trilobites continued to be very common, the cephalopods gradually became the masters of the seas. They grew to be much larger than any of the trilobites. Some of those with straight shells were 20 feet long. Since they were meat eaters, the cephalopods probably devoured enormous numbers of their trilobite neighbours. Like the trilobites, they ruled the seas for about a million centuries.

The trilobites lived on all through the reign of the cephalopods and for many millions of years after that. Then, approximately 200 million years ago, they died out completely. We say that they became extinct. Many kinds of early cephalopods became extinct, too.

It would be a mistake to think of these animals of the ancient seashores as living just where the seashores are today. Land and sea were not always as they are now. Long ago there were seashores in many parts of the world that today are far from the sea.

The reigns of the trilobites and the cephalopods are sometimes called "the heyday of animals without backbones." For the trilobites and cephalopods and their neighbours had no backbones. They had no bones of any kind. Their skeletons were on the outside.

Scientists divide the story of the earth into long stretches of time called "eras." As the chart on pages 208 and 209 shows, the so-called heyday of animals without backbones – the time sometimes spoken of as the "Age of Invertebrates" – was the first part of the Paleozoic Era. "Paleozoic" means "ancient life."

The early Paleozoic was a quiet time. Not an animal in the world had a voice. There were, moreover, no land animals to make a noise by running about. Almost the only sounds were thunder and the noises of wind and waves.

The first animals with backbones to appear on the earth were the fishes. They appeared back in the days when the cephalopods were the terrors of the seas. The early fishes were successful. Within 50 million years or so there were so many of them that they quite overshadowed the simpler animals. The time when they were the leading animals of the earth is called in everyday language the "Age of Fishes."

Many of the early fishes were covered with bony plates that made regular suits of armour for them. Some of the early fishes were jawless, as the hagfishes are now. Some of them were ancient relatives of our sharks. Some were lungfishes. Lungfishes breathe both with lungs and with gills. When there is plenty of water they breathe with gills just as ordinary fishes do. But when dry weather comes they bury themselves in mud and breathe with lungs.

Dinichthys was one of the armoured fishes. The first syllable of its name means "terrible"; the last two syllables mean "fish." It *was* a terrible fish. It measured 20 feet long and had jagged jaws that snapped shut with great force, like the jaws of a snapping turtle. It is queer that this big, ferocious fish could not hold its own. But in time it was crowded out by fishes more like those of today.

The sharks and lungfishes were not crowded out, but they became less common. Their heyday ended.

The Age of Fishes was followed by the Coal Age. It, too, was a part of the Paleozoic Era.

At the beginning of the Coal Age much of Europe was low and swampy. So were some other parts of the earth. Forests grew in the

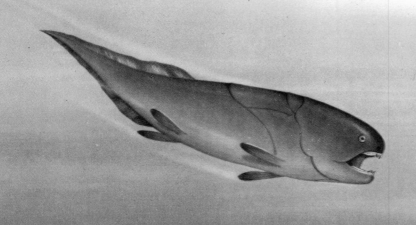

Dinichthys ($^1/_{60}$)

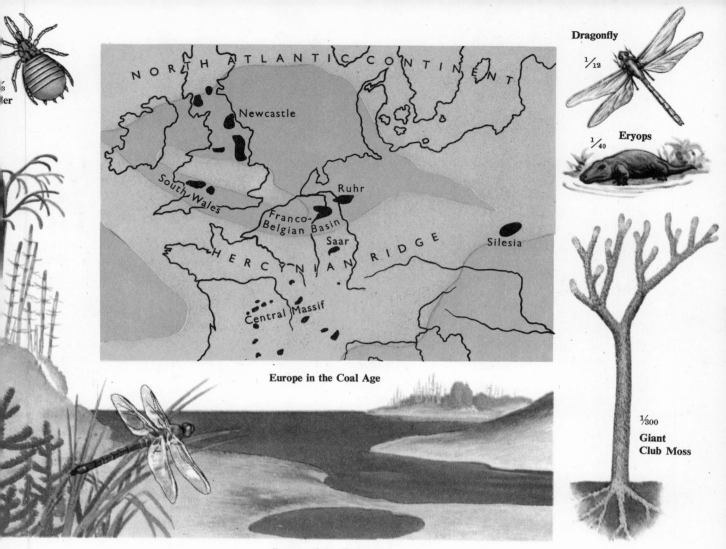

Dragonfly

1/12

Eryops

1/40

1/300
Giant Club Moss

Europe in the Coal Age

Swamp of the Coal Age

swamps. The forests were luxuriant, for the climate was mild, and the air as well as the ground was very moist. The trees that died and fell into the swamps did not rot away entirely. Instead, they formed a thick layer of plant material at the bottom of the swamps.

In many of the swamps the water gradually grew deeper. It may be that the land was slowly sinking. It may be that the seas were rising and overflowing into the swamps. The change was very slow, but at last the forests were drowned. The drowned trees were added to what was left of the trees that had died before. Mud was washed in over the thick layer of dead trees.

Later much of the water that covered the old swamps was drained away. Again there were many swamps with forests growing in them. In time these forests, too, were drowned and buried under mud. Time after time the same changes took place. At last in many regions there were several layers of buried forest. As millions of years went by, these layers were changed to coal.

The trees that made up the coal forests were not oaks and elms and pines. They were not any of the trees common in our forests now. Instead, they were giant club mosses, horsetails, and ferns.

The map above shows Europe as it was at one time during the Coal Age. As it shows, the sea at that time covered a large part of what is now dry land.

The animals pictured beside the map were common animals of the Coal Age. Clearly an important change in the animal world had taken place. For these three animals are land animals – at least they spent part of their lives on land. The moment when an animal first successfully crossed the dividing line between water and land was one of the very most important times in the earth's long history.

Probably the first animal to live on land was a scorpion. Back in the days of the trilobites there had been scorpion-like animals in the sea. At last there were scorpions on land. Spiders soon followed the scorpions. Later insects appeared.

Eryops (¹⁄₁₂)

Scorpions, spiders, and insects of several kinds were well established on land at the beginning of the Coal Age. They were common all during that long age.

Some of the insects that lived during the Coal Age were larger than any of the insects of today. There were dragonflies with wings that measured two feet across. There were giant cockroaches, too. In fact, cockroaches were so common that the Coal Age has sometimes been called the "Age of Cockroaches."

Scorpions, spiders, and insects have no backbones. The first backboned animals to live on land were amphibians. Toads and frogs are among our common amphibians of today. Toads and frogs begin their lives in water. The tadpoles that hatch from the eggs are very much like little fish. Later they become air-breathing animals and can live on land. The first amphibians also began their lives in water, but were able to live successfully on land when full-grown.

Scientists believe that the amphibians descended from the fishes. The first amphibian is sometimes called "the fish that walked."

One of the amphibians of the Coal Age was a giant named *Eryops*. *Eryops* was over eight feet long. It looked like a huge frog with a tail.

This big amphibian, so many scientists think, had three eyes – two in the normal places for eyes and one in the middle of its forehead. *Eryops* had an enormous mouth, so big that it could not have been any bigger unless the creature's head had been even bigger than it was.

Eryops could walk, but not at all fast. Its legs, although big, were so short that its stomach was close to the ground. It probably spent most of its time sunning itself at the edge of a swamp. Since it was the largest land animal, it did not have to run away from any enemies. It did not have to hurry to get food, either. Shellfish and water plants could be scooped up easily at the water's edge. Besides, *Eryops*, with its many sharp teeth, could capture some of its smaller amphibian relatives.

Although *Eryops* had a big skull, there was not much room inside it for brains. We can be sure this big fellow, as it sunned itself, did not do any thinking about the changes that were taking place on the earth.

Eryops could boast of something which no animal before the days of the amphibians had had – a voice. Probably, however, the only sound it could make was a hoarse croak.

Even though some amphibians lived on, *Eryops* disappeared long ago. In the end size did not mean success. The largest amphibians now are only about half the size of this early giant.

Rather late in the Paleozoic – some 275 million years ago – a new group of animals with backbones appeared on the earth. They were the reptiles. The early amphibians all began their lives in the water. The reptiles began theirs on land. The eggs of the amphibians were covered with a layer of jelly and were kept damp by being in water. The eggs of the reptiles had a shell around them. This shell protected them from drying out. The little reptiles that hatched from the eggs were not like little fish. They were very much like their parents. They could travel about on land from the beginning because they had lungs to breathe with, not gills.

One of the early reptiles was the sail-backed reptile. The sail-back was about the same size as *Eryops*. But it did not look like *Eryops* because, stretching down the middle of its back, it had a queer sail nearly a yard tall. This sail was made of tough skin stretched between long, bony spines that reached upward from the animal's backbone. Since the sail of the sail-back was somewhat like the fins of a fish, this early reptile is sometimes called the "fin-back."

The head of the sail-back was quite different from the head of *Eryops*, too. It was not nearly so broad and flat. The creature had many teeth. On each side of its mouth it had two daggerlike tusks. Clearly the sail-back was a meat eater. And clearly it ate animals bigger than insects.

In crushing the animals it caught, the sail-back probably often broke off some of its teeth. But it did not matter. The broken stumps fell out and new teeth grew in their places. The reptile might break off a certain tooth time after time, but always another tooth grew to replace it. It was a great advantage for a meat-eating animal never to be short of teeth.

No one can tell what the sail on the sail-back was good for. It must have been a nuisance as this reptile roamed in and out among the trees. But the sail-back was not the only early reptile that had a sail. Another early reptile is sometimes called the "ship lizard" because of its sail.

Sail-backed Reptiles (1/25)

Tyrannosaurus (1/120)

Triceratops (1/60)

Trachodon (1/90)

During the days of the early reptiles enormous changes were taking place on the earth. Great mountains were being pushed up in some places and new coast-lines were being formed in others. Arms of the sea became land and many swamps disappeared. The climate changed, too. It became cooler in many places. The great changes in the earth brought about great changes in the life on the earth. The Paleozoic Era – the era of ancient life – ended, and the Mesozoic, or middle-life, Era began.

This era, together with the last 35 million years or so of the Paleozoic, was the Age of Reptiles. In the Mesozoic reptiles flourished amazingly. They practically overran the earth.

On the land a great new group of reptiles called the "dinosaurs" appeared. The word "dinosaur" means "terrible lizard." The dinosaurs were not lizards, although they were reptiles just as lizards are. Neither were they all terrible. Some were rather small, and some, although big, were gentle plant eaters. But there were some dinosaurs that were really terrible.

The dinosaurs flourished for about 150 million years. In all, there were thousands of different kinds – probably at least 5,000. One kind would disappear and another kind would take its place. For most of the thousands of kinds of dinosaurs there are no common names. They have only the scientific names scientists of modern times have given them.

The reptiles pictured on these two pages did not all live at the same time. Neither did they all live in exactly the same parts of the world. But they were all land animals – all dinosaurs were.

Tyrannosaurus and *Allosaurus* are two of the dinosaurs that really deserve to be called terrible. They were both meat eaters. As the pictures show, they walked on their hind legs. Their front legs were so much smaller than their hind legs that they look as if they had not grown properly.

Tyrannosaurus – its name means "tyrant lizard" – grew to be from 18 to 20 feet tall. It was the largest flesh eater of all time. The head of this giant was enormous, and its jaws were so big that it could open its mouth more than a yard. Its mouth was filled with sharp teeth. On its toes it had sharp claws like an eagle's. The tail of *Tyrannosaurus* was very big and heavy. It helped this giant meat eater to walk upright.

Allosaurus means "leaping lizard." This meat-eating dinosaur used its powerful hind legs to go leaping about after its prey. *Allosaurus* was not quite so big or so dangerous as *Tyrannosaurus*, but it was far larger than any meat-eating animal of today.

With such animals as *Tyrannosaurus* and *Allosaurus* on the lookout for prey, life for other land animals was a dangerous undertaking. It is not surprising that some of the other dinosaurs developed armour to protect themselves. *Triceratops* was one of the armoured dinosaurs. *Triceratops* means "three-horned." As a part of its armour it had three sharp horns on its head. As a matter of fact, this armoured dinosaur had all its armour on its head. As long as it could face up to its enemy in a fight, it was well protected, but behind the great bony frill around its neck *Triceratops* had nothing but its thick skin to protect it.

No doubt *Triceratops* won some battles, but certainly, in spite of its armour, it often fell prey to the giant meat eaters.

Triceratops was a plant eater. *Brontosaurus* was another plant-eating dinosaur. *Brontosaurus* means "thunder lizard." This dinosaur was not given its name because it had a voice like thunder; it probably could not make much more than a squeal. The scientist who named it chose its name, it is said, because he thought that so huge an animal must have shaken the ground and made a noise like thunder when it walked about. It certainly was a giant animal. From the end of its nose to the tip of its tail it was about 70 feet long. It weighed about 35 tons.

Brontosaurus ate only tender plants. It did not eat grass – there was not yet any grass in the world for it to eat. Many of the plants it ate grew in the ponds and swamps of the time. The big thunder lizard gulped them in by the mouthful. But it must have taken the big animal most of its time to get enough food for its enormous body. Probably the thunder lizard spent almost all its time out in the ponds and swamps. Not only was food-getting easy there, but the water helped hold up the animal's huge body. Besides, being out in the middle of a pond was a good protection from the meat-eating dinosaurs. *Brontosaurus* had no other protection except its thick skin. It certainly could not run away easily. Its legs were like tree trunks, and its long tail was not by any means easy to pull along.

The head of *Brontosaurus* was small. There was not much room in it for brains. The brain of the thunder lizard weighed only about a pound – not much of a brain for a 35-*ton* body. The big animal must have been stupid.

Trachodon was another harmless plant-eating dinosaur. It was one of the duck-billed dinosaurs. Like the thunder lizard, it spent much of the time in water. It even had webbed feet. In the late part of the Age of Reptiles *Trachodon* was very common. It probably furnished many a meal for *Tyrannosaurus*.

Little dinosaurs furnished many meals for the meat eaters, too. Some of these small dinosaurs ran about on their hind legs. One of them can be seen in the picture below of a fight between *Triceratops* and *Tyrannosaurus*.

Some of the small dinosaurs that ran about on two legs could cover ground fast. Probably many of them got a part of their food by stealing eggs from the nests of other dinosaurs. If so, having two free feet to serve as hands must have been a great help to them in picking up the eggs. Their speed was needed to escape from the bigger dinosaurs whose nests they robbed.

Allosaurus (1/90)

Brontosaurus (1/125)

A Battle between Two Dinosaurs

The two dinosaurs pictured here were both plant eaters. *Diplodocus* looked much like *Brontosaurus*, but was longer and more slender. It was, in fact, the longest animal that ever walked on land; it measured nearly 90 feet from the end of its nose to the tip of its tail. If they were alive today, it would take only one of these giant reptiles to cover almost the length of one and a half cricket pitches. And as it walked down a street it could easily peer through second-storey windows. Like *Brontosaurus*, *Diplodocus* was clumsy and stupid. Its brain was about the same size as that of the thunder lizard.

Diplodocus, like all the dinosaurs, came from eggs. We know that the eggs of one nine-foot dinosaur were nine inches long. If *Diplodocus* followed the plan of an inch of egg for every foot of body, how enormous its eggs must have been!

Stegosaurus was another dinosaur that was built on the pattern of big bodies and small brains. Its brain was not much larger than a person's fist. This reptile was one of the armoured dinosaurs. *Stegosaurus* did not have its armour on its head. It had a double row of bony plates all down its back and sharp spikes on its tail. Swinging its tail from side to side was like swinging a gigantic battle-axe.

Stegosaurus had so tiny a brain that it could not control the muscles of its legs and tail with it. These muscles were controlled by an enlargement of the spinal cord at the base of its tail. This enlargement gave rise to the idea that *Stegosaurus* had two brains. One jingle tells that *Stegosaurus* could think on both sides of every question; it could think on one side of the question with the brain in its head and on the other side with the brain in its tail. It could, the jingle says, make both heads and tails of every problem. Actually *Stegosaurus* did none of what we call thinking. This armoured dinosaur, moreover, was not the only dinosaur with two "brains."

There were many other giant dinosaurs. *Brachiosaurus* was a great plant eater much like the thunder lizard but even heavier; it weighed some 50 tons. *Titanosaurus* also was much like *Brontosaurus*; its name tells that it was a giant. *Styracosaurus* looked like *Triceratops* but had an even more elaborate bony frill round its neck. *Corythosaurus*, a duck-billed dinosaur, had a crest on its head that was like an ancient Greek helmet. *Parasaurolophus*, another duck-billed dinosaur, had a bony frill down its neck the shape of an Indian chief's headdress. *Ceratosaurus* and *Deinodon* were other meat-eating giants. *Deinodon* was almost as big as *Tyrannosaurus*.

In reading of *Brontosaurus*, *Tyrannosaurus*, *Diplodocus* and their giant relatives it is easy to get one wrong impression about the dinosaurs. These big reptiles were truly huge. But they were not the biggest animals that have ever lived. No dinosaur was as big as a blue whale. But they were the biggest four-footed animals in history.

About 60 million years ago the dinosaurs disappeared. When they went out of the picture, the Age of Reptiles came to an end. Why, after they had been the lords of the land for 150 million years, the dinosaurs *all* died is a mystery.

Doubtless the reason many of the dinosaurs died is that their bodies were too big for their brains. With smaller bodies and bigger brains they might have lived on. They were successful for a very long time because conditions on the earth remained almost the same for millions of years. When conditions changed, they did not have sense enough to help themselves in any way.

Diplodocus (1/80)

One of the changes that helped bring about the end of the dinosaurs was the drying up of many of the ponds and swamps. There were fewer places in which the water could help the great plant-eating dinosaurs hold up their huge bodies. There were fewer water plants to serve as food for these great reptiles, too. As the huge plant-eating dinosaurs became fewer and fewer, there was less food for the big flesh eaters.

Changes in temperature were also against the dinosaurs. The dinosaurs, like all the reptiles of today, were cold-blooded. Their temperatures were the same as the temperatures of their surroundings. The climate became colder in many of the regions where the dinosaurs lived. The dinosaurs had no way of keeping their bodies warm in these cold surroundings. Getting cold made them become very sluggish and less able to fend for themselves. Moreover, the eggs of the dinosaurs probably did not hatch so well after the climate changed.

The habit of some dinosaurs of eating the eggs of others probably played a part in bringing an end to the dinosaurs. The rise of a great new group of animals, the mammals, doubtless played a part, too. But some of the dinosaurs' reptile relatives lived on. Why no dinosaurs at all did is still puzzling.

A Plesiosaur ($\frac{1}{40}$)

During the Age of Reptiles by no means all the reptiles lived on land. There were also many that lived in the sea.

Among the reptiles that lived in the sea were the plesiosaurs. They were descendants of early land reptiles, but they certainly did not look like land animals. They were very different even from the big plant-eating dinosaurs that spent most of the time in ponds.

The bodies of the plesiosaurs were rather flat, and their legs had become great paddles. Their necks were long and slender – somewhat like the necks of *Brontosaurus* and *Diplodocus* – but they had rather short, thick tails. Their mouths were full of sharp teeth – clearly they were meat eaters.

The largest plesiosaurs were about 50 feet long. Some of them had exceptionally long heads. The skull of one kind measured three yards!

Although they lived in the sea, the plesiosaurs kept one of the habits of their land ancestors. They laid their eggs on land. Little long-necked plesiosaurs finding their way down to the water after they were hatched must have looked a little like snakes that had changed their minds and decided to be turtles.

The ichthyosaurs formed another group of big reptiles of the sea. Their name means "fish lizard." This name was well chosen, for the ichthyosaurs certainly looked very much like big fishes.

The largest ichthyosaurs were shorter by 20 feet than the largest plesiosaurs. But of course much of the length of the plesiosaurs was in their very long necks.

The ichthyosaurs, like the plesiosaurs, were descendants of early reptiles. They still were air-breathing animals. They therefore could not stay under water for long at a time. But in many ways they had become well fitted for living in water. Their bodies were streamlined so that they could push their way through water easily. Their tails were not at all like the tails of the land reptiles or of the plesiosaurs. They were excellent oars. Their legs, moreover, had become paddles that were much the shape of fishes' fins.

These "fish lizards" had enormous eyes – bigger than those of any other animals of any time. An ichthyosaur's eye was as big as a man's head. It was so big that it could not have stood the pressure of the water if it had not been protected by a ring of bone. With its huge eyes an ichthyosaur could find prey even in very dim light. Ichthyosaurs ate chiefly fish.

Flopping their way up on shore to lay their eggs must have been hard for the plesiosaurs. It was impossible for the ichthyosaurs. But reptile eggs will not hatch in water. The ichthyosaurs solved the problem in the only possible way. They kept their eggs in their bodies until they hatched. Little ichthyosaurs were born alive.

The mosasaurs formed a third group of big sea reptiles. Mosasaurs came in many sizes – from 60 feet long down to 3 feet. They did not have the long necks of the plesiosaurs and were not nearly so fishlike as the ichthyosaurs. They looked like crocodiles with flippers in place of legs.

The plesiosaurs, ichthyosaurs, and mosasaurs died out at the end of the Age of Reptiles. The disappearance of the ichthyosaurs is especially puzzling. They had copied the fishes so well that it is hard to see why they did not live on. Fishes had been in the seas long before the ichthyosaurs, and the seas are still swarming with them today. Besides, the great changes in the earth that came at the end of the Age of Reptiles did not, as has been pointed out, bring an end to all the reptiles. Turtles and crocodiles, for instance, lived on. But, whatever the reason, the plesiosaurs, ichthyosaurs, and mosasaurs went the way of the dinosaurs.

Some of the descendants of the early reptiles, instead of taking to the sea, took to the air. These were the pterosaurs. "Pterosaur" means "winged lizard." The wings of the pterosaurs were made of sheets of skin, like the wings of bats. Each "hand" had one very long "finger," to which the front edge of the wing was fastened. Another name for many of the pterosaurs is "pterodactyls." "Pterodactyl" means "wing-finger."

Some of the pterosaurs were huge. The largest had a wingspread of nearly 30 feet. But there were little pterosaurs, too. Some were no bigger than our sparrows.

One of the rather early flying reptiles has a fairy-tale sounding name – *Rhamphorhynchus*. *Rhamphorhynchus* was about a foot and a half long. Its wingspread was nearly 10 feet. The most peculiar thing about this flying reptile was its long, thin tail that ended in a leaf-shaped piece of skin. Perhaps the end served as a kind of rudder as the pterosaur soared through the air.

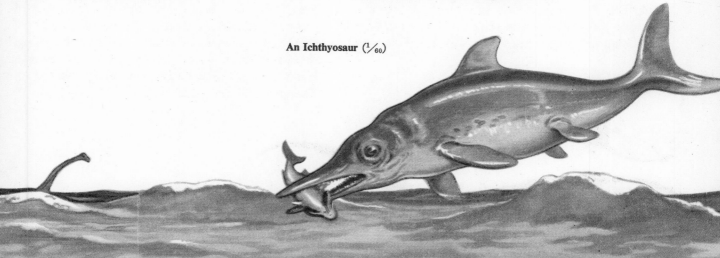

An Ichthyosaur ($\frac{1}{60}$)

Pteranodon (1/70)

Rhamphorhynchus never rested on the ground. Instead, it clung to the trunk or branch of a tree. Sometimes it hung head down, just as bats often do now. It could clamber around in trees easily because it had claws on its front wings. The skin of its wing was fastened to its fourth finger, leaving three fingers free for holding on.

Rhamphorhynchus had sharp teeth. Strangely enough, they pointed forward. Teeth pointing backward would, it would seem, have been much better for catching the fish that this flying reptile ate, but its forward-pointing teeth apparently served the purpose.

Pterodactylus was, as its name tells, a pterodactyl. It did not have the long tail of *Rhamphorhynchus*. Neither did it have so many sharp teeth.

Pteranodon was the giant of the pterodactyls. It was far larger, with its 13-foot wings, than any bird of today.

Pteranodon's head was big in proportion to its body. At a glance it would seem that this reptile was an exception to the fashion among big reptiles of having small brains. As a matter of fact, the brains of all the pterosaurs were rather large for reptiles. But *Pteranodon's* brain was not so large as one would guess from the size of its skull. Most of its queer, anvil-shaped head was full of air.

Scientists do not agree as to whether this giant flying reptile could fly well. Some think that it could fly wonderfully well – that its hollow bones, for many of the bones of the pterosaurs were hollow, and its great wings fitted it perfectly for flying. Others say that its wings were weak and that, in spite of its hollow bones, its body was too heavy to make flying easy. It is certain that a bad tear in a wing would make the wing useless. It would not be at all like the loss of a feather or two from the wing of a bird. It is certain, too, that, if *Pteranodon* in swooping down to catch a little reptile had to make an emergency landing on level ground, it would have a hard time getting into the air again.

Pteranodon may be thought of as a last fling of the pterosaurs. Its disappearance toward the close of the Age of Reptiles was the end of these creatures of the air.

The birds of today do not look much like snakes or turtles or alligators. But scientists believe that the ancestors of the birds were reptiles. They do not believe, however, that they were pterosaurs but rather small reptiles that ran about swiftly on their hind legs and were light enough to leap from the ground into the low branches of trees. Gradually, scientists think, the scales of these reptiles became feathers, and their front legs developed into wings. The reptiles that became birds changed in another important way, too. They became warm-blooded.

Rhamphorhynchus

Pterodactylus (1/12)

Archaeopteryx is the oldest bird we know about. Its name means "ancient wing." *Archaeopteryx* was very different from any bird of today. For one thing, it had claws on its wings just as the flying reptiles had. Probably it used its wings as well as its legs in climbing from branch to branch of the trees it lived in.

This ancient bird had no bill, but it did have jaws with teeth. Probably it was a meat eater – it may very well have lived on dead fish washed up on the shores of lakes and seas.

The bony part of the tail of a bird of today is very short. The tail feathers spread out from this bony part like the sticks of a fan. There were many bones in the long tail of *Archaeopteryx*. Along this bony tail, feathers were arranged in pairs, one pair for every joint in the tail.

Archaeopteryx was about the size of a crow. For all we know, it may have been as black as a crow. Artists have to simply guess at the colour of the animals of long ago.

Archaeopteryx appeared well back in the days of the dinosaurs – about 150 million years ago. Another bird that appeared in the Age of Reptiles, but later than *Archaeopteryx*, was *Hesperornis*.

Hesperornis was a big diving bird. It was probably better fitted for diving than any bird of today. Its body, which was more than four feet long, was very slender, and its beak was long and sharp. It had powerful legs that made excellent oars, and big webbed feet. Like *Archaeopteryx*, *Hesperornis* had many teeth; it could easily hold fast the fish it caught.

This big diving bird could not fly. The reason is simple: it had mere traces of wings. It could not walk well either; its legs were set too far back on its body.

Hesperornis was large, but the true feathered giants of the past were land birds somewhat like our ostriches. None of these truly giant birds could fly.

One of these ancient flightless giants was *Phororhacos*, a bird that lived in Patagonia some 20 million years ago. Although an ancient bird, it appeared long after the days of the dinosaurs. *Phororhacos* had a head that was as large as the head of a modern horse. Even though the bird was eight feet tall, its head was out of proportion. A sharp hook at the end of its beak served well to tear meat to bits.

The tallest birds that ever lived were the moas of New Zealand. Some of them were twelve feet tall. The moas were not very ancient. When the first white missionaries went to New Zealand, they heard stories of birds that were big enough to trample human beings to death. Apparently men had appeared on the earth before the moas disappeared. The early inhabitants of New Zealand may have helped to bring about the end of the moas by killing them for food.

Another of the ancient flightless giants is sometimes spoken of as the "elephant bird." Its scientific name is *Aepyornis*. This bird lived in Madagascar. It was not so large as the moa, but it laid eggs as big as footballs. One would have been equal to several dozen hen's eggs.

It has been suggested that the ancient flightless birds, as well as those we have now, descended from primitive birds that never learned to fly. But scientists do not agree. They say that in the beginning all birds could fly, but that some lost the power to do so. Perhaps they no longer needed to fly either to get food or to escape meat-eating enemies.

Archaeopteryx (⅙)

21

An Early Mammal (⅕)

The first mammals were not very important-looking creatures. Back in the Age of Reptiles no one, if he could have seen these little furry animals, most of them about the size of rats and mice, would have had any idea that their descendants would one day take the place of the reptiles as the lords of the earth. But they did. The era that followed the Age of Reptiles is called by scientists the Cenozoic Era. "Cenozoic" means "recent life." The common name for it is "Age of Mammals."

At the end of the Age of Reptiles the climate in many parts of the world had become much colder. This change worked against the cold-blooded reptiles. But it was not nearly so much of a hardship for the birds, which were warm-blooded, and for the mammals, which were warm-blooded, too. Their bodies stayed warm even in cold surroundings.

Their hair was a big help to the early mammals. Hair, or fur, is a very poor conductor of heat. It served well to keep the heat of their bodies from escaping. With hair to keep their bodies warm, they could be active the year round even during truly cold winters.

The early mammals, moreover, were built so that they could move very fast. They had to be able to move fast to keep out of the way of the great meat-eating dinosaurs. Besides, most of them, too, were meat eaters, and it was a great advantage to be able to move fast.

Another great advantage the early mammals had over the dinosaurs was the better care they took of their young. The reptiles laid their eggs and then went off and left them. The eggs and the young reptiles that hatched from them were at the mercy of meat-eating animals. The mammals on the other hand – at least most of them – were live-bearing. They carried their eggs in their bodies until they developed into young animals. After they were born the baby animals were fed with milk from the mother's body. They were guarded, too, until they were able to look after themselves.

Most important of all, the mammals had bigger brains in proportion to their sizes than the reptiles. They were better able to hold their own in a changing world.

During the Age of Mammals – the age we are still in, since we are mammals – mammals of thousands of kinds developed. As one would expect, since the Age of Mammals has lasted for some 60 million years, many kinds of mammals have appeared, flourished, and then disappeared. Some of the extinct mammals were very large. It was not long, as time goes in the story of the earth, after the great meat-eating dinosaurs disappeared before there were giants among the mammals.

One of the mammal giants was *Megatherium*. Its name means "giant beast." *Megatherium* was a ground sloth. The sloths of today are all tree dwellers. They are queer, clumsy beasts that hang from the limbs of trees almost without moving. Although they have four legs, these legs are not at all well fitted for walking. In contrast, *Megatherium* spent its whole life on the ground.

This sloth was a harmless vegetable eater. It had a thick tail and heavy hind legs. When it sat up on its back legs and tail, as it often did, it could use its front legs as arms to dig out roots or to break off branches of trees. Its arms were so strong that it could break down whole trees to get the leaves from them. When it sat up, it was about twice as tall as a tall man. It had a long, powerful tongue that it used to strip leaves off the trees. Its sharp, curved claws were helpful in digging up roots, but they were rather a nuisance when the animal walked. They had to be doubled under in an awkward way, since they could not be pulled in as a cat's can. Such handicaps may have caused *Megatherium* to disappear.

Glyptodon was one of the glyptodonts, ancient armadillo-like animals. They were mammals, though they were not at all furry.

Glyptodon sometimes grew to be as big as an ox. It was all wrapped up in armour. As the picture below shows, on its back it had a shield much like that of an armadillo of today. In addition it had a bony plate on its head, bony rings round its tail, and many spikes at the end of its tail.

In the end all *Glyptodon*'s armour did not help it. It disappeared, while some of its smaller, less well-armoured relatives lived on.

Uintatherium, *Titanotherium*, and *Baluchitherium* are three other mammal giants that deserve a place in a parade of ancient animals.

Uintatherium, the Uinta beast, gets its name from the Uinta Mountains, the region where it

Megatherium (¹⁄₃₀)

Glyptodon (¹⁄₃₀)

The horse as we know it developed through long ages from a little animal no bigger than a fox. The elephant (below) 50 million years ago looked somewhat like a pig.

Eohippus

Mesohippus

Protohippus

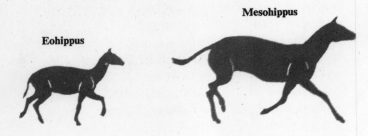
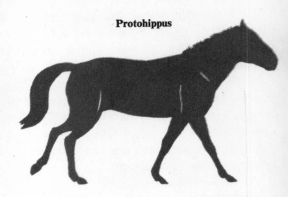

lived. This big animal specialized in horns. It had at least three pairs at various places on its homely face.

Titanotherium, the giant beast, specialized in horns, too. It had only one pair but they were very large and were just behind its nose. They extended forward and upward. This big animal's skull curved downward behind its nose so that its face was the shape of a soup dish. As one would guess, the giant beast was not the brainiest of animals.

Baluchitherium lived in Asia. It was a relative of the rhinoceroses of today, but it was much larger. It was, in fact, the largest *land mammal* of all time. At its shoulders it was as tall as a giraffe, and it was very heavy.

Not all the giant mammals that have disappeared lived on land. *Zeuglodon* was a relative of our whales of today. It grew to be 80 or 90 feet long but was very slender. If *Zeuglodon* had not disappeared long before there were any people, we would know where early sailors got their stories of enormous sea serpents.

We can trace the ancestry of some of our mammals back through millions of years. We can see what changes, in some cases very great ones, have taken place in them since they first appeared on the earth.

Modern Elephant

The horse is one of the mammals whose ancestry we can trace. The story begins with *Eohippus*, the dawn horse.

Eohippus was a little animal no bigger than a fox. It lived in the swampy woodlands of western North America and of Europe.

The dawn horse had only a few stiff hairs for a mane. It had a small tail, a short neck, and teeth that could chew only tender leaves. Most surprising of all, this little horse had no hoofs. It had four toes on each of its forefeet and three toes on each of its hind feet. Besides, this little dawn horse had extra bones in its feet to show that its ancestors had once been five-toed animals with feet that were flat like a bear's.

Eohippus was well fitted for living in swampy, wooded country. It could run in and out among the trees easily and could hide in the shadows from its meat-eating enemies. It could reach and eat the leaves on bushes and on low branches of trees. The feet of this little horse were good for walking on swampy land.

As time went by, conditions changed in the regions where *Eohippus* lived. The swamps dried up, and the ground was not so soft as it had been. Trees grew in many places where they had not grown before. Generation by generation *Eohippus* changed, too. After many centuries it had changed so much that scientists give it a new name – *Mesohippus*, the "in-between horse."

Modern Horse

Modern Horse

Mesohippus was about the size of a big gun dog. It had a small mane, and its tail was longer than the tail of the dawn horse. Its feet had also changed. *Mesohippus* had three toes on each foot, and the middle toe was larger than the other two. This big middle toe had a very thick nail. It was the beginning of a hoof.

Conditions on the earth kept on changing. The climate became much drier in the places where *Mesohippus* lived. Much of the woodland disappeared. In its place there was grassland. If *Mesohippus* had not been able to change, too, we would never have had our horses of today.

But generation by generation *Mesohippus* did change. With low-branching trees scarce, its teeth changed so that it could eat grass instead. It grew taller and swifter, and its neck grew longer. Size and speed were a help now that it could not hide in the woods. It could run much faster than its ancestors because it ran on only one toe on each foot. Its other toes did not touch the ground. On the toes it used, the nails were real hoofs. Such hoofs would have been a nuisance in swampy land, but they were excellent for dry, grassy plains. This first horse to run on its middle toenails is called *Protohippus*, the "just-before horse." It had a really horselike look.

Horses gradually grew still bigger, and they lost their useless toes. The horse of today carries about with it, however, a sign that its ancestors once had several toes. Hidden under the skin there are bits of bone left from the extra toes.

The story of the elephants is very much like the story of the horse. About 50 million years ago the ancestor of the elephants lived in Africa – perhaps in other places, too. It was a small animal that looked somewhat like a pig or a tapir. No person ever saw this little animal alive. If anyone had, he would never have guessed that its descendants would have long trunks, enormous ears, and great ivory tusks weighing more than 100 pounds apiece.

Mastodon (1/25)

The name of this small animal, which is believed to be the ancestor of all the elephants, is *Moeritherium*. Its name is taken from Lake Moeris, an ancient lake in Egypt.

Moeritherium was stocky. Its legs were thick and its neck was short. It had two small tusks – they were simply extra-large, sharp-pointed teeth – in its upper jaw. These tusks were useful in raking plant food into the animal's mouth.

Moeritherium

25

Mammoth (¹⁄₆₀)

Generation by generation the descendants of *Moeritherium* grew taller. As they did, some change had to take place to enable them to eat from the ground. Their necks became a little longer, but not enough. Most of the needed lengthening was done in their faces. Both jaws grew longer. Their tusks grew farther out from their upper jaws. Their noses and upper lips became longer, too. The elephant's trunk had begun.

The descendants of *Moeritherium* kept on growing taller. Their necks, strangely enough, became shorter once more. Their jaws and tusks and upper lips and noses stretched enough to make up not only for their longer legs but also for their shorter necks.

The elephants kept on growing. Then another strange thing happened to them. Just as their necks, after having stretched out, grew shorter, their lower jaws became very short. Their tusks, instead of growing straight down, curved upward. Then their upper lips and noses were left hanging down with no lower jaw to rest on. They had become real trunks.

A trunk proved to be an excellent way of gathering food from the ground or from branches of trees. It was such a success that it has changed very little in the past few million years.

About two million years ago the time that we call the "Ice Age" began. Vast sheets of ice spread from the regions around the North Pole down over much of Europe and North America. By this time the elephants had spread far and wide. Two of them were common in Europe and North America.

One was the mastodon. It had a woolly coat that protected it well from the cold. Its tusks were larger than the tusks of the elephants of today.

Cave Bear (¹⁄₂₅)

Sabre-tooth Tiger (¹⁄₃₀)

The other elephant that lived in Europe and North America during the great Ice Age was the mammoth. There were great herds of mammoths. They, too, were covered with coarse hair that protected them from the cold.

No one knows exactly when people first appeared on the earth. We do know that there were people living in Europe during the last part of the great Ice Age. These people lived in caves. The cave men knew the mammoths. They drew pictures of them on the walls of some of their caves.

The mammoths were a great help to the cave men. They furnished them with food. Perhaps some of the pictures of mammoths on the walls of caves were meant to be prayers for a successful mammoth hunt.

The cave men had other "friends" among the wild animals of the time. Many besides the mammoth furnished food. There were, among others, reindeer, musk oxen, and wild sheep.

But certainly not all the animals that lived in the days of the cave men could be called helpful. Some were really enemies.

One of the cave men's animal enemies was the cave bear. The cave men lived in caves during the winters to protect themselves from the cold. The cave bears sought shelter in the same caves. Many a fight was fought between a cave man and a cave bear. The cave bear was fierce when attacked. Of course, if a cave man won a fight with a cave bear, he had a warm bearskin for a blanket or for clothing. The cave men had to depend on wild animals for clothing as well as for food.

The picture above shows how some of the animals of the Ice Age met their death. The part of North America that is now the United States was not all covered with ice during the great Ice Age. In parts of the land not covered by ice, volcanoes were erupting. In other places tar welled up out of the ground and formed pools. After a rain, water would collect on top of the tar in these pools. Animals like mammoths, horses, and camels would wade out into the pools to get a drink. Then they would be trapped in the sticky tar.

The cries of the trapped animals would attract such meat eaters as the sabre-tooth tiger. The sabre-tooth tiger was a very fierce animal. It got the "sabre-tooth" part of its name from two enormous fangs, or teeth, in its upper jaw. With these great fangs it could kill another animal easily and slash the meat off its bones. But these weapons were of no use when a sabre-tooth found itself sinking into the tar, too. Many sabre-tooths were trapped along with many wolves and birds of prey. So many animals were caught in these tar pools that they are called the "death-trap tar pools."

We are still in the Cenozoic Era – the Age of Mammals. The great Ice Age and the time since then, often called the "Age of Man," form parts of it. Will mammals, one wonders, continue to be the earth's leading animals? Or, a hundred million years or so from now, will most of the mammals of today belong in a parade of ancient animals? No one can tell. At the moment there is little to make us think that man and his fellow mammals will be crowded off the earth.

The Earth's Rock Diary

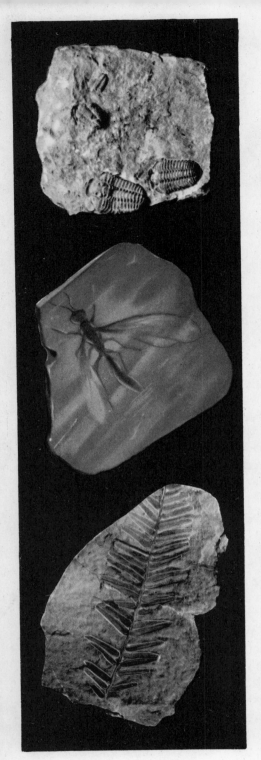

FOSSILS:
   Trilobite
   Insect in Amber
   Fern Leaf

Fossils tell us the story of the animals of long ago. If it were not for fossils, no one would know about trilobites, dinosaurs, and the many, many other kinds of animals that have become extinct. We know about ancient plants from fossils, too. Fossils are traces found in rocks of the living things of past ages.

There are fossils of many different kinds. A fossil may be a whole animal that was buried in such a way that the air was shut away from its body and its body could not decay. Many insects of long ago were trapped in the resin of ancient pine trees. The resin preserved them. Later the resin was buried underground and became amber. The insects remained unchanged. In many museums now there are pieces of amber that contain insects which still look very much as they did when they were trapped millions of years ago.

A few mammoths have been found in the Far North frozen in great blocks of ice left from the great Ice Age. Of course, these mammoths decayed very rapidly when they were broken out of the ice.

Many fossils are casts. One of the pictures shows a piece of rock on which there are several tribolite casts. The story of every trilobite cast is somewhat like this: A trilobite died, and its body fell to the muddy bottom of the sea. Soon the soft parts of its body decayed. Then the hard covering was like a mould. Limy mud filled it up. Later the hard covering itself decayed, and the space was filled with limy mud. Later, no one knows how much later, the limy mud hardened, just as did the mud round about, into solid rock.

The fossil leaves in the pictures are casts, too. The leaves were pressed down in some way into mud. They decayed, but left their imprint in the mud. More mud washed into the imprint. All the mud hardened into solid rock. When the rock was split apart later, there was a raised cast on one layer and the imprint in which it was made on the other.

Fossil footprints are imprints. Those in the picture were made when a dinosaur walked across a layer of soft mud. Ordinarily such prints

Skeleton of Diplodocus

would have been washed away or spoiled by other footprints on top of them. But conditions were such that these footprints were not destroyed. When later the mud hardened into solid rock, the footprints remained.

In our museums there are many skeletons of ancient animals. The skeleton of such an animal as *Diplodocus* weighs tons, for the bones it is built of are solid stone – they are petrified. A bone is petrified in this way: An animal that has bones dies. The soft parts of its body decay rather rapidly, but the bones are left. They are buried in sandy or limy mud. While they are buried, the water in the mud gradually dissolves the material they are made of and leaves some rock material in its place. Little by little, then, a true bone becomes a bone of stone. "Petrified" means "turned to stone." A petrified bone is not actually turned to stone. It is really rebuilt in stone. Petrified wood is made in the same way.

It takes an enormous amount of work to dig petrified bones out of the rocks in which they are found. It is also a difficult task to join them to form a skeleton like the one pictured.

Some fossils are simply the hard parts of plants or animals that have been kept as they were. A fossil may be, for instance, a shell or a bone that has remained unchanged. Prehistoric bones have been recovered from ancient beds of tar where they had been wonderfully preserved.

The outside "skin" or "crust" of the earth is made up of rocks of many different kinds. Some of them are made from the sand and mud and pebbles washed down by rivers and waves into lakes and seas. These rocks are often spoken of as water-made rocks. "Sedimentary" is another name for them. Other rocks are made from hot, liquid rock material that comes from deep down in the earth. Such rocks are called "igneous rocks." This name is from the Latin word for fire. Sometimes they are called "volcanic rocks." It is easy to see why, since hot, liquid rock often pours from the mouths, or craters, of volcanoes. There are also rocks that have been changed since they were first made. These are the metamorphic rocks. "Metamorphic" means "changed."

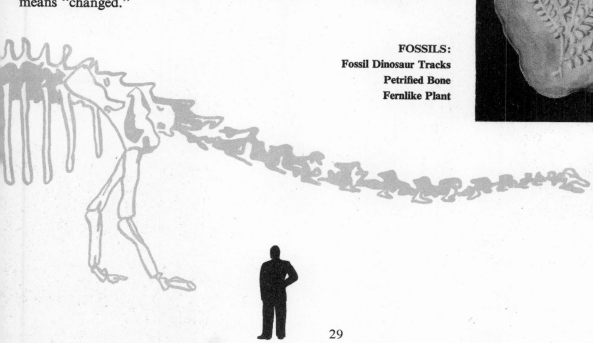

FOSSILS:
Fossil Dinosaur Tracks
Petrified Bone
Fernlike Plant

The different layers of rock that make up the earth's crust may be thought of as pages in the earth's diary. They tell the story of the earth during the long ages before there were any people anywhere in the world who could write of the changes that were going on. A deep gorge like the Grand Canyon shows many rock pages ready to be read.

The layers of water-made rocks are the pages that tell most of the story of the plants and animals of long ago. It is not surprising that they do, since mud and water play so important a part in the making of fossils.

Sandstone, limestone, and shale are three very common water-made rocks. Sandstone, as its name suggests, is made of grains of sand cemented together. Shale is made of mud. Limestone may be made of lime that settles to the bottom of a body of water from the water itself. Anyone who has seen the lime that collects on the inside of a kettle knows that water may have a great deal of lime in it. Limestone may, instead, be made of the shells of water animals. Vast numbers of animals take lime from the water of lakes and seas to make shells for themselves. When they die, their shells sink to the bottom of the water. Animals with shells have lived and died in such numbers that in many places thick layers of limestone have been built by them. A piece of limestone may be a great mass of fossil shells.

Conglomerate is another water-made rock. It is usually partly sandstone, but it contains pebbles, too. In the picture the pebbles show clearly.

Coal was made, not of sediments washed down into a lake or sea, but of buried forests. Many plant fossils are found in coal. From them we can tell what trees grew during the Coal Age.

Rock salt is another water-made rock. Since sea water contains salt, it is not surprising that in places layers of salt have been formed at the bottom of a sea. Rock salt is not likely to contain fossils.

The Grand Canyon

Igneous Rocks:

Pumice

Obsidian

Tuff

Basalt

Granite

Layers of water-made rocks tell much more about the earth's history than just what plants and animals once lived here. They tell where the old lakes and seas used to be. Land and sea have not remained the same through the ages.

The map on page 11 shows that Europe looked very different back in the days when coal was being made. Great arms of the sea spread over thousands of square miles of what is now land. Scientists are sure that this is true because they have found layers of water-made rocks there — rocks that were made back in the Age of Coal.

The layers of rocks through which the Colorado River in the United States has cut the Grand Canyon are, except for those at the very bottom of the gorge, water-made rocks. They tell that this part of the world was covered by water for countless centuries. Scientists can read the story of land and sea for every part of the world from the rocks underlying its surface.

Those who know how to read the earth's rock diary can also read from water-made rocks about changes in climate in ages past. Rock salt, for example, is much more likely to be formed when the climate is dry and water is evaporating fast from lakes and seas. The fossils found in water-made rocks help tell the stories of changes in climate. The discovery of fossils of the Osage orange and other southern plants in Greenland, for instance, shows that Greenland was once much warmer than it is now.

The diagrams below show how a volcano is built up. Hot rock comes to the surface from deep in the earth. While it is under the surface it is called "magma." When it pours out on the surface it is called "lava." Sometimes a volcano erupts with such force that bits of the liquid rock are shot

How a volcano is built up

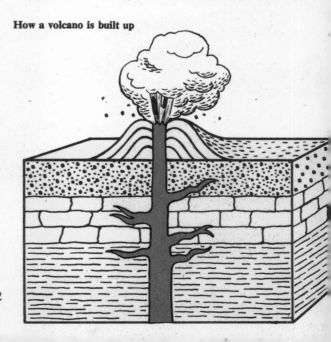

32

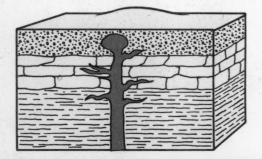

high into the air. They cool and harden and fall back as cinders and ashes close to the opening from which they came. Gradually they build a cone-shaped hill around the opening. Lava pouring from the volcano builds the hill higher. It becomes a mountain.

Lava that pours out of a volcano may cool very quickly. It may cool so fast it has many spaces in it just as slag does that comes from steel mills. These spaces were filled with gas as the lava poured out. The rock thus formed is called "pumice." Pumice is so light that it will float in water.

Obsidian is another rock that is formed from lava that cools quickly. Obsidian looks like glass. In fact, it is often called "volcanic glass." As a rule it is a shiny black.

Tuff, often called "volcanic tuff," is an igneous rock made of the ashes from a volcano. It looks much as the ashes from a coal-burning furnace would look if they were cemented together.

Basalt is formed from lava that cools rather slowly. It is a dull-black rock, as the picture shows. Basalt is common. In some places there are very thick layers of it. A layer of basalt may break up into six-sided columns. The Giant's Causeway in Ireland and the Devil's Postpile in California are made of basalt columns.

Magma may cool when it comes near the surface and harden into solid rock underground. A very common igneous rock, granite, is formed from magma that hardens beneath the surface. Some granite is red rather than grey like that in the picture. Granite always has dark crystals in it that make it speckled. Although formed underground, it is often found at the surface, because the rocks above it have been worn away. Granite is very hard; it has been called "the rock everlasting." This rock can be polished easily.

There are a great many other igneous rocks. Some, like granite, cool so slowly underground that crystals large enough to be easily seen form in them. Others, like pumice, obsidian, and basalt, are made from lava that pours out over the surface of the ground. The crystals, if there are any, in these rocks made from lava are very tiny.

From the igneous rock pages in the earth's diary scientists can tell that in parts of the world there were once active volcanoes where there are no active volcanoes today. They can tell, too, that there have been times in the past when great cracks opened up in the earth and allowed lava to pour from them.

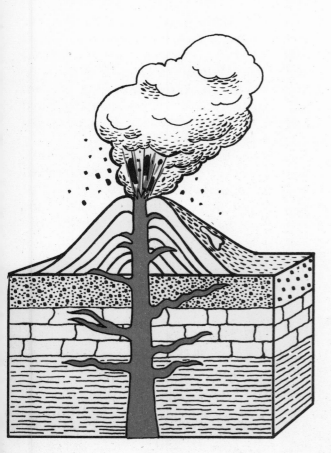

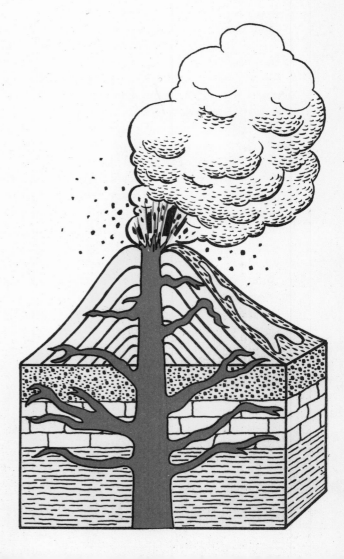

The metamorphic rocks in the earth's crust are like pages that have been rewritten. After layers of rock have been formed, they are sometimes squeezed up into great folds. They are sometimes pushed up by magma from below. The pushing and heating bring about changes in the rocks. Marble, slate, and quartzite are common metamorphic rocks. All marble was once limestone. All slate was once shale. All quartzite was once sandstone. In the same way hard coal was made from soft coal, mica schist from conglomerate or various other rocks, and gneiss from granite.

Quartzite is an extremely durable rock. Streets are sometimes paved with brick-shaped blocks of quartzite.

Almost everyone is familiar with slate. It has long been used for blackboards and for roofing shingles. Some slate can be split into very thin sheets with smooth surfaces. Not all slate is grey. Some is red, some green, and some purple.

Marble is the most beautiful of the metamorphic rocks. It can be given a high polish. The purest marble is white, but marble may be grey, green, pink, red, or black. Some coloured marble is streaked with white.

Hard coal is a much cleaner fuel than soft coal. It is not dusty, and it produces very little smoke as it burns.

Mica schist sparkles because of the mica in it. Garnets are often found embedded in this rock. The garnets pictured are in mica schist.

The effect of heat and pressure on granite is to make the dark speckles into streaks, or bands. "Banded granite" is another name for gneiss.

A pebble is a small piece of rock of one kind or another. A handful of pebbles one picks up on a beach usually includes some bits of sedimentary rock, some of igneous rock, and some of metamorphic rock. Many of them may have been carried a long way, perhaps by waves, perhaps by streams, or perhaps by the glaciers of the great Ice Age.

On their journeys pebbles get their rough edges worn smooth. Some pebbles are so waterworn that it is hard, unless they are cracked open, to tell what kind of rock they are made of. But even the tiniest pebble has a story to tell of ancient lakes or seas, of volcanoes or lava flows, or of the pushing up of the earth's crust into hills or mountains.

Rocks are made up of what scientists call minerals. A rock may be made up of only one mineral. Most rocks contain more than one. Often minerals form crystals.

Crystals are formed in many different shapes and sizes. Each kind of mineral has its own crystal pattern. The crystals of black mica, for example, are thin sheets. Quartz crystals are six-sided. Feldspar crystals are box-shaped, Tourmaline crystals are shaped like three-sided prisms. As the picture shows, garnet crystals have many faces; there are usually either 12 or 24.

Three of the minerals pictured are commonly found in granite. All granite has quartz and feldspar crystals in it. The dark crystals which make the speckles are, in many cases, black mica. But they may be some other dark mineral.

The crystals in granite are not large and perfect like those in the pictures. But it is not hard to pick out the three kinds. Granite, although it is a durable rock, can be broken up in time by wind and water. Much of the sand on our beaches comes from the breaking up of granite. The grains of sand are tiny crystals of quartz.

There are so many different minerals that it takes years of study to know them all well. The crystals of some of them are so beautiful that we use them as jewels. Diamonds, rubies, sapphires, emeralds, and amethysts are a few of them. Amethysts are among the less expensive of our precious stones. Amethysts are crystals of quartz coloured a beautiful violet by the presence of a tiny amount of manganese.

From minerals in the rocks of the earth's crust also come gold, silver, iron, tin, and many, many other metals. Clearly the earth's rocks are a true treasure house. Some of the layers have much more treasure than others. But they all play their part in telling the earth's story.

Quartzite

Slate

Marble

Hard Coal

Mica Schist

Black Mica

Tourmaline

Gneiss

Quartz

Feldspar

Garnet

35

Living Things

THE world of living things is made up of many, many thousands of kinds of plants and animals. Some of these, typhoid germs and paramecia, for example, are so tiny that they cannot be seen without a microscope. Others are so big that they weigh many tons. Some live their whole lives in less than a day. Others are not yet old when they have lived for a hundred years. But in certain ways all living things are alike.

They are all made in part of that mysterious living stuff called "protoplasm." They are built of tiny blocks of protoplasm called "cells." A typhoid germ (a plant) and a paramecium (an animal) are both single cells. So are many other plants and animals. Bigger plants and animals are made up of perhaps billions of cells.

All living things, even the very tiniest, show some organization into different parts for

Paramecium

different purposes. An oak tree has roots, a trunk, branches, leaves, flowers, and seeds. A tiger has a body, head, tail, legs, eyes, ears, and a mouth, to say nothing of the many organs inside its body. Even the paramecium has an opening through which it takes food, and hairlike cilia which drive it through the water.

All living things have much the same needs. They must all have food and water and oxygen.

Chemical changes go on in all living things. Food is used up to furnish energy. New living material is made. Old living material is worn out. Wastes are produced that must be got rid of.

All living things have the power of growth. They all have the power of producing or helping to produce other living things like themselves. They all have some power of movement. True, most plants and some animals stay in one place all their lives, but at least inside every living thing some movement goes on.

All living things, moreover, show change in response to changes that go on around them. The leaves of a sensitive plant fold up if something touches them. A kitten scratches when someone annoys it. A sunflower turns toward the sun. An elephant trumpets if it is frightened.

Clearly all plants and animals are alike in many ways. Strange as it may seem, it is not easy to tell how all plants are different from all animals. In fact, there is no hard and fast way of telling plants and animals apart. Of course, it would be simple to find twenty ways in which a toad is different from a toadstool. But these ways would not hold for all plants and animals.

One of the big differences between a toad and a toadstool is that a toad can hop about, while a toadstool must live its whole life in one place.

But not all animals can move about, while some plants can. A barnacle, for example, lives attached to a rock or something else solid, although it is an animal. A typhoid germ is a plant, but it can move through water by moving its tiny cilia.

A toad has eyes, ears, bones, muscles, and a brain. A toadstool has none of these things. But neither does the tiny paramecium.

A great many plants are green. But toadstools are plants and are not green.

Most animals change rather fast when there is a change in their surroundings. But a sensitive plant is faster than a snail.

The cells of most plants have walls made of a material called "cellulose." As a rule, the cells of animals do not have cellulose walls. But even this difference is not a sure way of telling plants from animals.

How then can scientists be sure whether a living thing is a plant or an animal? In some cases they cannot be. Slime moulds, for instance, are called plants by some scientists and animals by others. For part of their lives they move about and act like animals. Then they stop moving and act much like certain mould plants. There are other puzzling cases. Some living things have the same green colouring in them that all green plants have but are much like animals in other ways.

Such puzzling cases, however, are rather few as compared with all the hundreds of thousands of living things that are clearly either plants or animals. It is as easy to tell whether most living things are plants or animals as it is to tell that a toad is an animal and a toadstool a plant.

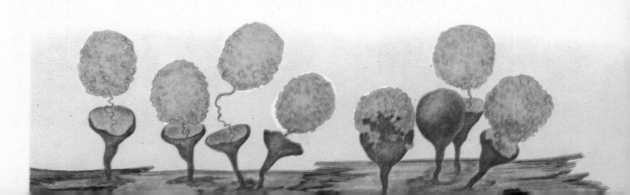

A Slime Mould

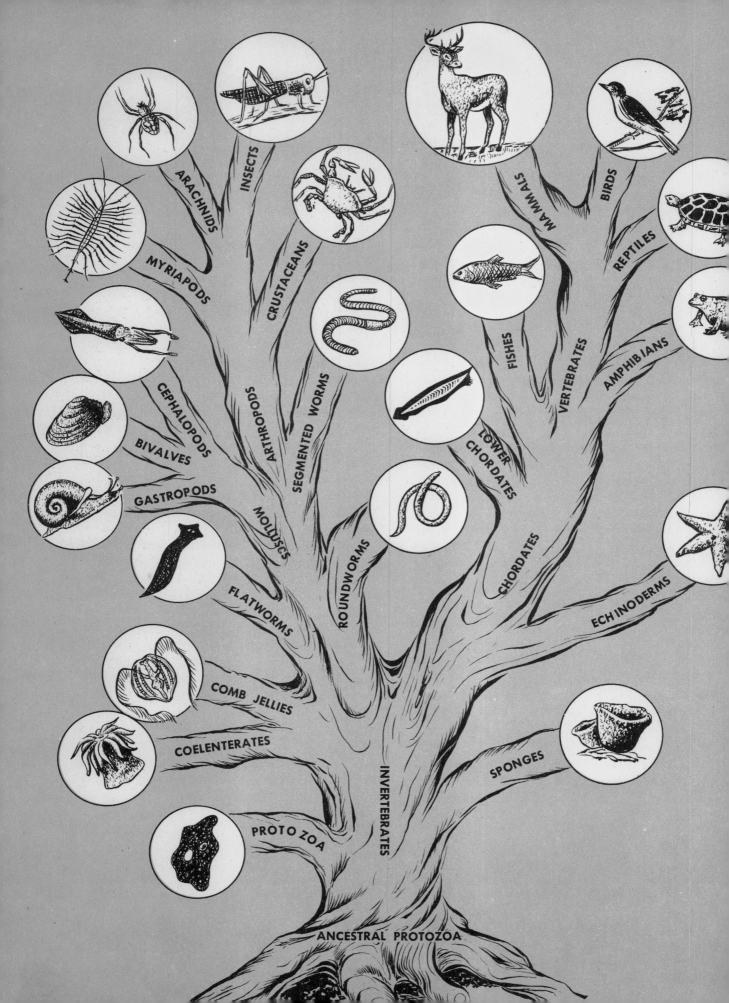

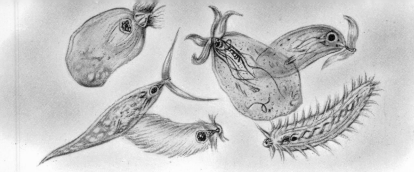

The Animal Kingdom

Lobster

ODAY almost a million kinds of animals are known. There may be many more not yet discovered. Since some animals are microscopic, it is not surprising that new ones are constantly being found.

Scientists, after comparing all the different animals with one another, have worked out a scheme for classifying them. The chief divisions of the animal kingdom are called "phyla." There are about 20 altogether, some made up of little-known animals. Phyla are divided into classes. Classes in turn are divided into orders, orders into families, families into genera, and genera into species.

The Red Admiral butterfly is one kind, or species, of animal. It belongs to the *Vanessa* genus. Every animal has a scientific name that tells its genus and its species. The scientific name of the Red Admiral is *Vanessa atalanta*. The name is a Latin one, as all scientific names are. The name of the Painted Lady butterfly, in the same genus, is *Vanessa cardui*.

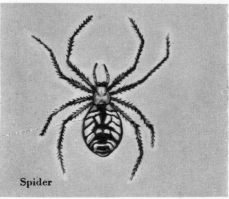

Spider

The Vanessa butterflies belong to the family of brush-footed butterflies. This family is in the order of scaly-winged insects, one division of the class of insects. The insects are a part of the phylum of jointed-legged animals, or arthropods.

Oyster

The chart on the opposite page gives a family tree of the animal kingdom. In this chart the simplest animals are at the bottom, the most advanced at the top. All the animals of today are supposed to have come from tiny one-celled animals of long ago – "ancestral protozoa," they are called.

The vertebrates – the animals with backbones – are the most conspicuous animals on the earth today. But in numbers they are still far, far behind the animals without backbones – the invertebrates. Even though they have lost the high place in the world they held for hundreds of millions of years, animals without backbones make up 95 per cent of all the kinds of animals. The animals pictured on this page are a few of the many invertebrates.

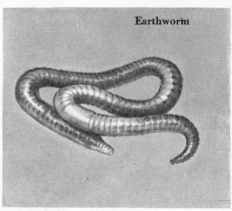

Earthworm

Red Admiral Butterfly

There are five big groups of animals with backbones. They are the fishes, the amphibians, the reptiles, the birds, and the mammals. Their backbones are made up of separate bones called "vertebrae." They get their name of "vertebrates" from these small bones. In addition to their backbones, these animals all have other bones. Their bones make up their skeletons, which form the framework of their bodies and give them their shape.

Three of these big groups of animals are cold-blooded. They must get the warmth they need from their surroundings. In this way they are like the animals without backbones. The three cold-blooded groups are the fishes, the amphibians, and the reptiles. The birds and the mammals are warm-blooded. They get most of their warmth from the burning of the food they eat. They are warm even when their surroundings are cold.

The trout, needless to say, is a fish. Fishes are all water animals. They have fins, not legs. Fishes breathe with gills. A few kinds have additional ways of getting oxygen. Most fishes, but not all, are covered with scales.

The green frog is an amphibian. Amphibians get their name from their life-histories. "Amphibian" means "living in two places." An amphibian, as a rule, starts its life in the water. It gets oxygen from the water with gills, just as a small fish does. It has no legs. Later it becomes an air-breathing creature. It develops legs as well as lungs. This is the general amphibian pattern. The amphibians have no scales. Their skins are bare. As a rule they are moist, too.

The crocodile is a reptile. The word "reptile" comes from a Latin word which means "to creep." Reptiles have short legs, if any. The snakes, which make up one group of reptiles, have none.

Most reptiles are land animals, even though the one pictured spends most of its time in the water. Even those that spend most of their time in the water come up on land to lay their eggs.

Reptiles are built somewhat like adult amphibians, but they differ from amphibians in these two important ways: they breathe with lungs all their lives, and, with very few exceptions, their skins are covered with scales. Contrary to the common idea, the scales are dry, not slimy.

The wood-pigeon, of course, is a bird. Birds can be told from all other animals by their feathers. Birds are truly warm-blooded. The body temperature of some species is as high as 112 degrees Fahrenheit.

All birds are air-breathing. They have lungs all their lives. The first birds had teeth, but the birds of today do not. Instead, they have a gizzard in which their food is ground up.

40

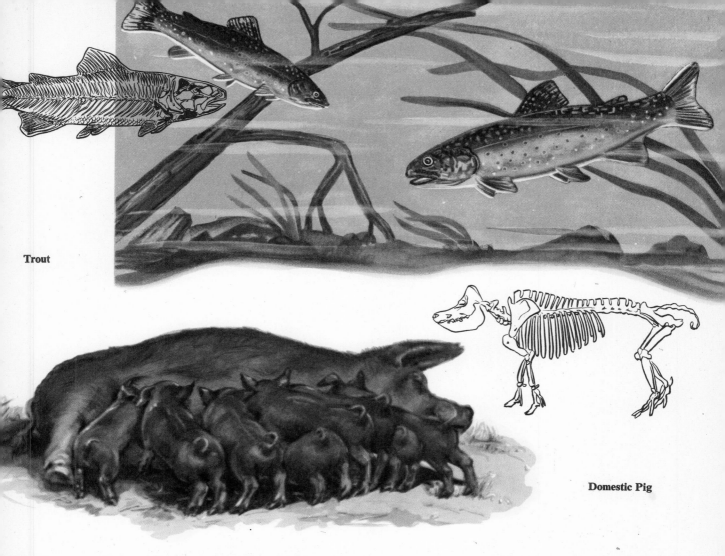

Trout

Domestic Pig

The pig is a mammal. Mammals get their name from their mammary, or milk, glands. All mammals feed their young with milk.

As has already been pointed out, mammals are warm-blooded. They are like the birds in this way. They breathe with lungs all their lives. In this way they are like both the birds and the reptiles. They all have some fur, or hair. Their hair, as well as their milk glands, serves to set the mammals apart from all other animals.

One might expect that each of these big groups of animals with backbones would be called a separate phylum. But in spite of their differences they are alike in so many ways that scientists group them all together in one phylum. The five do not even make up quite all of one phylum. They form a subphylum. The sea squirts and a few other little-known animals are grouped with the vertebrates to form the phylum of chordates. These "lower" chordates have no backbone, but they do have, for at least a part of their lives, a stiff rod down their backs which serves the same purpose. It is called a "notochord." Backboned animals have a notochord in their early stages.

Wood Pigeon

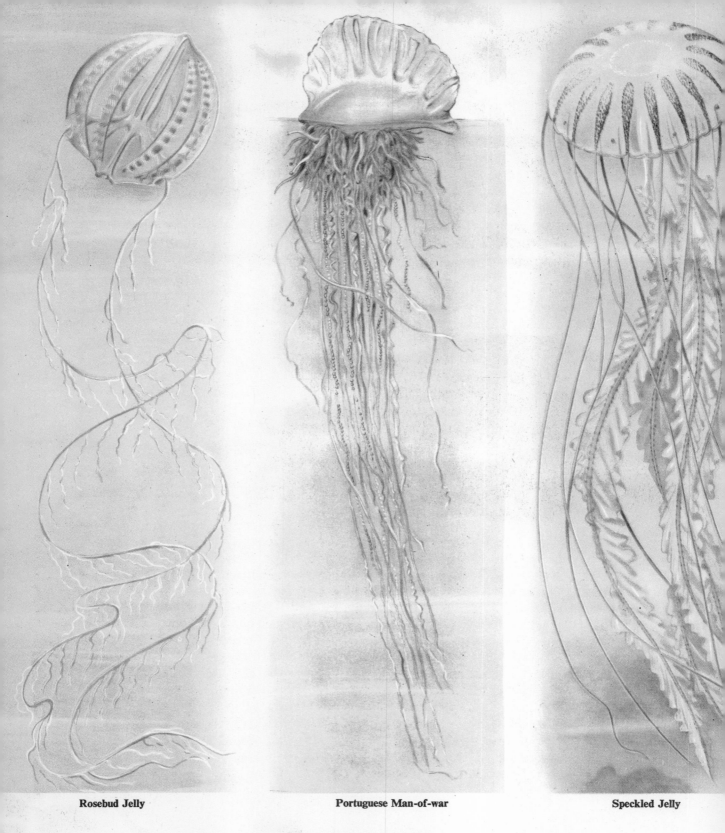

Rosebud Jelly

Portuguese Man-of-war

Speckled Jelly

Animals of the Seashore

THE seashores of the world are the homes of thousands of kinds of animals without backbones, just as they were half a billion years ago.

These animals live where the tides flow in and out and where great waves buffet the shores. Some of them move with the waves and the tides. Some bury themselves in the sand when the tides go out and wait for them to come in again. Some anchor themselves for life to rocks along the shore. A great many animals of the seashore are protected by hard coverings. But others, like the speckled jelly, the rosebud jelly, and the Portuguese man-of-war, have no hard parts at all.

The rosebud jelly is not a true jellyfish. It is one of the little comb jellies. Comb jellies form an important part of the "sea soup" on which many of the larger animals of the ocean live.

Comb jellies get their name from the "combs" with which they swim. These combs are made of tiny plates joined together like the teeth of a real comb. They are arranged in eight rows.

The softly coloured rosebud jelly is pretty at night as well as in the daytime. It shines in the dark.

This small animal catches its prey with its long tentacles. The tentacles are sticky.

The Portuguese man-of-war and the speckled jelly both belong to the group called by the long name of "coelenterates." The Portuguese man-of-war is not a single animal. Instead, it is a whole community of little animals. The little animals are all joined together. But they do not all look alike, and they do not all do the same kind of work. Some of the animals in the community do all the eating and digesting of food. Some act as fishing lines and also protect the colony from enemies. Others are good only for feeling. Still others form eggs.

The "sail" of the Portuguese man-of-war is a small bag filled with gas. It keeps the community afloat.

The Portuguese man-of-war got its name because it reminded people of a tiny battleship as it sailed along. Besides, it has poison darts with which it can kill even large fish. These darts probably made people think of the guns of a battleship.

Most Portuguese men-of-war float out at sea. But during heavy storms some are blown in close to shore. Often the Portuguese man-of-war has some little fish travelling with it. They are called man-of-war fish. These fish would seem to be in danger. But for some reason they are safe from the darts of their companion.

The speckled jelly is one of the many true jelly-fishes. It swims lazily about by opening and closing its umbrella. The mouth of the speckled jelly is on the underside of its umbrella body. Hanging down around its mouth are long, frilly mouth arms. They help the jellyfish catch the little animals it eats. The long feelers, or tentacles, also help the jellyfish catch its food. On them there are many tiny darts filled with poison. When a small animal happens to touch a feeler, it is shot at once with a poison dart. The speckled jelly then eats the animal. Like the rosebud jelly, this jelly-fish glows in the dark.

Graceful forms like the one pictured below are built by tiny animals called sea fans. These little animals do not move about freely; they stay in one place and wall themselves up with lime from the water. When they die they leave their rock houses behind them.

Sea fans are coelenterates just as the jellyfishes and the Portuguese man-of-war are. The corals and the flowerlike sea anemones are in this group of animals, too.

Sea Fan

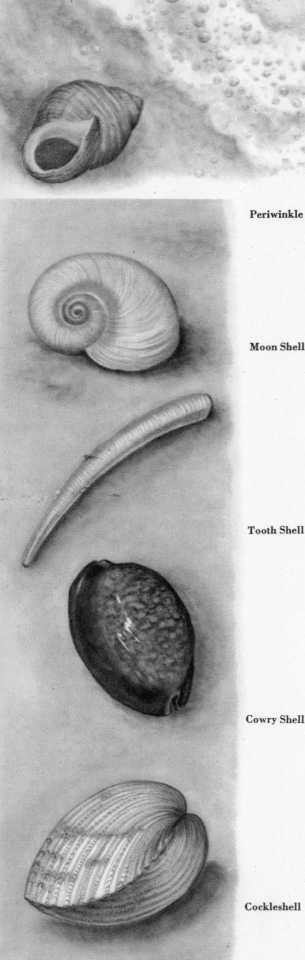

Periwinkle

Moon Shell

Tooth Shell

Cowry Shell

Cockleshell

Many of the animals of the seashore are molluscs. Molluscs get their name from a Latin word meaning "soft." Their bodies are soft; they have no bones of any kind. But almost all of them have hard shells.

The shells pictured here are all mollusc shells. It is clear that different molluscs follow different plans in making their shells.

The moon shell, the cowry, and the periwinkle belong to the group of molluscs called the "gastropods." Their name means "stomach-footed." The gastropods include the snails and their close relatives. They crawl along on a broad foot and carry their shells on their backs. They can pull themselves into their shells for protection.

The shell of a gastropod is all in one piece. Often it is coiled. Since a gastropod's shell has only one part, gastropods are sometimes called "univalves." "Univalve" means "one door."

All gastropods have a peculiar tongue; on it there are many rows of tiny teeth. With its tongue a mollusc of this group can scrape little plants off stones, tear larger plants to pieces, and even drill through the hard shell of another animal.

The tooth shells make up a different group of molluscs. It is not a large group. The tooth shells get their name from the shape of their shells. Tooth shells do not move about after they are full-grown. They live in one spot with their heads buried in sand and only their shells showing.

The cockles belong to a very large group of molluscs called the "pelecypods." "Pelecypod" means "hatchet-footed." The molluscs of this big group are often called "bivalves," for their shells always have two "doors" instead of one. In the group are all the clams, oysters, mussels, and scallops.

These hatchet-footed animals have no heads at all. Neither do most of them crawl about on their feet as the snails do. Instead, they use their feet as burrowing tools. Sometimes they pull themselves along with them.

Shells have been used by many peoples as money. Cowry shells, which are very hard and shiny, and tooth shells are among those that have been widely used. In the early days of America both white men and Indians used strings of shell beads as money. This shell money was called "wampum." Much of it was made from the shells of the hard-shell clam.

For millions of years cephalopods were the terrors of the sea. The chambered nautilus and the squids are modern cephalopods. "Cephalopod" means "head-footed." The head-footed animals make up the third of the main groups of molluscs.

In place of a broad foot, a cephalopod has a number of arms which surround its head. These arms are helpful in gathering in food. As a rule they are equipped with suckers. On their heads the cephalopods have the best eyes to be found among animals without backbones.

Squids are sometimes called "sea arrows" because of their shape. A squid has two fins. By moving these fins it can swim slowly. But it has a way of swimming much faster. Underneath its head it has a tube called a "funnel." The squid can make itself move very fast either forward or backward by squirting water out of this funnel.

Two of a squid's arms are much longer than the other eight. When a squid is after a fish to eat, it darts forward. It catches the fish with its two long arms. It pulls the fish back with these arms until the other arms can catch it and hold it while the squid eats it.

When a squid is trying to escape from an enemy, it usually darts backward. It has another good trick that helps it escape: it squirts out brown ink. Perhaps this ink hides the squid. Perhaps it merely surprises the enemy and lets the squid swim away safely.

The squid has still another way of protecting itself. Its colour changes to match the colour of its surroundings.

The squids along our seashores are less than two feet long. But there are giants 50 feet long. Their suckers are as big as teacups.

The squids have no shells that show in a picture. Buried in their soft body they have only a bit of horny shell. In contrast, the chambered nautilus has one of the most beautiful of all shells. A nautilus shell is made up of many rooms, or chambers. When the nautilus is young, its shell has only one room. As the animal grows larger, it adds one room after another. Finally it has a house of many rooms, but it lives in only the last room it has built.

Another well-known cephalopod, the octopus, has no shell at all. Octopuses are sometimes called "devilfish." The big ones – they may measure 16 feet with arms spread out – are probably as much a terror to their neighbours in the sea as were some of the cephalopods of long ago.

Squid

Chambered Nautilus

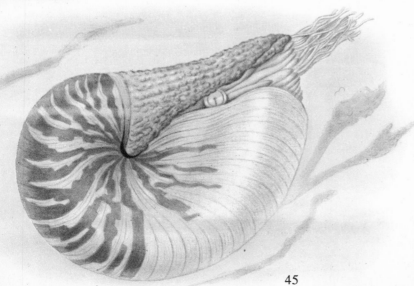

Spider Crab

Fiddler Crab

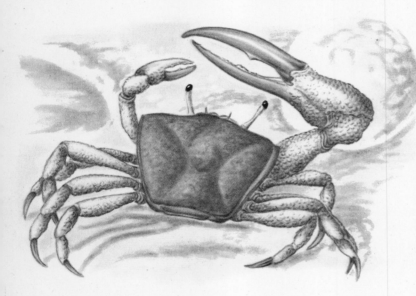

Crabs, shrimps, and lobsters are common animals of the seashore. They are rather closely related: they are all crustaceans. The crustaceans, as the animal tree on page 38 shows, form one of the divisions of the enormous group of jointed-legged animals called "arthropods." The trilobites, the world's leading animals for a hundred million years, were crustaceans.

All the crustaceans have a horny covering. It is quite different from the shells with which the molluscs protect themselves. The hermit crab appears to have a shell, but it simply borrows the shell of some mollusc. The hermit crab in the picture has taken over the shell of a moon snail. This kind of crab needs the protection of a shell. For some reason the back part of its body does not have any armour.

Shrimp

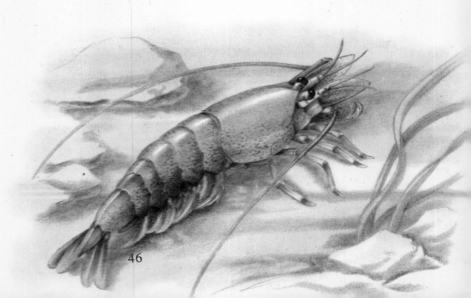

Blue Crab

A crustacean's suit of armour cannot stretch. The crustacean must change its suit as it grows.

All the crustaceans pictured have ten legs. Their two front legs end in stout claws, which are helpful in catching and crushing small animals. All of them have two pairs of feelers and eyes on stalks. They all breathe with gills. Five pairs of legs, two pairs of feelers, stalked eyes, gills, and a good suit of armour make up a common crustacean pattern.

In spite of their likenesses, the crabs are easy to tell from the shrimps and lobsters. They have no tails.

Sea crayfishes look so much like lobsters that it is easy to tell that they are crustaceans. Some crustaceans are not so easily recognized. Among them are the barnacles and the tiny beach fleas.

Hermit Crab

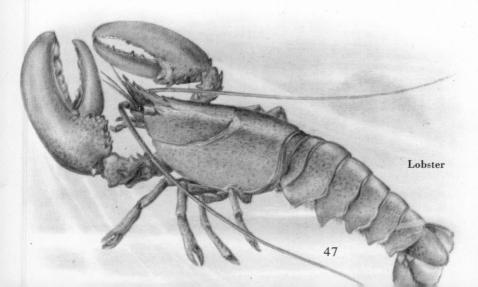

Lobster

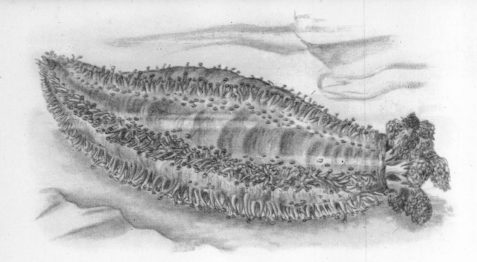

Molluscs furnish large amounts of food. People eat tons of clams, oysters, and scallops every year. Mollusc shells supply materials for pearl buttons. Besides, all true pearls come from clams or oysters. The molluscs would be a hard group for us to get along without.

It goes without saying that the crustaceans are also an important group of seashore animals. Lobsters, shrimps, and crabs are eaten by the million every year.

No one would guess from their looks that the animals pictured on these two pages are quite closely related. But they are all members of the group of spiny-skinned animals called "echinoderms." The echinoderms are far less important to us than the molluscs and the crustaceans. We do not get any food or any other valuable product from them. The best known of the spiny-skinned animals is one not pictured here – the starfish.

Some of the echinoderms have names that are misleading. The starfish is, of course, not a fish; the sea cucumber is not a vegetable; and the sea lily is not a flowering plant.

The animals in this group differ from all other animals in having inside their bodies a system of water canals. These canals are connected with tube feet which, as a rule, end in suction discs. Tube feet are helpful in moving about and breathing. They are also helpful in catching prey. A starfish, let us suppose, comes upon an oyster. It fastens one or more of its arms to each half of the oyster's shell. The suction discs hold its arms tightly to the shell. Then it tries to pull the shell open. At first the oyster can hold its own. But after a time it gets tired. The starfish is then able to pull the halves of the shell apart and eat the oyster.

The sea cucumber has a different way of catching its prey. Although it has tube feet, it does not use them to get its food. This animal is very sluggish. As a rule it waits for its food to come to it. Its mouth is surrounded by many feelers. Tiny animals are caught on them. When a feeler is loaded with food, the sea cucumber puts it in its mouth.

With its feelers the sea cucumber can catch only tiny animals. It has another method of catching prey with which it can catch animals as big as small crabs and lobsters. It throws out a mass of white threads that act as traps. These threads, when they are inside its body, help the sea cucumber breathe.

Sand Dollar

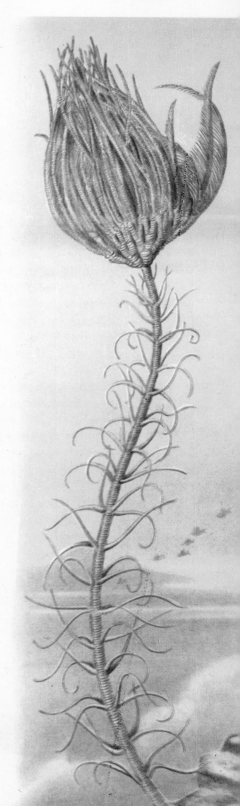

The sea cucumber cannot pull the threads in again after it has used them as a trap. They must grow again inside the animal's body. They soon do; like many of the lower animals, the sea cucumber is able to grow again a part of its body that has been lost or injured. In the same way, a lobster can grow a new claw and a starfish a new arm.

The sand dollar, which gets its name from its shape, lives on sandy sea bottoms in sheltered places. It moves about on its tube feet. If a sand dollar is turned over, it can turn a somersault to get right side up again. A sand dollar's spines are fine. They make the little animal look as if it were made of velvet. Its skeleton is made of lime. It gives the sand dollar its shape.

The sea urchin has a limy skeleton, too. A sea urchin's skeleton may be very pretty. The sea urchin shows more clearly than any other animal in the group how the echinoderms got their name. Its spines are conspicuous. These spines are sharp. A sea urchin may grind itself a home in a rock with its spines. You may have seen fossil sea urchins in chalk cliffs and cuttings.

The sea lily, like its relatives back in the days of the trilobites, anchors itself to rocks and stays in one place. It must wait for its food to come to it. The "flower" at the top of the stalk is made up of feelers with which it can catch small animals that come near.

Echinoderms have no heads or tails. A sea urchin or a sand dollar may move forward with any part of its circular body in front. These animals are built on what might be called a wheel plan, rather than on a two-sided plan. All the markings on their skeletons go out from the centre like the spokes of a wheel. All grown echinoderms are built on the same kind of plan. They are like the jelly fishes and comb jellies in this way. But, strangely enough, young echinoderms are not built on a wheel plan. They are two-sided, like all the higher animals. They are very much like the young of the simplest of the chordates, the big group of which the animals with backbones are a part.

Many animals of the seashore have quite close relatives that live in the fresh water of ponds and streams. There are, for instance, fresh-water crabs, clams, snails, and crayfishes. But there are no fresh-water echinoderms. All the echinoderms live in the sea.

MOON MOTH

Insects

IN the world today there are so many kinds of insects that some people think that this time in which we are living ought to be called the "Age of Insects" instead of the "Age of Man." More than half of all the species of animals are species of insects. There are about 600,000 kinds of insects in all.

It is not easy to get an idea of what as large a number as 600,000 means. Suppose the scientific names of all the kinds of insects were printed on a strip of paper one after another in type the size of the type in this book. The strip of paper would have to be 15 miles long! Suppose someone set out to learn about insects by studying a different one every day. He would have to live to be nearly 2,000 years old to study them all! Suppose, as another way of trying to get an idea of what 600,000 means, one were to picture a parade of all the kinds of animals in the world, with one kind of animal going by every minute day and night. The whole parade would last for nearly two years. It would take a year and a month for the insects to go by.

There are not only many kinds of insects; there are also many insects of a kind. A single tree may have 20 million plant lice on it. A swarm of gnats may be made up of hundreds of thousands of gnats. At times there are plagues of grasshoppers. If all the people on the earth were scattered evenly over the land, there would be about 50 people for every square mile. If the insects were scattered evenly, for every square mile there would be about 25 million! Insects thus outnumber people about half a million to one.

The insects form one division – of course, the largest – of the jointed-legged animals, or arthropods. Sometimes insects are called "hexapods." "Hexapod" means "six-legged." The name is a good one, for all insects have six legs. The commoner name "insects" comes from the word "incised," which means "divided." An insect's body is divided into three parts – the head, the thorax, and the abdomen.

In addition to having three pairs of legs and three body regions, all insects are alike in having one pair of feelers, or antennæ. They all have a covering of a remarkable substance called "chitin." Chitin is waterproof. It is very light, and it bends without breaking. Most of them have compound eyes – eyes made up of many tiny eyes. Most of them, moreover, have wings. Winged insects, as a rule, have two pairs of wings. But some have only one pair.

Insects can be told fairly easily from animals of other groups. But there is a great deal of variation, as the pictures on these two pages show, among the insects. Scientists have divided them into many orders. For example, termites belong to the order Isoptera, beetles to the Coleoptera, grasshoppers to the Orthoptera and mantids to the Mantodea. In some scientific lists you would find some of these orders combined. Many scientists, for example, put both the praying mantids and the stick insects in the order with the grasshoppers.

The moon moth, as its name tells, is a moth. Some people consider this the most beautiful of all insects. Its other popular name "luna" comes from the Latin word for "moon."

CRICKETS

KATYDIDS

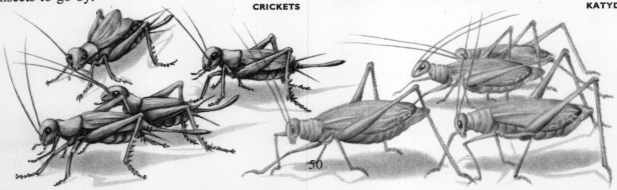

FIREFLY

The firefly is a beetle. It lives mainly in hot countries, and only its relation the glow-worm is found in the British Isles. The insect can turn its glow off and on so that the flashes are like tiny flashes of lightning. Fireflies have the secret of giving off light without giving off heat – at least heat enough to be noticeable. Scientists would like very much to have their secret of "cold light."

In the parade below there are five kinds of insects: crickets, katydids, grasshoppers, stick insects, and ladybirds. Ladybirds are beetles.

Insects live in more different kinds of places than do the animals of any other one group. By far the greater number of insects are land animals, but there are many insects in the fresh water of lakes and streams. Insects are not common in salt water, but even there there are some.

There is almost no place on land that is not well stocked with insects. The seashores and the mountains, the forests and the prairies, the hot lands near the Equator and the cold lands near the Poles have their insect populations. In the short Arctic summer myriads of mosquitoes appear, as big and vicious as any in the tropics.

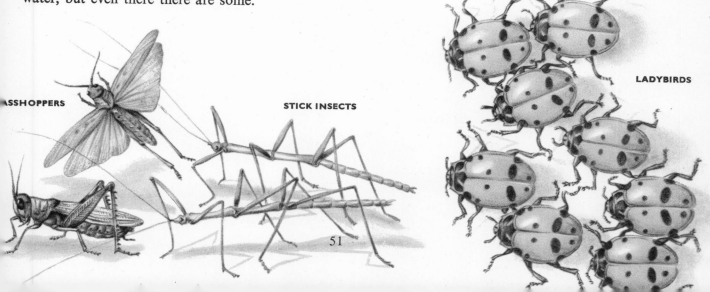

ASSHOPPERS

STICK INSECTS

LADYBIRDS

51

MUD DAUBER
WASP

The scientific names of many orders of insects end in "ptera." This ending means "wings." Wings are a big help in identifying insects.

The scientists' name for the moths and butterflies is Lepidoptera. The name means "scaly-wings." The wings of all moths and butterflies are covered with tiny scales that look like powder when they are rubbed off. The Camberwell Beauty butterfly does not look scaly. The separate scales are too small to be seen without a microscope.

The mud dauber wasp and the honeybee both belong to the Hymenoptera – the "membrane-winged" insects. The giant water bug illustrated here is a member of the Heteroptera, the "different-wings." But the British great water beetle is a member of the true beetle family, the Coleoptera or "sheath-wings."

The name for the order which includes the flies, gnats, and mosquitoes is Diptera. "Diptera" means "two-wings."

Every insect, to whatever order it belongs, has to have oxygen and food. Insects are like all other animals – like all other living things – in this way.

Most insects have a system of tubes which carry air to all parts of their bodies. The air comes in through tiny openings called "spiracles." Some insects have special breathing devices which fit their particular way of living. When young, for example, mosquitoes live in water and breathe through tubes which extend above the water.

The food of the many thousands of kinds of insects includes almost every variety of plant and animal material. Their mouth parts fit different insects for eating different kinds of food. The grasshopper, which eats leaves, has biting mouth parts. Its jaws grind up the plant material bitten off. In contrast, the giant water bug has sucking mouth parts. It has a stout beak which serves to make a hole in whatever this insect has captured for food.

The food of the four insects pictured here gives some idea of the variety of food insects eat. The water bug lives on small water animals. It captures tadpoles, snails, other insects, and even small fish. The mud dauber, which is a kind of wasp, is a meat eater when it is young, but becomes a "vegetarian" later. In its "babyhood" it eats almost nothing but spiders. The parent mud daubers provide spiders as food for their young. The mud dauber builds a nest of mud. In each room in the nest it lays an egg. Then in each room it packs a spider or two to be ready for the young wasp when it comes out of the egg. Adult wasps live on nectar, the sweet juice found in many flowers.

Honeybees eat honey made from the nectar of flowers and beebread made of nectar and pollen, the yellow dust found in flowers.

When young the Camberwell beauty butterfly eats the leaves of elm, poplar, or willow trees. When fully grown, it, too, lives on nectar. Clearly, a great water beetle would starve on the food a Camberwell beauty eats, and the other way round.

GIANT WATER BUG

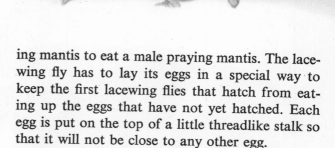

There is a race between people and insects for every bit of food that is raised. In a big field of sweet corn there is a great deal of food for people. But insects may get to the corn first and eat it up before people have a chance to eat it. The insects do not care whether the ears of corn are ripe or not. They may eat them while people are waiting for them to ripen. Every wormy apple or peach or pear, every weevil-eaten sack of flour or box of biscuits, and every jar of jelly damaged by ants means that insects won the race.

Every part of a forest tree may furnish food for some kind of insect. Some insects may drink the sap of the tree. Others may eat the leaves, the bark, the young twigs, or the roots. After the tree has been cut down, there are insects ready to eat both the green and the dried timber.

In the same way, there may be several different kinds of insects eating a cotton plant at the same time. There may be insects eating the young pods where the cotton is, others sucking the sap of the plant, others eating its leaves, others eating its roots, and still others eating its stalks.

Fur, woollen goods, and blood – these are a few of the other things insects eat. People spend a fortune every year putting their furs and woollen clothing in cold storage so that clothes moths will not damage them. No one needs to be told that mosquitoes suck blood. Many people do not know, however, that only the adult female mosquitoes live on blood. The male mosquitoes live on plant juices. Young mosquitoes live on tiny water plants and animals. Anyone who has a pet dog or cat knows how carefully dogs and cats have to be guarded against fleas, which are also blood suckers.

Some insects live part of their lives inside the bodies of other insects. An insect may, for example, lay its eggs inside the body of a fat caterpillar. When the eggs hatch, the young insects eat the caterpillar's body. The caterpillar, of course, dies.

Some insects are cannibals. They eat up one another. It is not at all unusual for a female pray-

ing mantis to eat a male praying mantis. The lacewing fly has to lay its eggs in a special way to keep the first lacewing flies that hatch from eating up the eggs that have not yet hatched. Each egg is put on the top of a little threadlike stalk so that it will not be close to any other egg.

The fact that some insects eat different food when they are young and when they are grown suggests that insects – at least some of them – change greatly as they grow up. They do. In fact, learning the names of the insects around us is complicated by the fact that young insects may bear almost no resemblance to the adults of the same kind. One might recognize a young grasshopper from knowing the adult, but certainly not a mud dauber wasp, a honeybee, or a Camberwell beauty butterfly.

CAMBERWELL BEAUTY BUTTERFLY

CECROPIA MOTH

The beautiful insect pictured above is a Cecropia moth. The Cecropia is one of the silk moths. The pictures on the opposite page show stages in the life-history of this insect.

The female Cecropia lays her eggs on the leaf of some plant. The moth is not particular, but she may very well choose the leaves of an apple tree or a cherry tree.

The eggs hatch into tiny black caterpillars, or larvæ, as scientists call them. A Cecropia caterpillar does not look in the least like a full-grown moth. It shows no signs of wings or feelers. It has six short legs close to its head, but it also has several false legs on which it crawls along. Its body is clearly divided into many parts, or segments. The caterpillar's skin is studded with little bumps, or tubercles.

Each caterpillar, or larva, begins at once to stuff itself with leaves. It grows fast and is soon too big for its skin. Its skin cannot stretch and has to be shed. Shedding one skin and getting another is called "moulting."

The black skin splits down the back, and out comes the caterpillar in a dull-orange skin. The young insect keeps on eating and growing and soon has to shed its orange skin.

The caterpillar's third dress is yellow. Some of its tubercles are brightly coloured. By the time it is dressed in yellow, the caterpillar is more than an inch long and can be seen very easily. But it is not nearly full-sized yet. It changes its skin twice more. After both moults it is green. In its final stage it has blue, red, and yellow tubercles. At least in colouring it is a handsome creature.

Of course, the caterpillar has to breathe while it is growing. It breathes just as most adult insects do – through spiracles. Almost every segment of its body has a pair of spiracles.

A full-grown Cecropia caterpillar is more than three inches long and is as big round as a person's finger. After it reaches its full size the caterpillar stops eating. It begins spinning a long thread of silk from its mouth. It winds this thread of silk round and round itself. At last the caterpillar is so well wrapped up that it cannot be seen at all. The moth is now no longer in its larva stage. It has become a pupa.

The silken case the caterpillar spins for itself is a cocoon. The caterpillar, as it makes its cocoon, fastens it firmly to a small branch or twig. The cocoon is even more cleverly made than it looks to be at first glance. At one end there is a weak spot, or door, through which the moth can push its way when it is ready. It is amazing that every Cecropia caterpillar "knows" enough to spin its cocoon with a door. Of course, it does not do any thinking about the matter. It inherits its way of making a cocoon, just as it inherits the beautiful colours of its wings.

The pupa stage of a Cecropia is often called its "resting stage." But really great changes are taking place inside the silken cocoon. The caterpillar is changing into an adult moth.

A Cecropia usually spends the whole winter in its cocoon. In the spring it pushes its way out. When it first comes out its big wings are crumpled and moist. But soon the moth pumps a liquid into its wings so that they spread out. Soon, too, they dry. The emerging of a Cecropia from its cocoon is a really wonderful sight.

By the time it emerges from its cocoon a Cecropia's life is almost over. It eats nothing at all. Shortly it finds a mate. After eggs are laid, both the male and the female die. They have started a new generation on its way.

The life-history of the Cecropia can really be told in four words: egg, larva, pupa, adult. The life-histories of many, many kinds of insects are made up of these same four stages. We say that these insects show "complete metamorphosis." "Metamorphosis" means "change."

All moths go through a complete metamorphosis. So do all butterflies, beetles, bees, wasps, ants, flies, mosquitoes, and others besides.

We have different common names for the larvæ of different kinds of insects. The larvæ of many beetles are called "grubs." The larvæ of flies are called "maggots." The larvæ of mosquitoes are called "wrigglers" or "wiggle-tails." And so on.

The pupa stage of an insect goes by different names, too. The pupa of a butterfly, for instance, is often called a "chrysalis."

After insects that have four stages in their life-histories reach the fourth stage, they do not grow. Many people who see big flies and little flies during the summer think that the little flies have simply not had enough time to grow big. This idea is wrong. Any fly one sees flying about is as large as it will ever be. In the same way, as soon as a moth, a butterfly, a beetle, a bee, or a wasp has wings, it has reached its full size.

LIFE HISTORY OF
THE CECROPIA MOTH

pupa

larva, or caterpillar

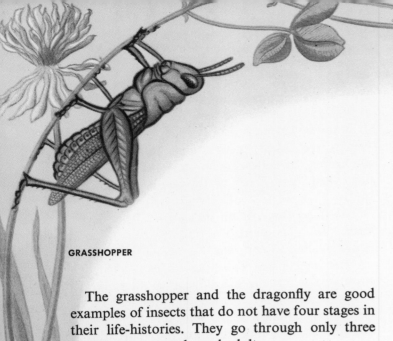

GRASSHOPPER

The grasshopper and the dragonfly are good examples of insects that do not have four stages in their life-histories. They go through only three stages – egg, nymph, and adult.

With her egg-laying organ – an "ovipositor," it is called – a female grasshopper lays a cluster of white eggs in a hole she makes in the ground or in rotten wood. She packs her eggs in the cavity very neatly, from 20 to 200 of them.

Little grasshoppers that look much like their parents hatch from the eggs and crawl out of the cavity. There are two big differences between these young grasshoppers, or grasshopper nymphs, and their parents. They are much smaller, and they have no wings.

As each nymph grows, it moults five or six times. When, after a few weeks, it changes its skin for the last time, it is full-grown and has two pairs of strong wings. Many people are surprised to find that a grasshopper has two pairs of wings. Only one pair shows unless the grasshopper is flying. The second pair is folded up under the pair that shows. The pair that folds up, as the picture of the flying grasshopper on page 51 shows, is larger than the first pair.

A full-grown grasshopper has one pair of long, strong legs. Even the youngest grasshopper nymph has back legs that are much longer and stronger than its four other legs. These back legs are excellent for jumping. They help the insect make the hops that give it its name.

A grasshopper has a pair of feelers, as all insects have. It has compound eyes just as most insects do. It has also, in between its compound eyes, three simple eyes. It has, besides, a way of finding out what is going on around it that few insects have: it has ears. Clearly, a grasshopper's ears are not in the usual place. Instead, they are under the insect's wings.

Grasshoppers do not have voice boxes of any kind in their throats, but the sound grasshoppers make is well known. The grasshoppers make this sound either by rubbing their two hind legs together or by rubbing a leg and a wing together.

As has been pointed out, grasshoppers are leaf-eating insects. They have jaws strong enough to chew even tough leaves. They eat tender leaves when they can get them, but they do not go hungry just because there are no tender leaves to be had. When a grasshopper is eating a leaf, it usually holds the leaf between its two front feet.

A grasshopper has two habits that anyone who watches grasshoppers soon learns to know. It keeps itself well groomed by cleaning itself up often. It "washes" its face with its front legs. It cleans each feeler by holding it down on the ground with one foot and then pulling it out from under the foot. It cleans its legs by rubbing them together.

Its second habit is less pleasant. At times it spits a brown liquid out of its mouth. This liquid is often spoken of as "tobacco juice." The "tobacco juice" has an unpleasant taste. Probably it helps protect this insect from birds that might otherwise relish a grasshopper dinner.

The grasshopper in the picture is a short-horned grasshopper. Its feelers are much shorter than its body. There are long-horned grasshoppers, too. Another name for this short-horned grasshopper is "American locust." Many people, when they hear the name "locust," think of the seventeen-year locust. That insect is not a real locust. A better name for it is "cicada."

GRASSHOPPER NYMPHS

The adult dragonfly has several nicknames. "Devil's darning needle" and "snake doctor" are two of them. Its long, slender body explains why it should be called a darning needle. With its needle-shaped body, however, the dragonfly never pricks or stings. Why it should have "devil" in its nickname and why it should be called a "snake doctor" are puzzles.

This insect begins its life in the water of some pond or stream. The female lays her eggs in the water. She may simply drop them in the water. She may fasten them to some plant.

The eggs hatch into nymphs that, unlike grasshopper nymphs, do not look at all like their parents. No one would guess from seeing a dragonfly nymph crawling up a plant in the water that it would grow up to be one of the handsomest of insects, with beautiful gauzy wings.

The most remarkable part of a dragonfly nymph is its lower lip. This lip is long and, queer as it sounds, jointed. The young insect hides in plants growing under water. When something the nymph might eat swims or floats by, out goes the long lip. As a rule it catches the bit of food and brings it back to the insect's mouth.

The dragonfly nymph grows and moults just as the grasshopper nymph does. But it grows up rather slowly. It remains in the water for two or three years. All the while it is in the water its lower intestine acts as a gill to take oxygen out of the water.

After two or three years under water, the dragonfly nymph climbs up above the surface. It sheds its skin for the last time, spreads its silvery new wings, and flies away – a full-grown dragonfly. In the picture a discarded skin is clinging like a ghost to a water plant.

A full-grown dragonfly is remarkable not only for the beauty of its wings but also for its huge eyes. Almost all insects have compound eyes, but the dragonfly has especially large ones. Each eye is made up of about 30,000 tiny eyes.

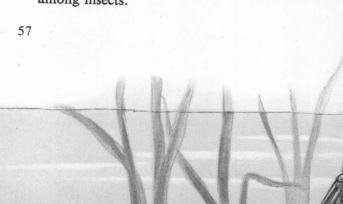

DRAGONFLY

The dragonfly does not lose its appetite when it emerges as an adult. It darts through the air, catching insects as it goes. It catches and eats many flies, gnats, and mosquitoes.

Many other insects have life-histories much like those of the grasshopper and the dragonfly. They show incomplete metamorphosis. Some of them change rather gradually to their adult form as the grasshopper does. Some change suddenly as the dragonfly does. But they do not have a stage that corresponds to the pupa of the insects with complete metamorphosis.

A few kinds of insects are born alive. The female keeps the eggs inside her body until the eggs grow into young insects. Some plant lice, for instance, are born instead of hatched. When they are born, they look very much as they do when they are full-grown. But such a life-history is not at all common among insects.

57

DRAGONFLY NYMPHS

MONARCH BUTTERFLY

CLOUDED YELLOW BUTTERFLY

Almost everyone can call some moths and butterflies by name. Those pictured on these two pages are not all well known, however.

On the British list there are about 70 kinds of butterflies and about 2,000 kinds of moths. Moths, therefore, outnumber butterflies, at least as far as kinds are concerned, nearly thirty to one. But moths, as a rule, fly by night, when they are not so likely to be seen, while butterflies flit about in the daytime. Most people feel better acquainted with butterflies than with moths.

There are several helps in telling whether a scaly-winged insect is a butterfly or a moth. Moths have rather thick bodies; butterflies have more slender ones. Moths usually rest with their wings spread out. Butterflies, when resting, usually fold their wings together so that they make a kind of sail above them. More helpful still, butterflies have clubbed antennæ – their antennæ, that is, are swollen into knobs at the ends. Moths do not have clubbed antennæ. Their feelers may look like feathers as those of the Cecropia moth do. They may, on the other hand, be plain. But they do not have clubs.

The scaly-wings differ greatly in size. They range, when full-grown, from a wingspread of only about half an inch to a wingspread of more than six inches. The largest moths are larger than the largest butterflies.

All moths and butterflies have four stages in their life-histories. They are all caterpillars when

COMMA BUTTERFLY

BLUES

SWALLOWTAIL

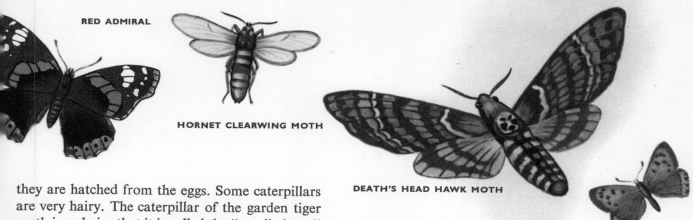

RED ADMIRAL

HORNET CLEARWING MOTH

DEATH'S HEAD HAWK MOTH

AMERICAN COPPER

they are hatched from the eggs. Some caterpillars are very hairy. The caterpillar of the garden tiger moth is so hairy that it is called the "woolly bear." The woolly bear with its thick brown coat is a pretty caterpillar. Some other caterpillars are pretty. But some are ugly. Some are so ugly that their looks may serve to protect them from their enemies.

The monarch butterfly of America is often called the "milkweed butterfly." It gets its name because the female often lays her eggs on the leaves of a milkweed. The caterpillars feed on milkweed leaves. The chrysalis of this butterfly is beautiful. It is green with golden dots. It has been called the "green house with golden nails."

Our swallowtail is one of many swallow-tails. They get their name from the projections on their back wings. The caterpillar of the tiger swallowtail has a false face. This face is on the third and fourth segments of its body. When the caterpillar needs to defend itself, it tucks its head under its body so that its false face, with two horns, appears to be its real face. Birds have been seen to fly away as if they were frightened when they got a glance at its false face.

The blues, the coppers and the bordered white get their names from their colour.

The clouded yellow is also named after its colour. Both this butterfly and the red admiral fly to England across the Channel. In 1941 so many clouded yellows arrived on the south coast that in places they carpeted fields like patches of yellow flowers.

The comma butterfly has a white mark on the underside of its wings, very much like a comma in appearance. You can see it in the picture.

The hornet clearwing moth looks like a real hornet, and so it escapes its enemies, who think it is a dangerous insect.

The two big moths in the pictures are both hawk moths. The death's head is so called because of the skull pattern on the back of its head. The privet hawk moth has earned its name because its caterpillars feed on privet leaves.

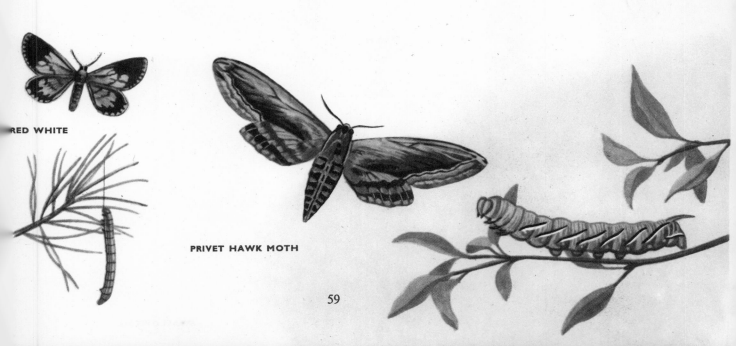

RED WHITE

PRIVET HAWK MOTH

Hawk moths appear even on bright summer days. They hover over honeysuckle or a favourite flower like some tiny humming-bird, while their long proboscis searches the flower for nectar.

There are a great many harmful insects. A common term for them is "insect pests." They harm us in different ways. Many of them are our enemies simply because they eat food that we want for ourselves or keep plants from producing the food we need. There are crop pests, orchard pests, garden pests, and insects that eat stored food. Some insects do great harm to our shade trees and forest trees. Some ruin buildings we have built and clothes we have made.

The most dangerous of our insect pests are those that carry disease. High on the list of these public enemies are mosquitoes of certain kinds. Malaria and yellow fever are two of the diseases they carry. In Britain the common housefly is not only a nuisance; it is also dangerous because it carries tuberculosis and typhoid germs. Some parts of Africa are almost empty of people because of the tsetse fly, which carries sleeping sickness. Fleas and body lice both carry typhus, a disease that may flourish in areas with little sanitation.

So many insects harm us that many people think of all insects as our enemies. To them, simply saying "It's a bug" is a legitimate excuse for killing any insect on sight. But we have many good friends among the insects, too.

Some insects help us by eating insect pests. The dragonfly eats many mosquitoes. The ladybird eats many plant lice. The praying mantis is such an enemy of harmful insects that some plant nurseries abroad have praying mantis eggs for sale.

Many insects are an enormous help, too, by visiting flowers and carrying pollen, the yellow dust found in flowers, from one flower to another. By carrying pollen they help seeds and fruits to form. Without insect pollen-carriers we would have no apples, no peaches, no clover seed – the list could be made long.

We get very valuable products from some insects. Honey and silk are probably the two most important. But shellac, which is widely used, is made from secretions of the lac insects. The red pigment, carmine, comes from the cochineal insect. And some insects furnish useful drugs.

As a rule only savages or semi-savages eat insects, but some insects have high food value. Carpenter ants, grasshoppers, water boatmen, and termites are among those that are eaten in different

BUMBLEBEES

GRASSHOPPER

parts of the world. The Arabs eat honeydew, the sweet secretion of certain tiny desert insects.

There are some important insect scavengers. Stable flies, ants, and burying beetles are among them. They eat up much dead animal matter and waste.

Some insects help us fight weeds. If a certain kind of insect eats a plant we want, it is an enemy. If it eats a weed, it is a friend. When the prickly pear cactus was introduced into Australia it spread rapidly and was soon a troublesome weed. As a way of fighting this weed, insects that feed on it were shipped to Australia. They were a great help.

Some insects have been good "guinea pigs" for scientists. One kind of fruit fly has been used very successfully in the study of heredity.

Of course, the insects that are our friends do not deserve any credit for being helpful. Neither do those that harm us deserve any blame for the damage they do. The insects are simply living their own lives. It happens that in living their lives some of them make things we want or help us in other ways. It happens that others, in living their lives, interfere with ours.

There were no insect pests and no insect friends before men lived on the earth. In the great Coal Age, for example, there were cockroaches five inches long. But they were not pests, for there were no people for them to interfere with. The first honeybees were not insect friends, for there were no people for them to help. When we think of insects as being friends or enemies, we are being selfish. We are thinking of ourselves and of how the insects help or harm us.

But we really cannot be unselfish in thinking of insects. They are our greatest rivals. To hold our own we have to carry on a never-ending fight against our insect enemies.

The four insects pictured on these two pages are evenly divided between friends and enemies. Bumblebees are important pollen-carriers. Our silk comes from the cocoons spun by the larvæ of the silkworm moth. The grasshopper attacks crop plants. The cabbage butterfly, when it is a caterpillar, eats cabbage. The cabbage butterfly is one of the few black sheep among the butterflies. Most butterflies are helpful or at least not harmful. We have a great many more enemies among the moths.

One of the pests most feared by Britain is the Colorado potato beetle. So far this creature has not established itself in our islands. It is really a stranger to Europe, as its true home is in North America. It first spread to France and later reached many parts of Europe, where it now ruins potato crops whenever it appears in large numbers. Sometimes one or two are found on this side of the Channel, but farmers are always on the watch to stamp out this pest whenever it shows itself.

CABBAGE BUTTERFLY

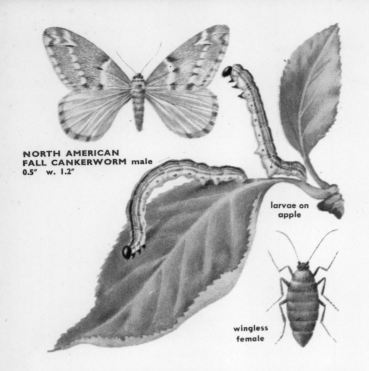

NORTH AMERICAN
FALL CANKERWORM male
0.5" w. 1.2"

larvae on
apple

wingless
female

The insects pictured on these two pages are among the pests that attack garden and crop plants both here and abroad. Some are more important than others. But we could do very well without them all.

It goes without saying that many ways of fighting our insect enemies have been worked out. But fighting insects is not easy. They are well protected by their covering of chitin.

We can set traps for some kinds of insects. A band of cotton around the trunk of a tree acts as a trap for caterpillars that try to climb the tree. It is one way of fighting the tussock moth, a serious enemy of oaks and other trees. A band of sticky gum around a tree trunk serves the same purpose. There are light traps that attract some

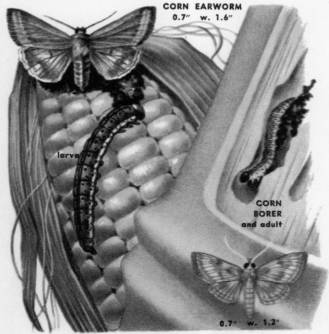

CORN EARWORM
0.7" w. 1.6"

larva

CORN
BORER
and adult

0.7" w. 1.2"

night-flying insects. Trenches filled with oil trap others. One has to know a great deal about an insect and its habits before one can plan a good trap for it. The army worm, which is the larva of a moth, gets its name because it moves in great armies from one field to another. A trench filled with oil is a good trap for a marching army of army worms. It would be of no use in fighting mosquitoes.

Removing breeding places is an excellent way of fighting some insects. It makes better sense to try to keep them from multiplying than to kill them after they are at work against us. Draining swamps is one way of lessening mosquitoes. Breaking up soil by ploughing helps keep down the numbers of the Hessian fly, a serious enemy of wheat. Clearing away garbage and manure piles takes away the chief breeding places of the common housefly.

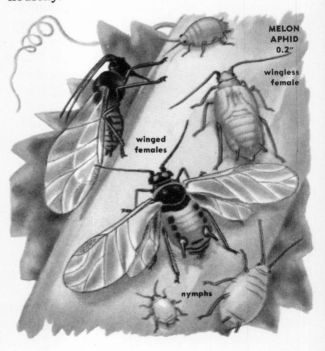

MELON
APHID
0.2"

wingless
female

winged
females

nymphs

Chemicals are widely used in fighting insects. No one chemical is helpful in fighting all kinds of insect pests. The chemicals used can be divided into two groups: stomach poisons and contact poisons.

As its name suggests, a stomach poison must reach the insect's stomach if it is to do the insect any harm. A contact poison need not be eaten by an insect. It does its work when it comes in contact with the outside of an insect's body. It may harm the insect by stopping up its breathing pores. It may eat its way into the insect's body through thin spots in the chitin.

Chewing insects such as the corn earworm can best be fought with stomach poisons. Sucking insects such as the aphids are more easily killed with contact poisons.

Unfortunately, insects build up a resistance to chemicals used in fighting them. DDT, when it was first used, was thought to be the final answer to many of our insect problems. It has killed many insects of many kinds, but there are now strains of the same kinds of insects that are not affected by it. The makers of insecticides must be constantly at work developing new ones.

Inside buildings poison gas is sometimes used instead of liquid or powdered poisons. The use of poison gas to kill insects is called "fumigation."

A region in which there is a serious insect pest is sometimes quarantined to keep the pest from spreading. The Mediterranean fruit fly was kept from spreading from Florida by quarantine. Of course, no one person can manage a quarantine. It has to be set up by a government.

One of the very best means of fighting insect pests is to encourage their natural enemies. Birds are among the natural enemies of insects. We should have done more than we have to encourage birds that are insect eaters. Frogs, toads, lizards, snakes, and certain fishes are other insect eaters of importance. A small minnow, for example, is now being raised and shipped far and wide over the earth as a way of fighting mosquitoes. Some insects are very successful in keeping down other insects. Praying mantis eggs, it has already been said, are sold by some nurserymen abroad. A kind of ladybird beetle brought from Australia saved the California orange orchards when it looked as if the cottony cushion scale would completely ruin them.

Developing plants and animals that can better stand the attacks of insects is another hopeful way of fighting insect pests. Changing crops often in a field – crop rotation – is still another way. But the problem of holding our own against our insect enemies is so big that every once in a while someone asks the question, "Will the insects win?"

Long ago people learned to live in groups. They learned to help one another and to divide up the kinds of work to be done. Far, far longer ago some kinds of insects learned to live in groups, to work together, and to divide up the work to be done. The insects which form groups in which there are both co-operation and division of labour are called "social insects."

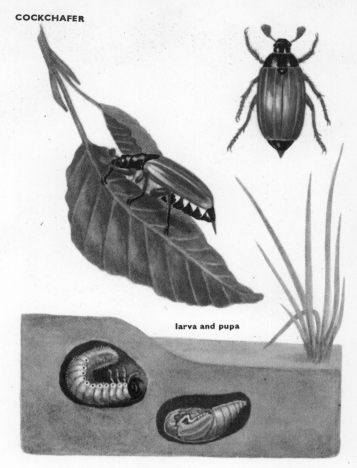

COCKCHAFER

larva and pupa

COLORADO POTATO BEETLE

larva

adult
0.4"

eggs

STRIPED BLISTER BEETLE 0.7"

ANTS:

queen

male

worker

Many animals are social to some extent. Wolves hunt in packs and kill animals too big for a single wolf to kill. Beavers work together to build dams that would be out of the question for a single beaver. These animals co-operate. But they do not divide up among themselves the different jobs to be done. Only people and the social insects are really social.

All the insect societies are to be found among just four groups of insects. They are the wasps, the bees, the ants, and the termites.

Not all wasps are social. Some are solitary — that is, they have not formed themselves into societies. The sand wasp is a solitary wasp. The paper wasp, on the other hand, is social. Its colonies, however, are small. A colony is made up of the queen, a female that lays eggs, a few male wasps, and a number of worker wasps. The workers are females that do not lay eggs. They find food and take care of the queen and the young wasps. The different kinds of individuals in an insect society are called "castes." There are three castes in a society of paper wasps.

There are three castes in a colony of honeybees, too – the queen; the males, or drones; and the workers, females that do not lay eggs. But a hive of honeybees is far larger than a colony of paper wasps. There may be as many as 80,000 workers. Unlike the paper wasps, many of the workers in a hive, as well as the queen, live through the winter. They live on the honey they have stored up.

The making of honey is complicated. It involves several different kinds of work – hunting for flowers, gathering nectar from them, building comb, filling it with honey made from the nectar, and capping the cells to seal the honey in. There are many housekeeping chores to be done in a hive, too. Among them are taking care of the queen bee, keeping the hive clean, ventilating it by fanning fresh air in, feeding the baby bees, and mending any cracks that appear in the hive. Worker bees also protect the hive from intruders. They have good weapons – stings. But if a worker has to sting an enemy, she is giving up her life for the group. For she cannot pull out her sting, and without it she dies.

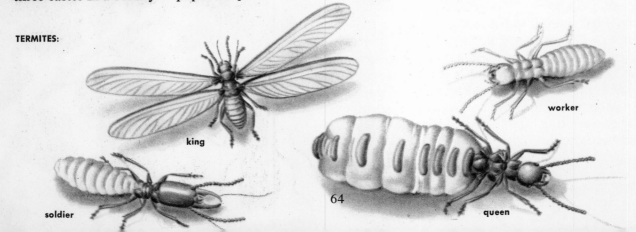

TERMITES:

king

soldier

worker

queen

64

Bumblebees are social, too, but their societies are simple. There are seldom more than 500 workers. Only queen bumblebees live through the winter. There are some solitary bees, just as there are solitary wasps.

All ants are social. Some live in rather simple societies. But some are very complex.

In many ant societies there are several castes of workers. In some there is a special caste called "soldiers." As one would guess, their work is to protect the colony from enemies that attack it. They have especially powerful jaws.

Among the most interesting ants are the army ants and the fungus-growing ants.

Army ants move about in large armies. They eat other insects. They move slowly, searching for food beneath the litter on the floor of a forest. When the trail is rough, the workers make it smooth by filling in the hollows with their own bodies. When there is a gap in the trail, worker ants hang on to one another and build themselves into a bridge over the gap. When an army stops to rest, the workers may even build themselves into a nest with many rooms. When the army is ready to move on, the walls fall apart to become the separate workers that formed them.

Fungus-growing ants raise gardens of fungus plants that are much like tiny mushrooms. They cut leaves and bring them to their gardens for the fungus plants to feed on.

Some ants have domesticated animals, among them "ant cows." The "cows" are aphids, or plant lice. The ants take care of the aphids. They protect them from their enemies. The aphids in turn give off honeydew when the ants stroke them with their feelers. The ants eat the honeydew.

PAPER WASP

All termites are social, too. The castes of the termites differ in one way from the castes of wasps, bees, and ants. All the workers among the wasps, bees, and ants are females that do not lay eggs. The workers among the termites, even the soldiers, are some male and some female.

The biggest colonies of termites make even the biggest colonies of ants seem small. A single termite colony may have several million workers in it. A termite queen has been known to lay 8,000 eggs in one day. It is no wonder that the colonies are large. It is no wonder either that such an egg-laying machine has a large body.

In some ways an insect society is far ahead of a community of people. Every individual that is old enough to work has work to do; there is no unemployment. Every insect knows exactly how to carry on its work in the community; it does not have to be taught. There are practically no quarrels between members of the group. But neither is there any freedom. We like our own societies, in spite of their faults, much better.

HONEYBEES:

queen

worker

drone

Spiders

SPIDERS are often called insects. But their eight legs show that they are not. Instead, they are arachnids. To this group also belong the mites, ticks, scorpions, and daddy-long-legs. The spiders are no more closely related to the insects than they are to the centipedes and millipedes.

The number of legs is by no means the only way of telling spiders from insects. An insect's body is divided into three regions, a spider's into only two. Insects have feelers, or antennæ; spiders have none. Most insects have two big eyes made up of many little eyes. Many of them have simple eyes, too. Spiders have only simple eyes. As a rule they have eight. Insects have jaws; spiders do not. A spider has to have food soft enough to be sucked up. At each side of a spider's small mouth there is a poison fang. At each side, too, there is a "feeler-leg," or pedipalp. Most spiders have spinnerets. Many young insects can spin silk from their mouths, but full-grown insects cannot spin silk.

There is still one more way in which spiders are different from insects. Most insects have wings. No spiders have.

There are thousands of kinds of spiders. They differ greatly in size. The picture of the golden garden spider is greatly enlarged, but there are some big hairy spiders called "tarantulas" that are really as large as the spider in the picture. Spiders differ in colour and shape, too. But the strange long-legged harvestman is not a true spider, although the others pictured with him are.

Spiders are scattered far and wide over the earth. There are the most different varieties in the warm lands near the equator. But there are many kinds that live where it is cold, some in the Far North and some on mountain-tops. Some spiders are more common in buildings than out of doors. The common house spider – the spider to blame for most of our cobwebs – is one of them.

Most spiders are land animals. But there are some water spiders. The fresh-water spider carries air down to a silken sac under the water so that it can breathe there. For all spiders are air breathers. They do not, however, all breathe the same way. Some have air tubes inside their bodies. Some have book lungs, air sacs filled with thin flaps of skin. Many spiders have both air tubes and book lungs.

Spiders eat only the juices of living animals. Insects are the commonest spider food. But large spiders near water may eat tadpoles or even small fish. One big tarantula is well named the "bird-catching spider." The webs they spin help many spiders get food. Their poison fangs help, too.

All spiders come from eggs. A female spider may lay more than a thousand eggs at a time. As a rule she spins a silken case for them. When little spiders hatch they look like full-grown spiders except that they are smaller and are very pale. There is never any food for baby spiders inside the egg case. At times little spiders turn cannibal and eat one another.

Many people think of spiders as enemies to be killed on sight. Actually most of them are harmless, and some are very useful. Spider silk is used in telescopes and other scientific instruments. It is fine and smooth and is stronger than steel wire of the same size. Some spiders kill harmful insects. There are a few poisonous spiders, among them the black widow and some of the tarantulas. But there are so few that spiders have been called the most unfairly treated of all groups of animals.

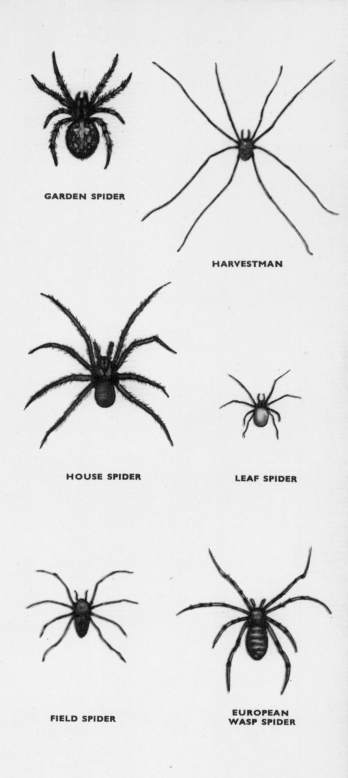

GARDEN SPIDER

HARVESTMAN

HOUSE SPIDER

LEAF SPIDER

FIELD SPIDER

EUROPEAN WASP SPIDER

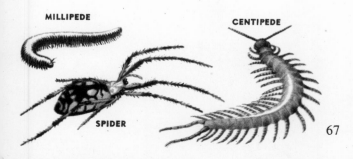

MILLIPEDE

CENTIPEDE

SPIDER

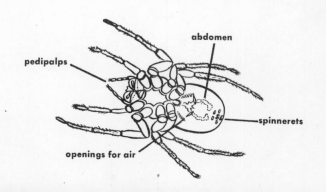

pedipalps

abdomen

spinnerets

openings for air

Fishes

Swordfish (1/40)

To many people any animal that lives in water all its life is a fish. For this reason names with the word "fish" in them have been given to many water animals that are not really fish. The jellyfish, starfish, crayfish, and cuttlefish are not real fishes. Neither are the many kinds of shellfish. All these animals are invertebrates.

Even though there are many "fish" that are not fish, there is great variety among the fishes. The black bass is a typical fish. It has two pairs of fins which correspond to the legs of a four-legged animal, an unpaired, almost-divided fin on its back, one under its body near its tail, and one on its tail. Just behind its head are its gill covers. They protect the gills with which it breathes. It has the shape which we usually think of as the fish shape. But all the other animals pictured here are fishes, too. Clearly, fishes may differ greatly in appearance.

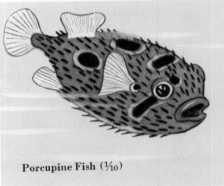

Porcupine Fish (1/10)

The saying "as lost as a fish out of water" is sound; all fishes are water animals. But a few fishes, while they are not fitted for living on land, can take short excursions out of water. The flying fish, for instance, can leap from the water and sail through the air for hundreds of feet. The mudskipper often crawls up on land or on the root of a tree and lies with only the end of its tail in the water. Out of water it cannot breathe with its gills, but it can get oxygen from the water through the skin of its tail.

In contrast with most fishes, the sea horse swims head up. It also has a tail very different from the tails of other fishes. Its tail can be twisted around the stem of a plant. The sea horse differs from most fishes in still another way: the male fish has a pouch on its stomach in which it carries the eggs the female lays.

Flying Fish (1/5)

Some fishes have conspicuous ways of protecting themselves. The "sword" of a swordfish is an excellent weapon. The porcupine fish has spines all over it. It also protects itself by puffing itself up when an enemy comes near. The sting ray has a sharp dart on its long tail. Some fishes have armour—bony scales that make a good protection. But hundreds of kinds of fishes have no armour and no weapons. Moreover,

Sea Horse (1/2)

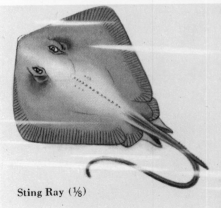

Sting Ray (1/8)

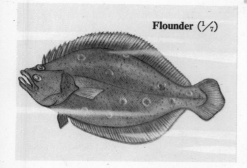

Flounder $(\frac{1}{7})$

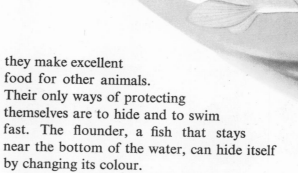

Black Bass $(\frac{1}{3})$

Angler $(\frac{1}{12})$

Goatfish $(\frac{1}{6})$

Hammerhead Shark $(\frac{1}{60})$

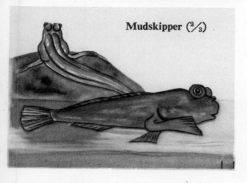

Mudskipper $(\frac{2}{3})$

they make excellent
food for other animals.
Their only ways of protecting
themselves are to hide and to swim
fast. The flounder, a fish that stays
near the bottom of the water, can hide itself
by changing its colour.

Even though some fishes when they are full-grown have good ways of protecting themselves, little fish are almost defenceless. They are, moreover, such good food for other water animals and for larger fishes, too, that a baby fish does not have a very good chance of growing up. It is easy to see, then, why some fishes lay millions of eggs at a time.

Some fishes are meat eaters. Others are plant eaters. The black bass is one of the meat eaters. It may eat animals as large as snakes. No one knows whether fishes have a sense of taste. But at least some of them appear to have a keen sense of smell. They have nostrils which they use only in smelling. Probably they choose their food chiefly by smell.

Three other senses help fishes tell what is going on around them. All fishes have eyes. As a rule a fish has one eye on each side of its head. Most fish can never see the same thing with both eyes at the same time. But there are exceptions. The flat-fishes, of which the flounder is one, swim on their sides and have both their eyes on the upper side. Deep down in the sea it is very dark. Some of the fishes there have "lanterns" that may help them see. The angler is one of the fishes that carry a "lantern." It is on the rod that extends out from the fish's head. It glows just as a firefly glows in the dark. The hammerhead shark has its eyes in a queer place, as the picture shows. The eyes of all fishes are alike in one way. They are always open. Fishes have no eyelids.

Many fishes have a very good sense of touch. Some of them have feelers. The goatfish is one. Its feelers hang down from its chin and help it explore the bottom of the sea.

Almost all fishes have ears of a kind, but their ears do not show. They are buried deep in their heads. Probably fishes hear very little.

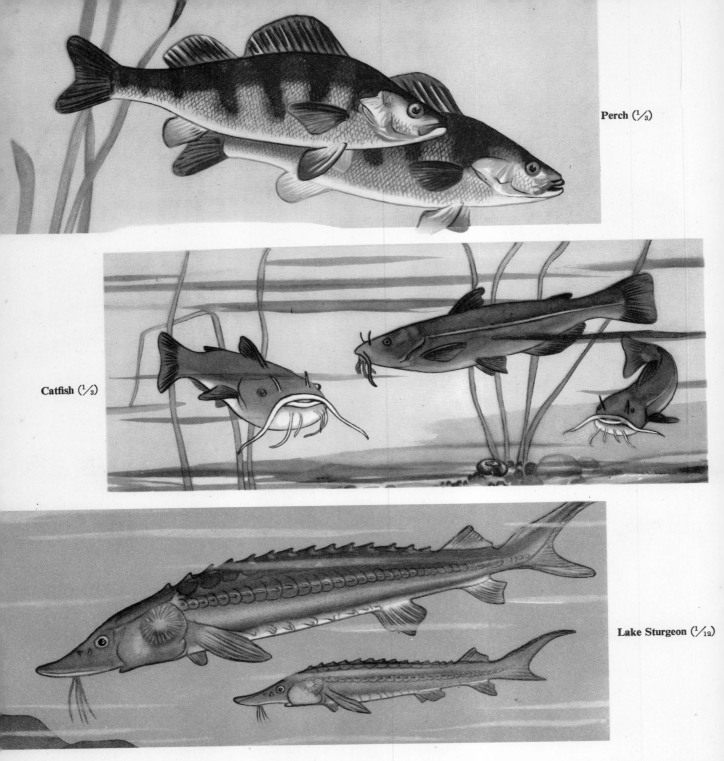

Perch (1/3)

Catfish (1/3)

Lake Sturgeon (1/12)

"He can swim like a fish" is high praise for a swimmer. For most fishes are wonderfully built for swimming. Their tails make good oars for pushing their streamlined bodies forward. Their other fins help them keep their balance and guide themselves. Swim bladders – air-filled sacs inside their bodies – make it easy for them to go up or down as they please in the water. To sink, a fish expels some of the air from its swim bladder. To rise, it forces more air into it.

The fishes pictured on these two pages, except perhaps the eel, are easily recognized as fishes. But they can readily be told from one another. And they would never all be found in the same body of water. The perch, lake sturgeon, and catfish are fresh-water fishes. The cod and herring are salt-water fishes. The eel spends part of its life in fresh water and part in salt water. It travels from coastal rivers far out to sea to lay its eggs.

70

Herring

Eel (⅕)

Cod (⅙)

The perch is so common in lakes and streams that it is sometimes called "everybody's fish." The perch, the herring, and the cod are all built on the typical fish plan. The lake sturgeon is a reminder of the fishes of ancient times. Its scales are bony, as were the scales of many ancient fishes. In contrast, the catfish has no scales at all. The eel is rather snakelike. The cod is different from the other fishes, in being able to live only in cold water.

All of these fishes are good food fishes. Some of them are in danger of disappearing because so many have been used as food. Of them all the cod is perhaps the most important. It has made the Atlantic near Newfoundland one of the greatest fishing regions in the world. And the North Sea provides us with great harvests of fish. Millions of herrings are caught there annually by trawlers, which travel as far afield as Norway and Iceland in search of their huge shoals.

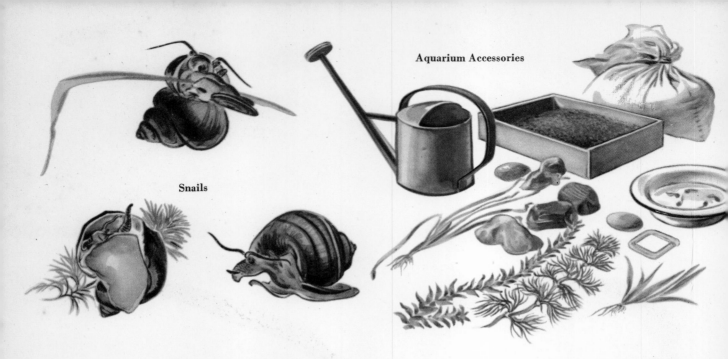

Snails

Aquarium Accessories

Aquariums are now very popular in homes. Many kinds of fishes can be kept successfully in them. The secret of having a good aquarium is to have an aquarium tank that is large enough for the number of fish one plans to keep, to have plenty of green plants in it, and to have enough snails or other scavengers to keep the aquarium clean.

If there are plenty of green plants and scavengers, the water does not have to be changed often. The plants are important because, when they are in the sunlight, they use up carbon dioxide and throw away oxygen. Fish, like all animals, are constantly using up oxygen and throwing away carbon dioxide. Plants in the water help to keep it fit for the fish by keeping the carbon dioxide content low and the oxygen content high.

Among the most popular fishes for aquariums now are tropical fishes such as guppies, swordtails, angelfish, and zebra fish. They are small, interestingly coloured, and fun to watch. Many of these tiny tropical fishes are live-bearing. The female, that is, keeps the eggs in her body until the young fishes develop from them. One problem in raising these tiny live-bearing fishes is to keep the adult fishes from eating up the young. An aquarium for live-bearing fishes should have plenty of plants to afford hiding places. Keeping the water warm enough during the winter months and providing the right kind of food may be problems in keeping tropical fishes, too.

The goldfish is by far the most popular of all our aquarium fishes. Goldfish may now be bought in a great variety of colours. They may be bought with bulging "telescope" eyes and with very long, flowing tails. They may be bought with scales or

Assembling an Aquarium

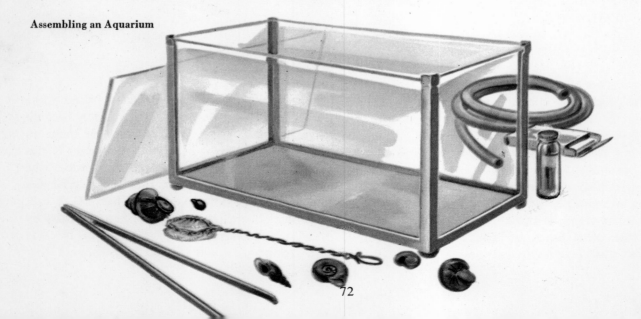

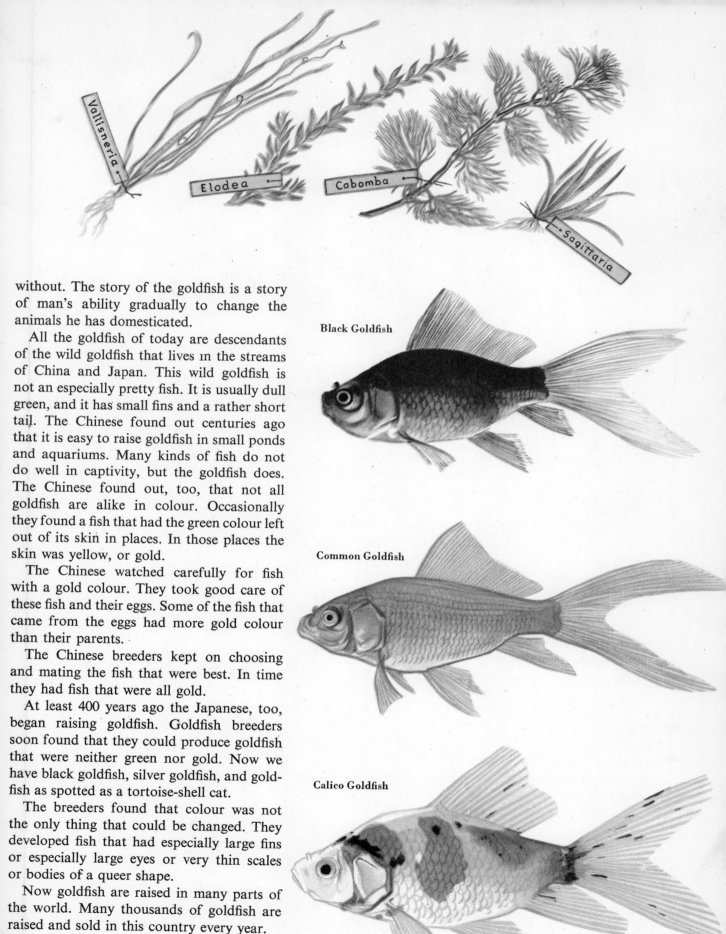

Vallisneria

Elodea

Cabomba

Sagittaria

Black Goldfish

Common Goldfish

Calico Goldfish

without. The story of the goldfish is a story of man's ability gradually to change the animals he has domesticated.

All the goldfish of today are descendants of the wild goldfish that lives in the streams of China and Japan. This wild goldfish is not an especially pretty fish. It is usually dull green, and it has small fins and a rather short tail. The Chinese found out centuries ago that it is easy to raise goldfish in small ponds and aquariums. Many kinds of fish do not do well in captivity, but the goldfish does. The Chinese found out, too, that not all goldfish are alike in colour. Occasionally they found a fish that had the green colour left out of its skin in places. In those places the skin was yellow, or gold.

The Chinese watched carefully for fish with a gold colour. They took good care of these fish and their eggs. Some of the fish that came from the eggs had more gold colour than their parents.

The Chinese breeders kept on choosing and mating the fish that were best. In time they had fish that were all gold.

At least 400 years ago the Japanese, too, began raising goldfish. Goldfish breeders soon found that they could produce goldfish that were neither green nor gold. Now we have black goldfish, silver goldfish, and goldfish as spotted as a tortoise-shell cat.

The breeders found that colour was not the only thing that could be changed. They developed fish that had especially large fins or especially large eyes or very thin scales or bodies of a queer shape.

Now goldfish are raised in many parts of the world. Many thousands of goldfish are raised and sold in this country every year.

73

Bullfrog

Amphibians

THE bullfrog is a typical amphibian. Its life-history shows how the amphibians got their name.

Early in the spring a female bullfrog lays her eggs in the water near the edge of a pond or a quiet stream. Each egg is surrounded by a layer of clear, tough jelly. This jelly holds the eggs together. There are so many of them that they form a pancake some two feet across.

As soon as they are laid, the eggs begin to develop. Each egg elongates till it is bean-shaped. One end is larger than the other. The larger end will become the head; the smaller, the tail.

In about a week the eggs hatch. A tiny tadpole wriggles out of each jelly covering. The tadpole is less than half an inch long. It has no eyes and no mouth. There are tiny bumps where the eyes are going to be. Instead of a mouth, it has a sucker which enables it to hold on to the jelly it wriggled out of. Its tail looks much like a fish's tail.

Very soon tiny fringes grow out of the sides of the tadpole's head. These are gills for breathing. A tadpole is truly a water animal.

By the time it is a day old, the tadpole can swim a little. But whenever it runs into a stick or a plant it holds on by means of its sucker and rests for a while.

In two or three days the tadpole has eyes and a mouth. Now it can see where it is going. It can nibble tiny plants off the stones and sticks in the water, too.

The tadpole's body soon bulges out so that it is much bigger in proportion to the tail. The baby amphibian looks less like a little fish.

The tadpole's sucker completely disappears. Its gills, too, disappear from sight, although the tadpole still has them. Skin grows over them.

To breathe, the tadpole takes gulps of water into its mouth. The water passes over its gills. Then it goes out through a little hole on the left side of the tadpole's body. This hole is called the "breathing hole."

The tadpole eats a great deal. It eats mostly tiny green water plants. Sometimes it eats scraps of food left by the bigger animals that share the pond or stream.

In time two legs begin growing out from near the base of the tadpole's tail. In a few weeks these legs are long and strong.

Inside the tadpole's body front legs now begin to develop. The left one pushes its way out of the tadpole's body first. It comes out through the breathing hole.

Soon afterward the right front leg pushes its way out. The tadpole has become a four-legged animal. But it still has a long tail.

Other changes are now going on in the tadpole's body. Lungs are developing; the tadpole is on its way to being an air-breathing animal. Its mouth is changing, too; it is getting much wider, and a long, sticky tongue is developing inside it.

While its mouth is changing, the tadpole cannot eat. It has to live on its tail. Its tail gradually shrinks as the food in it is absorbed in the tadpole's blood and carried to the part of the tadpole's body where it is needed. The tadpole's tail serves the same purpose as a camel's hump.

The tadpole's eyes become much more bulging. They take on the look which we associate with the eyes of toads and frogs.

Before its tail has completely disappeared, the little frog takes excursions out of the water. With its long tongue it now catches insects. It has become a meat eater at the same time that it has become an air-breathing animal. The little frog has developed a voice by this time, and its croak mingles with the voices of its neighbours in the pond or stream.

The young bullfrog finally loses its tail completely. It has the shape it will keep for the rest of its life. Now it begins growing fast. It grows so fast that it has to shed its skin several times.

At last the frog is really an adult frog. It is ready to mate and start many thousands of new bullfrogs on their way.

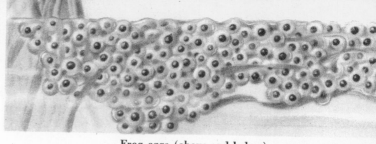
Frog eggs (above and below)

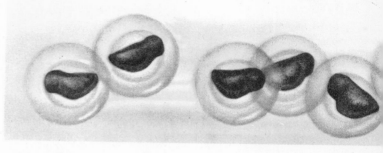

Newly hatched tadpole

Tadpole with hind legs

Tadpole with four legs

Frog, tail disappearing

75

It may take as much as four years for a bullfrog to grow up. Its growing up is interrupted by winters spent in the mud at the bottom of the pond.

This story of the life-history of a bullfrog makes the life of a bullfrog seem much safer than it is. Actually very, very few of the eggs a female bullfrog lays go through all these stages and become adult frogs. Tadpoles have many enemies. They furnish food for many of their neighbours in the water.

The frogs and their very close relatives, the toads, are to most people the best known of the amphibians. They are sometimes spoken of as the tailless amphibians since, when they are full-grown, they have no tails. Their life-histories, as a rule, are very much the same as the life-history of the bullfrog. But in many cases some of the stages last for a much shorter time. Many frog and toad tadpoles get their four legs and lose their tails during their first summer.

In addition to the frogs and toads, there are two other groups of amphibians: the newts and salamanders, and the legless caecilians. Newts are common in our country, but we have no salamanders. Both these amphibians have legs and tails when they are full-grown. Caecilians are found chiefly in tropical regions. They have no legs and practically no tails. They look like big earthworms.

Newts and salamanders, when they are first hatched, look much like tadpoles. They grow up in much the same way that toads and frogs grow up. The axolotl, however, although it belongs to the group of newts and salamanders, is an exception to the usual amphibian plan of life. It never becomes an air-breathing animal. It lives under water all its life and never loses its gills. They make conspicuous red fringes at its neck.

Although most amphibians are able to live on land for part of their lives, they cannot stand extreme dryness. They have no protecting scales or fur or feathers; their skins are bare. They must stay close to water or moist places. The part of their lives they spend in water is spent in fresh water. There are no marine amphibians.

Like fishes, all amphibians are cold-blooded. Those that live in regions of cold winters, as many of them do, protect themselves from the cold by hibernating.

European Fire Toad

Edible Frog

Green Tree Frog

Midwife Toad

Red Salamander

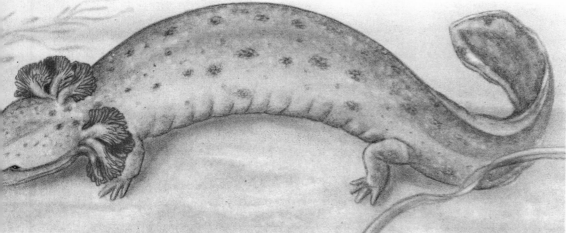

Axolotl

Smooth Newt

There are only a very few kinds of amphibians that do not lay their eggs in water. In the cases of those few kinds, the early stages are passed inside the egg. One kind of amphibian – a kind of salamander – is live-bearing.

Most amphibians take little care of their eggs after they are laid. But here, too, there are exceptions. The midwife toad – the male – winds the long string of eggs the female lays around his body. He carries them with him until they hatch, never letting them get dry. At hatching time he stays in the water. There are other such cases in which the eggs are carefully guarded.

Amphibians vary greatly in size. They go from the tiny tree frogs such as the little green tree frog, shown in the picture, to the giant salamander of Japan. But not even the giant salamander is much of a giant. It is only about two feet long. The largest amphibians of today are much smaller than some of their ancestors back in the Age of Coal.

Toad

Toad Croaking

Fowler's Toad

Wood Frog

Frogs and toads are so much alike that it is not easy to tell them apart. The kinds pictured illustrate the general differences between toads and frogs. Frogs have soft, moist, smooth skins. Most toads have tough, dry skins covered by little bumps that are often spoken of as warts. Frogs as a rule are slender; toads have broad bodies. Toads look clumsy. Their front legs are very short. Frogs look much more graceful.

When they are moving, frogs are certainly more graceful. They move much faster, too. A difference that does not show in the pictures is that frogs have small teeth, while most toads have none.

Leopard Frog

All frogs and toads are meat eaters. When they are eating such a tasty morsel as an earthworm, they may use their front feet to help push it into their mouths. Their tongues are a big help in catching their food. They have tongues that are fastened in the front, not at the back as ours are. A toad or frog can flip out its long tongue, catch an insect on its sticky surface, and bring it back into its mouth. These amphibians will catch nothing that is not moving. They will, therefore, not eat dead animals.

When a toad or frog swallows its food, it closes its eyes. Closing its eyes helps it to push food from its mouth into its stomach. For closing its eyes means pulling its big bulging eyes inward.

Frogs and toads have big appetites. A toad may eat 50 insect larvæ at a single meal.

Many of the insects and other animals toads and frogs eat are harmful to us. For this reason, among others, they deserve our protection.

The croaking of toads and frogs is a familiar sound. The croaking is done by the males. Each male has a vocal sac. He fills this with air. Then he pushes the air out past his vocal cords.

The warts on toads are not like the warts people sometimes have on their skins. They are small glands. When an enemy comes near, these glands give off a milky fluid. This fluid is poisonous to some animals. It is likely, for example, to make a dog sick.

Most amphibians must depend on hiding, jumping away, or blowing themselves up to protect themselves from their enemies. The leopard frog is one that puffs itself up when it is caught. The wood frog can turn itself around in mid-air when it is jumping away from an enemy. It lands facing its enemy. Many amphibians find it easy to hide because their colours are so much like those of their surroundings.

There are some queer superstitions about amphibians. One is that handling toads causes warts. Another is that salamanders can stay at the centre of a fire. There is no truth at all in either superstition about these creatures of two worlds.

Reptiles

THE great days of the reptiles are over. They ended millions of years ago, when the last dinosaurs died. But there are still about 5,000 kinds. The reptiles of today are in four groups: the turtles, the alligators and crocodiles, the lizards and snakes, and, all by itself in one group, the rare tuatara.

Turtles can be told by their shells. No other reptiles have shells. All turtles do. There are fresh-water turtles, sea turtles, and land turtles.

The little painted turtle is a pond turtle, or fresh-water turtle. It spends part of its time in water and part out of water. Since it breathes with lungs, as all reptiles do, it must be out of water to breathe. But, strangely enough, it cannot swallow any food unless its head is under water. The painted turtle is sometimes called the "painted terrapin."

The snapping turtle is another fresh-water turtle. It gets its name from the way it snaps at anything that disturbs it. It has no teeth – no turtles have any teeth – but its jaws are sharp enough to bite off a person's finger.

Turtles that live on land all their lives are often called "tortoises." Tortoises are famous for their slow movement; almost everyone has heard the fable of the hare and the tortoise. They are also famous for their long lives. Some giant tortoises live to be more than 100 years old. These tortoises earn their name of "giant." They may weigh more than 500 pounds.

The gopher tortoise is a medium-sized tortoise found in the New World. It lives in dry, sandy regions. The box tortoise can pull in its legs, head, and tail and shut itself up completely in its shell. The lower part of the box tortoise's shell has a hinge across it.

The green turtle lives in the sea. Its legs, as the picture shows, are shaped like paddles. Sea turtles do not come out of the water except to lay their eggs. Green turtles are caught for food in some countries. A full-grown turtle furnishes a great deal of food, for it may be four feet long and weigh as much as 400 pounds.

Alligators and crocodiles are our largest reptiles. The longest measure about 20 feet. These big reptiles look much alike, but alligators have broader heads and rounder snouts. Both alligators and crocodiles spend most of their time in the water. They have webbed feet, but they do not use their feet in swimming.

80

Painted Turtle (⅓)

Gopher Tortoise (¹⁄₄)

Box Tortoise (²⁄₅)

Green Turtle (¹⁄₁₂)

Giant Tortoise (¹⁄₁₅)

Alligator Hatching

Alligators and crocodiles eat nothing but meat. They have strong jaws and sharp teeth.

The eggs of alligators and crocodiles have hard shells. Every young alligator or crocodile has a point on its head that helps it break out of its shell. This point is called an "egg tooth."

Alligators and crocodiles have very tough skin. It can be used to make beautiful leather for bags and shoes. So many of these big reptiles have been caught that there is danger that they will be killed off. Some alligators are now being raised on alligator farms.

The tuatara, the reptile that is in a group all by itself, looks somewhat like a lizard. It lives nowhere in the world except on some small islands near New Zealand. This little reptile is sometimes called a "living fossil." It has been on the earth for many millions of years – since before the days of the dinosaurs. The tuatara lives in burrows in the ground. But usually it does not make its own burrows. As a rule it lives in those made by a bird called the "petrel." A petrel and a tuatara share the burrow.

The tuatara is being carefully guarded. People do not want this living fossil to disappear.

They swim with their tails. Thick folds of skin over their ears shut out the water when the alligators and crocodiles are below the surface.

The nostrils and eyes of an alligator or a crocodile stand up from its face. The reptiles often lie with only their eyes and nostrils above water. They are under water, and yet can breathe and see what is going on around them.

Alligators and crocodiles cannot stand cold weather. Most of them live in warm waters near the equator. With one exception, crocodiles are only found in the Old World.

Alligators often tell where they are by bellowing. Their bellows can be heard a mile away. They are the only reptiles with loud voices.

Alligator (1/15)

Tuatara (1/4)

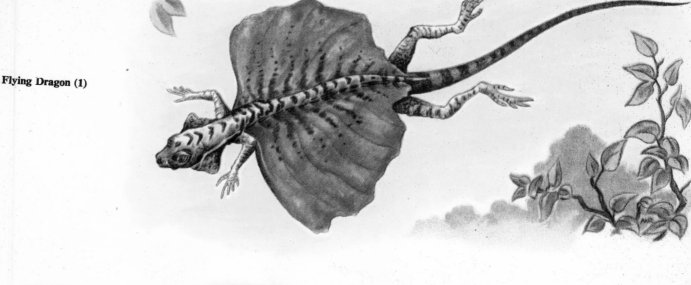

Flying Dragon (1)

Gila Monster ($\frac{1}{3}$)

There are lizards of many different sizes and colours and shapes. The sand lizard is the shape we think of as the typical lizard shape. It is a tiny lizard. The flying dragon is about the same size, but its wings, which are simply folds of skin that act as parachutes, make it very different in shape. The Gila monster is much larger. This lizard is a native of Mexico. It is poisonous. Small animals may die from its bite.

Even larger lizards are found in parts of Asia. Some of them weigh as much as 250 pounds.

Most lizards run or crawl on four short legs. But some can run on their hind legs like kangaroos. And some lizards have no legs. The glass snake is not a snake but a legless lizard.

Lizards eat food ranging in size from tiny insects to wild pigs. Some have remarkable tongues. A lizard eight inches long may be able to shoot its tongue out for seven or eight inches to catch an insect. Some lizards have a remarkable means of protection, too. If caught they may escape by breaking off their tails.

Sand Lizard (1)

Bull Snake (⅓)

Blacksnake (⅙)

Adder, or Viper (⅓)

There are about 2,300 kinds of snakes altogether. In our country there are only three: the adder, the grass snake, and the smooth snake.

Some snakes are many times larger than others, but they are all much the same shape. The only other reptiles that look at all like them are the legless lizards. No snakes have legs.

Since they have no legs, snakes cannot move in the way most other reptiles move. Many of them really walk on their ribs. The snake grips the ground with the sharp edges of the scales on the lower side of its body. Then muscles inside the snake's body pull it along the ground. Snakes can move faster on rough ground than on smooth ground because their scales can catch on the rough ground more easily.

Some snakes throw loops of their bodies forward to first one side and then the other to move

themselves along. Many desert snakes by moving in this way keep from sinking into the sand. Some snakes move so fast that they are called "racers." The blacksnake is a racer. The blacksnake can also swim and climb well. Many snakes can.

The skin of all snakes is covered with scales. The colours of the skin and scales in many cases are beautiful.

Snakes have many teeth, but they do not use them for chewing. Their teeth point backward toward their throats. Some of the teeth of certain snakes are poison fangs. These teeth are hollow. When a snake sinks its poison fangs into an animal, poison runs through the hollow teeth into the animal.

Snakes have long, slender tongues that are forked near the ends. They may be black, red and

Coral Snake (½)

black, yellow, green, or even some other colour. A snake uses its tongue for touching things. With its tongue a snake can also feel a breeze made by something moving. Its tongue helps it find food and avoid its enemies. It can dart in and out of a snake's mouth with remarkable speed.

Most snakes lay eggs. Some snakes, however, bear their young alive. The adder, or viper, is an example.

All snakes swallow their food whole. Many of them eat animals that look much too big to be swallowed by a snake. The secret is that its jaws are fastened together in such a way that a snake can open its mouth very wide. A snake's skin stretches like rubber, too.

As they grow, snakes have to shed their skins. Getting rid of an old skin is not always easy.

Most snakes do not hurt people. Some, indeed, are helpful. The adder, for instance, eats many mice. But, of course, it is also a poisonous snake and should be treated with respect.

The snakes which we can count as enemies are, for the most part, dangerous because of their poison. The boa constrictor is an exception. It kills animals by throwing its coils around them and squeezing them so that they cannot breathe.

Among the world's deadliest snakes are the cobra, the puff-adder and the coral snake. But all these fearsome reptiles are found in hot countries. The adder is our only poisonous snake, and its bite rarely proves fatal.

Many people are so afraid of poisonous snakes that they kill every snake they can. These people are being unfair to snakes in general.

Water Moccasin (¼)

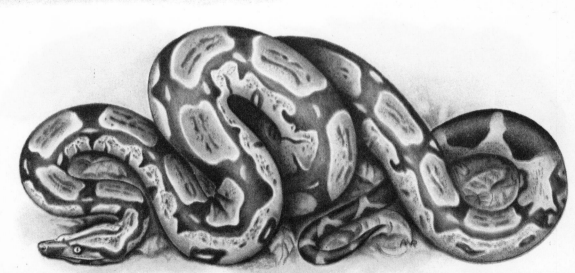

Boa Constrictor (⅛)

Swift

Birds

ALMOST all the animals that fly are in two great groups, one without and the other with backbones. The two groups are, of course, the insects and the birds. In the days of the dinosaurs the birds had backboned rivals in the air; there were many flying reptiles. But times have changed. Birds now outnumber the other vertebrates that can fly several hundred to one.

Just as there are a few flying vertebrates that are not birds, there are a few birds that cannot fly. Since far back in the time when birds were new on the earth there have been some flightless birds. Among the flightless birds of today are the ostriches, kiwis, and cassowaries. Most birds, however, can fly at least for a short way, and many are remarkable fliers – they fly both fast and for long distances.

Scientists have timed some birds to find out exactly how fast they can fly. The robin's speed is about 30 miles an hour. The swift can fly more than twice as fast!

Having wings is one of the most important ways in which birds are fitted for flying. A flying fish can soar through the air for a little way. A flying squirrel can glide down from one branch to another. But only creatures with true wings can really fly.

A typical bird's wings are powered by strong wing muscles. On the breastbone there is a projection called a "keel" to which the wing muscles are fastened. As it flies, a bird beats its wings against the air and pushes itself forward.

A bird's light weight is a help in flying. A swift weighs less than a mouse or a lizard or a toad of the same size. One reason why a bird is so light is that many of its bones are hollow. They are

Robin

filled with air. Connected with its lungs a bird
also has tiny air sacs scattered through its body.
These tiny air sacs act like little hot-air balloons.

A streamlined body is another help in flying.
One nickname of the swift reminds us that this
bird's body is streamlined. The nickname is
"flying bow and arrow."

Feathers are a very satisfactory covering for
creatures of the air. They are light, tough, and
strong. Besides, they make an excellent protection
for a bird's body. They shed rain because they
are a little oily and because the parts of each
feather and the feathers themselves are very
cleverly fitted together. Feathers, moreover, help
keep a bird's body warm. Since birds are warm-
blooded animals, it is important for them to have
a covering that will keep the heat of their bodies
from escaping. Feathers, largely because air is
trapped between them, serve this purpose very well.

Many birds use their power of flying to spend
their winters in one part of the world and their
summers in another. In this country the chiff-chaff
is one of the first signs of spring. For the chiff-
chaff goes south in the autumn and returns early
in the spring. The swift is a traveller, too. It leaves
earlier than the chiff-chaff in the autumn, comes
back later in the spring, and travels farther.

By no means all birds, however, have homes
in two different parts of the world. Some live in
one region all their lives.

Without any exceptions birds come from eggs. The eggs all have hard shells very much like the shell of a common hen's egg. But they vary greatly in size. An ostrich's egg is about six inches long. The tiny humming-bird's egg, in contrast, is only as big as a pea. As a rule, the eggs are laid in nests built by one or both of the parents.

Some nests are wonderfully made. The tiny humming-bird builds a beautiful little nest. It is about the size of half a walnut. The nest is lined with soft plant down; the outside is covered with moss, cobwebs, and lichens. It is built on a low branch.

The little yellow warbler builds a small, stout nest of grasses and plant fibres. Some warbler nests, like the one in the picture, have several stories. The cowbird often lays its eggs in the nests of other birds – sometimes in the nest of a yellow warbler. When the yellow warbler finds a cowbird's egg in its nest, it may build a new nest on top of its old one.

Birds have been on the earth far longer than people. The early birds could not build their nests near people's homes. But now many birds seem to prefer to do so. The wren is one of them. This little bird will build its nest in an old tin can, a hole in a fence post, or the pocket of a discarded coat. It will also accept a man-made birdhouse. The amount of sticks and string and grass this small bird will carry into a birdhouse is amazing. A pair of wrens may come back to the same nesting place year after year.

Yellow Warbler

Each kind of bird has its own special kind of nest. A humming-bird never builds a nest like a wren's, or the other way round. A bird inherits its way of nest-building. It does not have to be taught how to build a nest, just as we do not have to be taught how to use our eyes.

In contrast with the eggs of lower animals, bird eggs have to be kept very warm in order to hatch. As a rule, the female bird sits on the eggs to keep them warm. With some kinds of birds the male shares this duty. Many male birds are much brighter in colour than their mates. It is an advantage, if the female is to sit on the eggs, for her to be rather dull-coloured. She does not show so clearly as she stays quietly on the nest.

Some little birds are strong enough to run about almost as soon as they are hatched. They are covered with soft feathers, or down. Baby chickens and ducks are popular Easter pets because they are so pleasant both to look at and to feel. On the other hand, many birds are naked when they are hatched. They are so weak that they cannot stand up. Their eyes are shut, just as kittens' eyes are. Such baby birds have to be kept warm and have to be very well cared for.

Baby birds eat an amazing amount of food for their size. Since they are warm-blooded, they have to eat not only enough to grow but also enough to keep themselves warm. Many little birds seem to be hungry all the time they are awake. A young bird, in fact, may eat its weight in food every day.

Some adult birds first swallow the food they get for the baby birds. Then they pump it up out of their stomachs into the wide-open mouths of the babies.

Baby birds, even when they are males, often look more like their mothers than like their fathers. Probably a dull colour lessens the danger of their being caught by an enemy. A male scarlet tanager does not take on its bright red-and-black coat until it is several months old. Young ruby-throated humming-birds do not have ruby throats.

Scarlet Tanager

Great Spotted Woodpecker

There are about 14,000 kinds of birds altogether. Feathers make it easy to tell them from other animals. Bills, wings, and number of legs are a help, too, in telling whether an animal is a bird. But, although all birds are enough alike to be easily told from other animals, there are many differences within the group.

Birds range in size from the tiny humming-bird, which weighs less than a penny, to the ostrich, which may weigh 300 pounds. There have been, in past ages, birds even larger than the ostrich, but those bird giants are now extinct.

All birds have two legs, but the legs of one kind may be very different from the legs of another.

Some are long, some short; some are strong, others weak; some are fastened farther back on the bird's body than others.

The feet of birds are as different as their legs. Most birds have four toes. As a rule, three of a four-toed bird's toes point forward and one backward. But some birds – the great spotted woodpecker, for example – have two toes that point forward and two backward. Some birds have webbed feet. Some, like the hawks, have very sharp, strong claws at the ends of their toes.

All birds have wings, but, as has already been pointed out, not all birds can fly. The wings of a penguin make paddles for swimming.

The bills of birds differ greatly, too. Some are long and slender. Some are short and stout. Some are curved and end in very sharp points. Bills are much more than mere mouths. They are also "hands." By imagining building a house and getting dinner with your hands tied behind your back, you can get a picture of how important to a bird its bill is.

The feathers of birds also differ. As the pictures show, the tail feathers of the great spotted woodpecker are pointed, while those of the hawk and kingfisher are rounded.

The common names of birds show what a big range in colour there is. We have, for example, the redstart, the blue tit, the greenfinch, the whitethroat, the yellow wagtail, the golden eagle and the blackbird.

Many of the differences in birds are related to the places where the birds live. Webbed feet help water birds swim. Long legs help shore birds wade. Strong legs like those of the robin are good for hopping about on the ground. Some birds dig their nests in tree trunks. Tails with pointed feathers act as braces as the birds work. Sharp, strong bills are good digging tools.

Other differences in birds have to do with the different kinds of food the birds eat. There are insect eaters, seed eaters, birds of prey, scavengers that eat dead animals, and birds whose tastes include many different foods. The sharp, strong bill of the woodpeckers is good not only for digging nests in wood but also for digging out insects from tree trunks. The curved beak of a hawk is excellent for tearing up a small animal such as a field-mouse. Its sharp claws are a help in catching small animals, too. The kingfisher has a bill suited for fishing.

Many birds eat seeds. Short, stout bills are good for cracking seeds open. Some birds catch insects in the air. They open their mouths wide and scoop up insects in them very much as a fisherman gathers in fish with a net. A broad mouth and a short bill are best for catching insects in this way. Other birds have bills that are especially good for finding worms in the ground or for eating fruit. Scavengers need bills that can tear meat, just as do birds of prey.

Scientists have divided birds, on the basis of how they are built, into more than 20 orders. The woodpeckers are in an order that also includes the toucans, birds that live only in warm regions. The sparrowhawk belongs with the buzzards and eagles in another order. The kingfishers belong with the hornbills in a third.

As the chart on page 211 suggests, the perching birds make up by far the largest order. It includes almost all the good songsters.

Sparrowhawk

Buzzard

Kingfisher

91

Pheasant

Cuckoo

These birds belong to seven different orders. Although two of them are shown perching, none of them is in the order of perching birds.

The pheasant is a game bird. In the order with it are the grouse, quail, turkeys, and chickens. The young birds of this group are able to run about soon after they are hatched. Pheasants can fly, but they cannot fly far. Like their relatives, they nest on the ground.

The pheasant is not a native of Great Britain. It came originally from China.

The heron is grouped with the storks, flamingos, and bitterns. The heron is a bird of rivers and lakes. With its long bill it catches insects, small fish and snakes.

The stork is well known as a bringer of luck in Europe. In Germany and Denmark, especially, the people are very pleased when this bird builds its huge nest among their chimney-tops. In England storks are rarely seen. But many of us have watched a heron, flying high above the countryside. Herons never build their nests on house-tops, and are more shy than their European relation, the stork.

The cuckoo, which visits our country from Africa each spring, has relatives in many parts of the world. It is notorious for laying its eggs in other birds' nests—especially those of the hedge-sparrow and pied wagtail. Cuckoos are often mobbed by small birds. This is probably because they look like hawks, not because the small birds recognize them for what they really are.

Heron

Stork

92

Snipe

Screech Owl

The snipe belongs to the order which includes all the gulls, terns and sandpipers. The snipe is a wading bird, and searches for insects in shallow pools and marshes. Gulls are birds of the sea, but the snipe and the sandpipers are usually found inland. Sportsmen find snipe difficult to shoot because they rise in a zigzag flight.

Nightjars have been nicknamed "goatsuckers." There is an old superstition that they milk goats at night, but in reality nightjars live entirely on insects. They hunt chiefly at dusk, when you may hear their churring cry. This has earned them their name. Their American cousin, the whip-poor-will, is also named after its call. Nightjars winter in Africa, flying to our country to breed in May.

One order of birds is made up entirely of owls. The little screech owl shown here is one of them. Many owls, like the screech owl, have ear tufts. They are not ears at all but simply bunches of feathers. British owls with these "ears" are the long-eared and the short-eared owls. Owls are birds of the night; bright sunlight blinds them. At night their eyesight is so keen that it enables them to catch such animals as field-mice.

The Canada goose is one of the order that includes all the ducks, geese, and swans. They are all water birds. Their webbed feet help them swim. They are also very good fliers: some of them can fly 60 miles an hour. The Canada goose is one of the largest of our naturalized wild birds.

Whip-poor-will

Canada Goose

The perching birds are divided into many families. There are, for instance, the thrushes, the finches and the wrens. There are the swallows, the waxwings and the flycatchers, the titmice and the crows.

The blackbird is one of our commonest perching birds. It belongs to the thrush family. Other members of the same family which we all know well are the song- and the missel-thrushes. These three birds are with us all the year round. But two other members of the family, redwings and fieldfares, arrive from Norway and Sweden every autumn and stay with us until March, when they fly back across the North Sea to nest in their own countries.

The five birds just mentioned all look rather alike – except that the blackbird is black, of course. It may surprise you to know, then, that the robin, the redstart, the nightingale and the wheatear are also placed in the thrush family.

The blackbird is not related to the crows. These birds may share the same colours, but that does not put them in the same family. Magpies and jays, which are in the crow family, are not black at all.

The rook can usually be distinguished from the carrion crow by three features. It is gregarious: that is, it lives in flocks. The crow, on the other hand, is solitary. Also rooks have a bald patch at the base of their beak. There is no such bald patch on the carrion crow. A third way of telling these birds apart is their voice. Neither can claim to be a songster like the thrushes. But the carrion crow caws even less musically than the rook, making a far harsher, more raucous sound.

Jays and magpies are very colourful members of the crow family. Jays are cunning birds, and spend much of their life lurking in woods. But they sneak out to raid gardens and orchards. Magpies also have a bad reputation, and have been known to attack new-born lambs. But it must be admitted that they are very attractive in their smart "uniform" of blue-black and white.

Ravens and choughs were once common British crows, but unless you live near one of our rocky western coasts you are unlikely to see them today. Ravens, are much bigger than crows and rooks. Their croak sounds like a pig's grunt.

The chough is a slender bird – smaller than the rook. Its bill is long and down-curved. Both bill and legs are a bright coral red. The chough is indeed a striking bird. It is a pity that it has become so uncommon.

The golden oriole in the picture has relations in most parts of the world. But in Britain it is an unusual sight. However, golden orioles do sometimes reach our southern counties. The oriole is a shy bird and hides in clumps of trees. But it has a loud, flute-like whistle which is easily recognized before the bird is seen.

Our starlings have relations in Asia and Africa. The myna of India is one member of the family which can be taught to speak. Even from the starlings we hear every day we know how fond they are of imitating sounds.

We have often seen flocks of starlings busily engaged in searching lawns for "leatherjackets." Another species of starling, the African ox-pecker, does the same thing. But instead of examining lawns, it searches the backs of elephants, rhinos and cattle, removing the ticks which burrow in their skin.

Flycatchers are an interesting group of perching birds. The two which usually visit our country in the summer are the spotted flycatcher and the pied flycatcher. Spotted flycatchers are by far the more common of the two. Both these birds come from Africa with the other summer migrants. They spend most of their time perched on a post or some similar position, where they can spy on all the insects which pass. When the bird spots an insect it flies quickly from the perch, seizes its victim, and returns at once to its original post. The whole action takes place in a matter of moments – a swoop from the perch and the flycatcher is back again.

It seems strange that there should usually be more pied flycatchers nesting in Wales than in the south of England. You would imagine that their long flight from Africa would make them glad to stop as soon as they reached the other side of the English Channel.

The brilliantly marked waxwings, which we have also mentioned as members of the family of perching birds, only pay rare visits to Britain. They live north of our islands, in Scandinavia, and only fly across the North Sea in intensely cold winters. They even become bold enough to visit large gardens to find the yews and other trees which provide the berry fruits they need.

Rooks

Golden Oriole

Starling

Bullfinch

fond of pecking the buds of fruit trees. It is often shot because of this unfortunate habit. Bullfinches are usually quite shy birds and you may see no more of them than a flash of white and wine-red as they fly into a wood or hedge.

The chaffinch is perhaps the commonest of all British birds. It is not, like the sparrow, restricted to living near houses. It is found all over the country except in the most rugged areas. In the early spring the males are quite striking in appearance. They begin singing early in February, and nesting takes place from April onwards.

The goldfinch has a twittering call. It flies in short "loops." Goldfinches build delicate nests lined with thistledown, and thistle seeds are their favourite food.

The birds on these pages are all perching birds. The bullfinch, chaffinch and goldfinch are all members of the very large finch family.

The nightingale has already been mentioned – it is one of the thrushes.

The nuthatch belongs to the small nuthatch family. There are few kinds of nuthatch compared with the many varieties of thrush and finch. But they are distributed over much of the world.

The long-tailed tits are the most delicate of our tits, which are generally a hardy race. Other British titmice include the great tit, blue tit, coal tit, marsh tit and crested tit – the last of these being found only in Scotland.

Of the three finches shown on this page, the bullfinch is an enemy to fruit growers, since it is very

Chaffinc

Goldfinch

The nightingale is the only bird shown on these pages which is a migrant. Like the warblers, it comes to us from Africa, arriving in the middle of April. Its song is world-famous, but you might not be impressed by it until you hear it at night. During the day it is drowned by birds with louder voices.

Often the nuthatch can be heard when it cannot be seen. Its call has been described as sounding like a pebble bouncing over a stretch of ice. Like the tree-creepers, nuthatches spend their lives searching for insects on trees. And like the woodpeckers, they nest in a hole in a tree trunk. Nuthatches plaster the edges of the hole with mud until only they themselves can squeeze through – otherwise they would soon lose their nest to some greedy starling, too lazy to build its own.

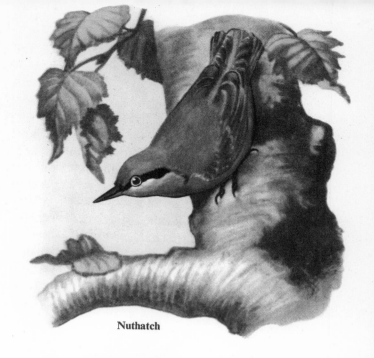

Nuthatch

Nightingale

The long-tailed tit's nest is round, with a hole at the side, and made almost entirely of feathers and lichen. Both the nest and its builder are delicate – whenever there is a hard winter many of these small birds die. But long-tailed tits have large families and this soon helps to bring their numbers up to normal. When the young ones are fledged they keep together until the following spring. Sometimes you may come upon a party of them, calling to one another as they travel along a hedgerow searching busily for insects. These parties always seem to be on the move, like bands of bird gypsies. Although these tits are not so bold as the great tit and the blue tit, they are just as interesting to watch. But you will have to look for them first.

Long-tailed Tits

All the best songsters are found among the perching birds. But by no means every bird of this group has a beautiful song. No one would call the starling, the crow, or the magpie a good singer, although they are all perching birds.

The best songsters generally seem to be small, rather dull-coloured birds. Most of the warblers certainly come into this group, which includes the chiff-chaff, willow warbler, wood wren, white-throats, garden warbler and blackcap. Warblers are found throughout much of the world.

The chiff-chaff is usually the first summer migrant to be heard. It arrives and starts to sing towards the end of March. When the woods are still, the chiff-chaff's jerky call carries for quite a long way. The willow warbler is very much like the chiff-chaff. If you can't hear it singing you can hardly tell which it is. But if you can see its legs you will notice that they are brown, whereas those of the chiff-chaff are black.

Both these warblers and the whitethroat are very common with us during the summer. The whitethroat arrives during April and nests early in May. It has an odd way of singing as it flies up from a bush, and drops quickly down into it again.

Two of the best songsters among the warblers are the blackcap and garden warbler. The blackcap pours forth a liquid torrent of sound, and can sometimes be mistaken for the nightingale.

Willow warblers have nothing to do with willows. But sedge warblers and reed warblers are always found by the edge of a pond or lake. Sedge warblers are very careful to keep out of sight in low bushes. You may creep up quietly to them, but they disappear as soon as you get near, and continue singing inside their bush.

One of the best American songsters is the mockingbird. It pours out a torrent of song at any time of the day or night, and at any time of the year. It belongs to a family related to the thrushes, but its habits of mimicking other birds are more like a starling's. The mockingbird has a mimic among its relations too – the catbird. This also has a fine song but its call note is a mew that sounds like a cat and has given this bird its name. Another native of the catbird's part of the world is the chickadee, which is the equivalent of our titmouse. The chickadee in the illustration would look very much like our marsh tit if it weren't for its black throat. This little bird is not a great singer but its cheerful piping must be as welcome in winter as that of our tits.

Mockingbird

Black-capped Chickadee

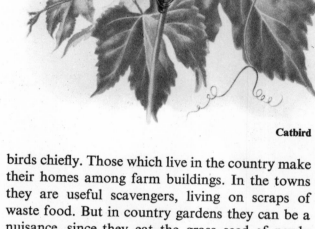

Catbird

Scientists have studied the food of birds carefully. Some birds are our friends and others are our enemies because of the kinds of food they eat.

Birds help us by eating four kinds of food. The four are weed seeds, small animals such as field-mice, dead animals, and insect pests – insects that do harm to ornamental trees, fruit trees, crop plants, and even to ourselves.

On the other side of the ledger is the harm which birds do us by eating fruit, grain, and helpful insects. Some birds harm us, moreover, by eating the eggs of other birds and even small birds themselves. A few kinds of birds eat the buds of trees – like the bullfinch, for example.

Of course, no bird is ever consciously helping us or harming us. We should not blame the birds that harm us any more than we should praise those that help us. They are simply eating the food they are fitted for eating.

Sparrows depend almost wholly on human beings for their food in Britain. They are town birds chiefly. Those which live in the country make their homes among farm buildings. In the towns they are useful scavengers, living on scraps of waste food. But in country gardens they can be a nuisance, since they eat the grass seed of newly sown lawns; and on farms at harvest time they collect in huge flocks to feed on the ripe grain.

But wood pigeons are the farmer's serious enemy. They start eating the corn as soon as it is planted and do not wait for harvest time.

Rooks, on the other hand, probably do as much good as harm. It is true that they do eat some grain, but they are also fond of pests like wireworms and leatherjackets. So farmers have as much reason to be pleased with rooks as they have to dislike them.

Sparrow

Farmers have no complaints about the swallows. Swallows and martins live entirely on insects. Many of the insects they eat are harmful to crops and fruit trees. In Britain there are two varieties of martin – the house martin, and the sand martin. House martins build nests under the eaves of buildings but the sand martins make tunnels in soft cliffs and banks, and live in those.

The purple martin of America, pictured above, is such a good hunter of mosquitoes and insects harmful to fruit trees that many people encourage them to nest by building birdhouses for them. As these martins live in groups, each birdhouse has lots of separate nesting rooms.

The cardinal ranks high as a friend to American farmers. It eats a little grain. But it does many times as much good by eating insect pests as it does harm by eating grain. In the Southern States it is a great enemy of the cotton worm.

Beneficial birds by no means all belong to the perching birds. Among the other birds which are man's very good friends are the vultures, good scavengers; the partridge, a very valuable bird to the farmer because of the insects and weed seeds it eats; and the barn owl, our best bird helper in fighting rats and mice.

Some birds have a bad reputation which they do not deserve. The buzzard is a good example.

This bird occasionally kills chickens when its usual food of mice and rabbits is scarce. But it catches so few chickens in proportion to the mice and rabbits it eats that it does not deserve to be persecuted. It was trapped and shot so extensively at one time that it disappeared from most of Britain. But protection has helped it to start spreading once more.

Of course, some birds are beneficial to us not because of the food they eat but because they furnish food for us. Centuries ago men found the meat of birds so pleasant that they began domesticating wild fowl of several kinds. We now raise millions of ducks, chickens, and turkeys. Eggs, too, have become so important a food that they are a part of almost everyone's diet. There are, in addition to the birds we raise for food, still many wild game birds.

Other birds are valued for their feathers. The snowy egret used to be killed for its beautiful white feathers. Ostrich feathers are popular now. Fortunately, getting ostrich feathers does not mean killing the ostriches.

Very soon game birds and many other beneficial birds might disappear if there were no laws to protect them. Some already have disappeared.

The passenger pigeon, of which there were once enormous flocks, has been killed off. The great auk, which used to be common along the shores of North America, has become extinct, too. A number of kinds of birds are now in danger. Most of our birds are very much worth saving, and everyone should play his part in seeing that the laws that protect them are obeyed.

We have done harm to some of our native birds, not by killing them, but by destroying their homes. At one time the great bustard roamed our chalk uplands. But fences and ploughing drove it away. Mowing machines are helping to wipe out the corncrake, which is becoming less common every year. These machines kill the crouching birds before they can escape, and smash their nests. By draining fenlands we have also lost many interesting birds of the marshes.

Cardinal

Mammals

THE opossum is a mammal. Its fur proclaims that it is. The duckbill, the koala, and the kangaroo are clearly furry and are therefore clearly mammals, too. The echidna is also a mammal, although no one would call it furry. Its hairs are stiff, sharp spines, or bristles. Another name for this queer-looking animal is "spiny anteater."

These five mammals are all primitive. On the mammal branch of the animal tree they belong at the bottom, or close to it. They can be thought of as left over from the days when Nature was experimenting with warm-blooded, hairy animals that nourished their babies with milk.

The duckbill and the spiny anteater rank below the opossum, the kangaroo, and the koala. They belong to an order of mammals called "monotremes." The monotremes differ from all other mammals in that they lay eggs. All other mammals are born alive. After monotreme babies are hatched, however, they are fed with milk from the mother, just as all other mammal babies are.

Another name for the duckbill is "platypus." This peculiar animal lives in Australia. When some of the early English settlers in Australia sent some platypus skins back to England, English scientists thought that someone was playing a joke on them. They thought that the bills of real ducks had been sewed to the skins of some furry animal.

The duckbill is like a duck not only in having a bill and laying eggs but also in having webbed

102

feet. Duckbills are very much at home in the water. They use their stout bills to dig worms and shellfish out of the mud at the bottom of streams.

Duckbills live in burrows dug in the banks of streams. A burrow may be 30 feet long. In a room at the far end the female makes a nest of weeds and lays one, two, or three eggs. The young duckbills are naked when they hatch and very helpless. The mother holds them to her with her tail at nursing time.

On their hind legs male duckbills have hollow spurs connected with poison glands. Duckbills are the only poisonous mammals.

The echidna lays eggs just as the duckbill does, but she places them at once in a pouch on the underside of her body. They stay there until they hatch and then for a few weeks afterward. The mother has two babies in her pouch at once.

Duckbill

The echidna is well built to be an anteater. It has stout claws that are useful in tearing ant nests apart, a long beak, and an even longer, sticky tongue. There are other anteaters among the mammals, but they are not closely related to this spiny anteater. This anteater is found only in Australia and some of the islands not far away.

The opossum, koala, and kangaroo are pouched mammals, or marsupials. They do not lay eggs. Their babies are born alive, but they are very, very small and undeveloped. The mother marsupial carries them in a pouch until they are well covered with fur and are able to look after themselves. Even after a baby marsupial is able to leave its mother's pouch it may climb back into the pouch when it needs protection.

The koala, or Australian native bear, lives in trees. It eats chiefly eucalyptus leaves. Only one koala baby is born at a time. It stays in the mother's pouch for a while – about three months – and then climbs on her back and rides pick-a-back for several months longer. Its rides on its mother's back should be rather exciting, for koalas, although they spend most of the day sleeping quietly among the lower branches of trees, go hopping about in the trees at dusk, often making jumps of several feet.

Koala

A young kangaroo rides always in its mother's pouch rather than on her back. But even so the rides should be thrilling, for kangaroos are famous for the long leaps they make. The leaps often measure 25 feet. Kangaroos live in the dry regions of Australia, where the plants on which they feed are rather scarce. It is an advantage to be able to cover ground fast.

There are many other marsupials in Australia and the islands round about. Among them are the honey mouse, the Tasmanian devil, the wombat, and the bandicoot.

The opossum is the one North American marsupial. In contrast with most marsupials, the opossum has several babies at a time, sometimes as many as 15. Like little koalas, baby opossums ride around on their mother's back after they have left her pouch.

It is not surprising that most of the very primitive mammals are to be found in Australia and the islands near by. This region has been separated by the sea from the rest of the world for a very, very long time. Otherwise the marsupials and monotremes would probably have been crowded out by more advanced mammals. The wonder is that the opossum has been able to hold its own.

Kangaroo

　　Echidna

Giant Panda

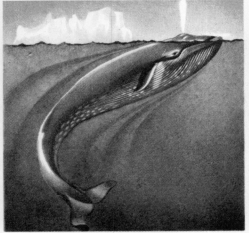
Blue Whale

Leopard

The monotremes and marsupials form two of the orders of mammals. There are some 4,000 other kinds of mammals, which are divided into many orders, as one of the charts on page 211 shows.

Scientists call all the mammals except the monotremes and marsupials "placental mammals." The young of placental mammals develop within the mother's body until they are much less tiny and helpless than baby marsupials. For each species there is a definite period of time during which the mother carries the young inside her body. Although the babies at birth are not so helpless as baby marsupials, they need care for weeks, months, or even years after they are born.

"As big as an elephant" is a common saying, but there are mammals much larger. A blue whale is far larger – the largest animal, so far as anyone knows, that ever lived. The chart on page 210 shows how much bigger this animal of today is than the land giants of all time – the dinosaurs. Mammals go down in size from the blue whales to the pygmy shrews, little insect eaters that are smaller than mice. Mammals live in a great variety of places and eat a great variety of foods.

Hair is one test of whether an animal is a mammal. Hair seems to be lacking on both the elephant and the whale, but they both have a little. Hair, or fur, makes an excellent covering for a warm-blooded animal. It shuts heat in.

The giant panda is certainly well supplied with hair. This mammal was little known until quite recently. It lives in forests in China near Tibet. It was real news when, in 1937, the first giant panda was brought to one of our zoos.

The giant panda belongs to the order of carnivores. "Carnivore" means meat eater. The teeth of the carnivores are specially fitted for tearing

Elephant

meat apart. Most carnivores do eat other animals, but the panda in its natural home eats nothing but bamboo sprouts.

The blue whale, strange as it seems, eats plankton, made of tiny plants and animals. This whale does not have teeth. Instead, it has plates of whalebone. On the edges of the plates there are long bristles which strain the little plants and animals out of the water. Imagine how many tiny living things a blue whale eats in just one day!

Whales, since they breathe air as all mammals do, must come to the surface of the water from time to time to expel the air from their lungs and fill them with fresh air. The warm, moist air a whale breathes out looks like a fountain. Blowing out air is called "spouting."

Whales and the other animals in the same order are often wrongly called fish.

The tiger has the reputation of being the fiercest of all meat-eating mammals. But its fellow carnivore the leopard is fully as ferocious.

The elephants are in an order all by themselves. No other mammals are very much like them. The elephants in the picture are Indian elephants. African elephants are larger and have much larger ears.

Feeding peanuts to the elephants is part of the fun of going to a zoo or a circus. But wild elephants feed on grass and roots instead. Their strong tusks are a big help in digging up roots. Inside its mouth an elephant has four huge teeth, good for chewing tough plants.

It is a common idea that elephants live to be very much older than people. On the contrary, few elephants live to be more than 70.

Bats are the only mammals that can truly fly. They fly very well. There are many kinds. The bats common in Great Britain are insect eaters. In Asia fruit bats are common. In the forests of tropical America there are vampire bats that bite animals and lap up the blood.

Bat

The order which includes the great anteater, the sloths, and the armadillos is a queer assortment of animals. The anteater has claws so long that they interfere with walking. But these claws are excellent for ripping up nests of ants and termites. The anteater has, as one would guess from its snout, a very long tongue. It serves to lick up insects by the thousands. An anteater may eat 150,000 termites at a time.

The walrus is another of the carnivores. Its tusks are used in digging up clams. Walruses live in the Far North. They have been called the monarchs of the arctic seas. Walrus hunts are an important part of the life of the Eskimos.

We like to think of the primates as being at the very top of the animal kingdom, for this is the order of mammals to which human beings belong. The gorilla is in this group, too. So are all the other apes, the monkeys, and the lemurs.

The gorilla is one of the manlike apes. It is the largest ape of all, considerably larger than its more teachable relative, the chimpanzee.

Gorillas live in family groups in the forests of equatorial Africa. A typical gorilla family group is made up of a male, a female, and children of assorted ages. The female and the children sleep at night on a platform built in a tree. The male stands guard below.

Apes and monkeys are always favourites in a zoo. People apparently are always interested in the antics of these relatives of theirs.

Great Anteater

Walrus

Gorilla

Grizzly Bear

Tracks of Black Bear

Tracks of Grizzly Bear (below)

Raccoon

All the mammals pictured on these two pages belong to the order of carnivores. And they all live up to their name.

In every region many food chains can be traced. In a region where there are oak trees, acorns are eaten by mice, and mice are eaten by owls. In parts of Africa grass is eaten by zebras, and zebras are eaten by lions. In the Arctic, plants are eaten by insects, insects by the snowy ptarmigan, and the snowy ptarmigan by the Arctic fox.

A food chain always begins with plants. It almost always ends with a meat-eating animal – in many cases one of the carnivores. Several of the carnivores pictured here are the chief meat eaters in their home regions.

As a rule, there are not many big carnivores in a region. There is not enough food to support very many. If a lion were to eat nothing but zebras, it would need about 50 a year. And 50 zebras eat a great deal of grass.

There are many families of carnivores. One is the cat family. The tiger and the mountain lion are big cats. The lion, the leopard, the bobcat, and the jaguar are also in this family.

The dog family is large, too. It includes the coyotes, the foxes, and the wolves.

The marten and the skunk belong to the marten family, which includes the otter, the mink, and the weasel as well. The raccoon is in a family closely related to the martens. The bears make up a family of their own.

There are a great many other carnivores. The walrus is by no means the only carnivore of the sea. The fur seal, the sea lion, and the elephant seal are carnivores, too.

The hyena is a carnivore, but as a rule it does not kill animals for itself. It eats what other carnivores leave behind. Although it has a bad reputation, it is a good scavenger.

Scattered over the world there are many little-known carnivores. Their names are as strange to us as their looks. Among them are the coati, the cacomistle, and the kinkajou.

Tiger

Marten

Coyote

Skunk

Mountain Lion

Hippopotamus

Horses have hoofs. The story has already been told of how the horse, through millions of years of change, became a large animal that ran about on its middle toenails, which had developed into stout hoofs. There are many other hoofed mammals. Scientists call them "ungulates."

Some animals with hoofs have an odd number of toes, just as the horse has. They are the odd-toed ungulates. Of the ungulates pictured here, the zebra and the rhinoceros are odd-toed.

The hippopotamus, elk, and giraffe are even-toed ungulates. Many of our big-game animals belong in this group. Sheep, cattle, pigs, goats, and camels are among the many other even-toed ungulates.

All the hoofed animals live on the ground. There would be no point to their having hoofs if they did not do their travelling by walking or running about on the ground.

They are all plant eaters. Plant-eating animals could be called "herbivores." No order of mammals, however, is given the name "herbivores."

The hoofed animals furnish a great deal of food for the meat eaters. They furnish a great deal of food for us, too. In Nature's scheme there have to be many herbivores to keep the carnivores alive.

"Hippopotamus" means "water horse." It is not a close relative of the horse, but it does spend most of its time in the water.

The hippopotamus is one of the least beautiful of all mammals. Like the whale and the elephant, it has almost no hair. But it has a little, and it follows the mammal pattern of feeding its babies with milk from the milk glands in its body.

The mouth of this big plant eater is enormous. And the animal has an appetite to match. Strong tusks help it dig up plants to eat.

"Hippos," like many hoofed animals, form herds. A herd spends the daytime in the water, as a rule. It comes out at night to feed in the lowlands.

A hippopotamus often lies with only its face above water. Its beady eyes are raised above its face. So are its nostrils. Its ears stick up above the water, too. It is easy for the animal to hear and see what is going on round about and also to breathe.

A baby hippopotamus is always a big attraction in a zoo. It looks tiny beside its mother. But actually it is not small. It weighs about as much as a colt.

The widespread hoofs of the hippopotamus are very different from those of the horse. They are better suited for walking on muddy river bottoms. The hippopotamus can also swim well. As it swims it closes its nostrils to shut out the water.

The zebra is a neighbour of the hippopotamus in Africa. But it lives in the grasslands. This animal is famous for its stripes. Herds of zebras feed at night, and their stripes may make them less conspicuous in the moonlight. But their stripes do not keep them from being one of the chief foods of the lions of Africa.

The tapir, a relative of the zebra, does not look at all like a zebra when full-grown. But baby tapirs are covered with a curious assortment of spots and stripes.

The deer family is a large one, well represented in North America. The elk, or wapiti, is a big deer. It has especially large antlers. A relative of the American elk once lived in Ireland. As generations went by, the antlers of this elk became larger and larger. At last they were so large that they were a serious hindrance. Two males fighting one another often got their antlers interlocked and could not separate themselves. The Irish elk became extinct.

Deer chew a cud. These animals depend chiefly on their speed to protect themselves from their carnivore enemies. A deer sometimes has to get its food "on the run." It swallows the food without chewing it. The food goes down into one division of the animal's stomach. There it is softened somewhat. Later, when the animal has a chance to rest, the food it has swallowed comes back into its mouth as a cud. Many other hoofed animals chew a cud. A cow chewing its cud in the shade in a pasture is a common sight. The cow follows the practice of its wild relatives even though, in a fenced-in pasture with no carnivore enemies to escape, it need not hurry about its eating.

The rhinoceros ranks third in size among the land mammals; only the elephant and the hippopotamus are larger. This animal has a long history. There were, for instance, many woolly rhinoceroses in North America in the days of the mammoths and mastodons. Now the only rhinoceroses are found in Asia and Africa.

The rhinoceros is easily told by the horn or horns on its nose. The horn of a rhinoceros is not made of real horn – the material a cow's horn is made of. It is a closely packed bundle of hair instead. The skin of a rhinoceros is very tough, so much so that "as tough as rhinoceros hide" is a common expression.

A mother rhinoceros always keeps her baby ahead of her as she walks along. She runs with her head close to the ground. It is easy for her to urge the baby along by giving it a little push with her horn.

A giraffe is an unbelievable kind of animal. Its legs and its neck are so long that they make the giraffe the tallest animal in the world today. A giraffe grows to be 18 or 19 feet tall.

A giraffe looks very awkward as it eats plants growing in the ground. It has to spread its front legs apart to get its head down to the plants. But its long legs are a big help in eating leaves from trees.

This long-legged animal has a remarkable ability to go without water. Of course, it gets some water in the leaves it eats.

The checkerboard pattern on the giraffe's skin helps the animal hide. It looks a little like the pattern made by sunlight or moonlight shining down through trees. The lion is the chief enemy of the giraffe, just as it is of the zebra. The giraffe sometimes defends itself by kicking with its hard hoofs. But its better ways of protecting itself are hiding and running away.

Almost every zoo has its giraffes. Zoo keepers worry for fear these "animals on stilts" will break their long necks.

Zebra

Elk

Rhinoceros

Porcupine

Chipmunk

Muskrat

The rodents make up a very large and very successful order of mammals. They are the gnawing mammals. Some of them can gnaw through hard nutshells and even through tree trunks.

These animals are well fitted for gnawing. They can move their jaws sideways as well as up and down. Their front teeth, moreover, have sharp edges like chisels. Their back teeth grind up the food their front teeth have cut off. Even chisels wear down. The rodents would soon wear down their front teeth if their teeth were like ours. But they are not. They keep on growing at the roots.

Rodents are found almost everywhere except in the seas. Some live on the ground, some under the ground, and some in the tops of trees. Some live in the water of swamps and streams. And some, like the kangaroo rat, are so well fitted for living in desert lands that they never have to have any water to drink. The flying squirrels even have flaps of skin which let them glide through the air.

The largest of all the gnawing animals is the capybara. It grows to be as large as a pig. This rodent lives in the streams of Central and South America. It eats plants that grow in the water and along the banks of the streams.

The squirrels, with their bushy tails, are perhaps the prettiest of the group. These tree-dwelling rodents are well known and well liked, even though, whenever they can, they steal nuts we have gathered for ourselves and may rob birds' nests.

The squirrel pictured is a red squirrel. Red squirrels have pointed tufts of hair on their ears which make them look quite elfin. The grey squirrel's head is more rat-like, and its grey colour makes this similarity especially noticeable. Since the grey squirrel was introduced to this country it has driven away the red squirrel from many of its old haunts.

Chipmunks are delightful little rodents which you may have seen on the films or at the zoo. Unlike squirrels they live in burrows under the ground. Often these are several yards long. Chipmunks have large cheek-pouches for storing their food.

The porcupine would never win any prizes for beauty or for its playful ways. If differs from all the other rodents in having quills – sharp spines with barbs on them. It is a very common belief that a porcupine shoots its quills at an enemy that comes near. It has no way of doing so. But the quills come loose easily. An enemy that attacks a porcupine finds itself full of the barbed quills, which are almost impossible to pull out. With such good weapons for defending itself, a porcupine can be very slow-moving, and it is.

Some of the rodents are valuable fur bearers. The fur of squirrels is pretty but not very durable. Ranking higher as fur bearers are the muskrat and the beaver. Rabbits, which some scientists put in an order of their own, have pretty fur, too. Much of it masquerades under some other name.

The rabbit is valuable for its meat as well as for its fur. Hunting rabbits has long been a favourite sport with men and boys. It is a wonder, with so many hunters as there are, that the rabbit had not disappeared before the disease myxomatosis broke out. The reason was that rabbits bred faster than they could be killed.

The villains among the rodents are the mice and rats. They destroy an enormous amount of food every year. Home owners have to

Red Squirrel

wage a never-ending war against them in their houses. Farmers have to fight them in their storage barns and fields. Rats not only destroy property but they also carry disease. To keep rats from travelling by ship and carrying diseases from one country to another, all big ships are equipped with rat guards, that prevent rats from running along the ropes that moor a vessel to its dock.

Man is proud of the great dams he has built. He has a right to be. But he cannot claim to be the first dam builder. Beavers were building dams long before there were any people to build them. By damming small streams they make the streams spread out into ponds and provide building places for beaver homes. Beavers live in colonies. They work together in building dams. With their sharp, strong teeth they fell trees near the water's edge, cut them into pieces, and float them into place. They then plaster the logs together with mud.

The beavers build their homes in the pond out of mud and sticks. The entrance to a beaver's home, or lodge, is under water. The living room of the lodge, however, is above the water-line. Beavers may also dig homes in the bank. The openings to these homes are also under water. But the tunnels slope upward so that the living space is above water-level.

Muskrats build their homes in water, too, most often in marshes. Their houses, like those of the beavers, have under-water entrances. Muskrats do not build dams to create ponds, as the beavers do.

It seemed to the early settlers of North America that there were enough fur bearers and enough big-game animals to last forever. But this idea proved to be altogether wrong. The four animals pictured here are all far, far scarcer than they once were. Probably all of them would have disappeared if the Americans had not woken up in time.

Early trappers made fortunes from beaver skins. They killed beavers by the millions. The killing of these fur bearers had some results which people did not connect with beavers for some time. By damming up small streams to form ponds beavers make the water from heavy rains and melting snow run off much more slowly than it would otherwise. With few beavers left to build dams, the water

many people warm in the winter. The meat of the buffalo made good food. The tongue was considered a special delicacy. Sometimes, in fact, people felt so sure that there would always be a supply of buffalo meat that when a buffalo was killed only the tongue was eaten.

At the same time that buffaloes were being killed by the thousands for their hides and their meat, their homes and their food were being taken away from them by the ploughing up of the plains where they roamed.

It is not surprising that the big herds were brought down to little herds and that the little herds were brought down to nothing. But just in time reservations were set up for them where they

Beaver

raced down the streams into the rivers, carrying much good soil and causing floods in the lowlands. The value of the land ruined was far greater than the value of the beaver skins. Now beavers are being encouraged in many places as a way of saving soil and preventing floods.

The story of the American bison is another story man cannot be proud of. When, on their westward journeys, early explorers reached the Great Plains, they found enormous herds of bison, or, as they were more commonly called, "buffaloes." They were in such big herds that a stampede of these animals was something to be dreaded. Then the killing began. Buffalo robes kept

could live undisturbed. The last great bison hunt was in 1883. Now there are thousands of bison in the herds on the reservations.

The pronghorn was once almost as common as the bison. It, too, was barely saved.

The moose, although never in such numbers as the beaver, bison, and pronghorn, used to be much more common than it is now. It lives in open woodlands. Cutting down forests has taken away many of its homes, and hunters have killed too many.

Other American wild mammals have been killed in great numbers for fun or for fur or for food. Fortunately, there are now game laws, and they are helping the wild mammals hold their own.

Pronghorn

Bison

Moose

Sheep and Lambs

Our early cave-man ancestors lived very simply. Their best weapons were crude axes made of stone, they depended on the skins of wild animals for clothing, and their only way of getting food was to gather wild plants and hunt wild animals. But at last they made a discovery that changed their whole way of living. They found that they could domesticate wild plants and animals and raise them as they needed them. No longer did they have to spend practically the whole of every day in search of food.

Many of the animals domesticated were mammals. Without question most of them were first thought of as a source of food. Even the horse may have been raised first for its meat and milk. But they served many other purposes, too. They furnished skins and wool for

Cow and Pigs

Horse and Colt

clothing, they helped with hunting and tilling the soil, and they carried people and their burdens from place to place. Besides, they guarded property and were friends and companions.

No one knows the exact order in which animals were domesticated. The order in which our most common domesticated mammals were tamed is believed by many to be this: dog, pig, cow, sheep, goat, donkey, horse, cat.

In the several thousand years since these animals were first domesticated man has done much to change them. He has developed different breeds

of each one, each breed to serve some special purpose or to be suited for some particular region.

Some sheep are raised chiefly for their wool, others chiefly for their meat. The fat-tails, raised in Asia, furnish the Persian lamb, caracul, and broadtail used in fur coats.

There are two general types of hogs: the lard type and the bacon type. The Hampshire, easily told by its white band, is one of the lard-type breeds. The bacon breeds are longer and leaner.

Cattle have been developed along two lines: better meat production and better milk produc-

White Rabbit

tion. Three popular breeds of dairy cattle are the Jersey, the Guernsey, and the Ayrshire. The oldest breed, however, is the Brown Swiss. Its ancestry can be traced back to the cattle raised by the Swiss Lake Dwellers of the New Stone Age. The Shorthorn and Hereford are beef breeds.

The many breeds of horses can be classed as draught-horses, developed for size and strength; light horses, developed for speed and beauty; and small horses, or ponies. With the coming of the motor car, horses lost some of their importance. There is much less need for heavy draught-horses than there once was. Horses for driving have lost much of their importance, too. Today's horse breeders are most interested in racehorses, and in hunters and jumpers.

Arabian horses are the oldest of the breeds of light horses. Almost all our modern breeds have Arabian horses somewhere in their ancestry. Many people, when they hear that a horse is a Thoroughbred, think that it is simply a horse with good breeding. But "Thoroughbred" is the name of one distinct breed of horse. The horses that take part in running races are Thoroughbreds. Nearco and Hyperion are famous racehorses of the past.

There are more breeds of dogs than of any other domesticated animal. Visitors at dog shows are almost always surprised at the number of breeds on exhibit. The wolf, scientists think, was the wild ancestor of our dogs of today. Some of our modern breeds look more like wolves than they look like their modern cousins.

Probably we have so many breeds of dogs because dogs serve so many different purposes. They

St. Bernard

Boxer

Scottie

Greyhound

English Setter

Dachshund

Guinea Pig

guard property, help in hunting, pull loads, guide the blind, destroy rats, herd sheep and cattle, help find persons that are lost, and make wonderful pets. Some are bred specially for racing. There are big dogs and little ones, long-haired and short-haired dogs, sedate dogs and playful ones. There is a dog to suit almost everyone's taste. All the many breeds are classified into six groups: working dogs, toy dogs, sporting dogs, non-sporting dogs, hounds, and terriers.

Cats have been developed almost entirely as pets. They are also good mouse catchers, but breeders have done nothing to develop better mousers. They have put all their efforts on getting more interesting-looking and more beautiful cats. Cats can be divided into long-haired and short-haired varieties.

The long-haired cats are the Persians. Some of them are often called "angoras." They have been developed in many different colours. Our common house cats are domestic short-hairs. The Maltese is a blue-grey variety. Many domestic short-hairs have stripes called "tabby" markings. Among the other short-haired breeds are the Manx, which is tailless, and the aristocratic Siamese, with its light coat and dark face.

Many breeds of rabbits have been developed as food animals. Rabbits are popular pets, too. The white rabbit often seen as a pet is an albino. An albino is an animal which for some reason has its natural pigment, or colouring, missing. As a rule the eyes of an albino are pink, just as the eyes of white rabbits are.

Guinea pigs, which are much more closely related to rabbits than to pigs, are small tailless rodents that make good pets. They are also used by doctors in experiments. They have been so much used in this way that "being a guinea pig" means "being used in an experiment."

Among the domesticated animals found in other parts of the world are the camel, the yak, the llama, and the reindeer. Some attempts to tame animals have failed. The zebra, for example, proved too difficult to train.

Domestic Short-hair

Persians

Siamese

Camel (1/25)

Animal Adaptations

EVERY animal has its natural home It is fitted for living there. The ways it is fitt d for living there may make it entirely unfitted for living anywhere else. A camel is not fitted for living in marshland any better than a sandhill crane is fitted for spending its life in a hot desert. A bat and a mole would certainly be misfits if they changed their places of living.

An animal's natural place of living is called its "habitat." The ways the animal is especially fitted for living in that habitat are called its adaptations to its environment.

A camel is fitted in many ways for life in a desert. It has been used for travelling across deserts for so long that it is often called the "ship of the desert." Travel in a desert is not easy. The places where there is water to drink are far apart. It is hard to walk in loose sand, and sometimes sand is blown about in terrible sandstorms. Most desert plants are small, with many spines, or hooks. But these hardships of the desert are not too great for a camel.

A camel does not have to have water so often as most mammals do. It can drink a great deal at one time. There are records showing that a thirsty camel may drink as much as 20 gallons. Some of the water a camel drinks is stored in special parts of its body for later use. After a camel has had all the water it wants, it can get along for several days without drinking.

Sandhill Crane

A camel can store up food, too. Its food storehouse is its hump. It stores up food mostly in the form of fat. A camel's hump is made chiefly of fat. If a camel could not find anything to eat, it could live for days on its hump.

The lips of this desert animal are covered with tough skin, and its teeth are strong. Camels are able to eat tough, spiny plants which most animals would not be able to eat.

A camel has thick pads on its feet. The pads keep its feet from sinking into loose sand. If the sand and rocks of the desert are hot, the pads also protect the camel's feet from the heat.

The hair that covers the camel's body protects it from heat and from sandstorms. A camel has long eyelashes that keep sand out of its eyes. It has hairs in its ears that shut out sand. It can close its nose during a sandstorm.

The sandhill crane has none of these adaptations. They would not fit it for its habitat. Its chief adaptations are long legs that allow it to wade in the water of marshes, a long neck, a long, strong bill suitable for catching fish and frogs and water insects, and strong wings that carry the bird over the water.

A bat is fitted for life in the air. It is so well fitted for the air that it is helpless when by accident it is on the ground. Its wings are made of tough skin. They are big in proportion to the size of its body.

Its legs are weak. But they have sharp little claws on them. To sleep, a bat hangs itself upside down by its back feet from the wall or ceiling of a cave or an old building or a cavity in a tree trunk.

Its beady little eyes enable a bat to see well in dim light. They enable it to fly about at dusk hunting for the insects it needs for food. Although bats do not see well in bright light, there is no truth to the saying "blind as a bat."

But probably the bat's most astonishing adaptation is its radar system. Even when it is pitch dark, a bat can fly without bumping into anything. The voice of the bat can make sounds too high in pitch

Bat (½)

for human ears to hear. But the bat can hear them, and the echoes of these sounds the bat keeps making as it flies about keep the little animal from flying into anything.

Moles spend practically all their time underground, a little way beneath the surface. A mole has fur that is like thick velvet. This fur can be brushed forward or backward and still look smooth. It lets the mole move either forward or backward through the ground easily.

From its home in the ground a mole digs tunnels in all directions. It can dig a tunnel with no difficulty. Its pointed nose works a little like a snowplough. Its big front feet are excellent shovels. The long, strong claws on its front feet are a big help in digging, too. In a single night a mole, which is only about six inches long, has been known to dig a tunnel nearly 100 yards long. As it digs its tunnels, the mole finds insects and earthworms for food.

A mole has two eyes, but they are very small. Good eyes would not be useful to an animal that spends practically its whole life in the dark.

A camel's habitat differs from a sandhill crane's chiefly in the amount of moisture present. A bat's habitat differs from a mole's chiefly in its relation to the surface of the earth. There are many other important ways in which habitats can differ. Temperature, light, pressure, and amount of oxygen present are among them. Plant and animal populations vary, too. It makes a great deal of difference to an animal what plants and animals share its place of living. Different as different parts of the earth are, there are some animals fitted for all but the very coldest, the very driest, the deepest down, and the highest up.

Mole (½)

White Pelican

Green Frog

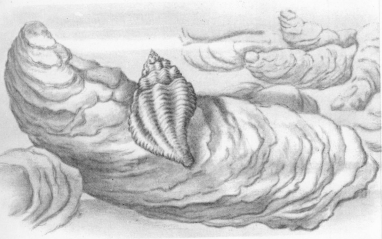

Oyster Drill

Animals are built to live in different kinds of places. They are also built to eat different kinds of food and to get it in different ways.

The white pelican eats fish. It has a built-in fishing net. As it swims through the water, it scoops up small fish with the pouch fastened to its lower bill. It lets the water drain away and then swallows its fish dinner.

The pouch on its bill also serves as a soup bowl for the baby pelicans. The adult birds fill their pouches with a sort of fish soup from their stomachs. The baby birds stick their bills into the bills of the parent birds to drink the fish soup. A baby bird's head may be almost completely hidden inside a parent's bill.

The pelican has webbed feet that enable it to swim fast enough to catch fish. Its strong wings carry it to good feeding grounds.

Toads and frogs, as has been pointed out, have long, sticky tongues that are excellent for catching insects. The tongues are fastened at the front rather than at the back. They can therefore be flipped out a long way. When a toad or frog flips its tongue back with an insect sticking to it, the insect is carried well down its throat so that it is easy to swallow. A toad's or frog's eyes are a help in swallowing a big mouthful.

The oyster drill is a kind of sea snail. It has a tongue that is covered with teeth and is like a small, sharp file. By means of this tongue it can drill holes through oyster shells. Starfish are great enemies of oysters. With their tube feet they pull open an oyster's shell and eat the soft body of the animal. The oyster drill has quite a different way. It does not have to pull open the oyster's shell. It could not possibly do so. But after it has drilled a hole through the shell it scrapes up the soft part of the oyster's body little by little and eats it.

A sea anemone is one of the animals that must wait for their food to come to them. Very early in their lives sea anemones anchor themselves to shells or rocks in shallow water along the seashore. They do not lose entirely their power of moving about, but they can move only slowly. An animal that moves so slowly could not catch much food for itself if it had to scoop it up as the pelican does. Instead, the sea anemone catches its food with its feelers. These feelers surround its mouth, which is at the top of its thick, stemlike body. From its feelers an anemone shoots out poison darts at the ends of long white threads. When an animal has been hit by a dart, the sea anemone's

Sea Anemone

120

Ruby-throated Humming-bird

feelers bend around the animal and bring it to the sea anemone's mouth. A sea anemone can even catch fish in this way.

Not all animals that are anchored in one spot have feelers with poison darts. A rock barnacle, for example, has featherlike legs that "kick" tiny animals into its mouth. An oyster strains small plants and animals from the water that flows in and out of its shell.

A humming-bird's bill is about as different from a pelican's as a bill could be. It is fitted for eating an entirely different kind of food. Most birds eat seeds or animals such as insects, fish, or toads. They have bills that fit them for getting such food. The humming-bird drinks the nectar from flowers. Some of the flowers that produce nectar have their petals joined to form a tube. The nectar is to be found at the bottom of the tube. The humming-bird's bill is long enough and slender enough to reach down into such flowers. The tongue has its edges rolled inward so that it becomes like two straws. The bird sucks the nectar up through it. The humming-bird often gets some tiny insects along with the nectar.

To drink the nectar the humming-bird must stay at almost the same spot for a time. It is able to do so by beating its wings up and down very fast — so fast that they make the hum that gives the bird its name. This bird can not only hover over a flower; it can also perform a feat very rare in the bird kingdom: it can fly backwards.

Among animals we find countless other adaptations for food-getting. The long neck of the giraffe, the big pincers of the lobster, the trunk of the elephant, the great anteater's long snout and very long, sticky tongue, and the spinnerets with which spiders spin webs that serve as insect traps are only a few of them.

Many animals have habits which can be thought of as adaptations. Migration is one of them.

Ever so many birds, as has been said before, have summer homes in one part of the world and winter homes in another. They make the journey between summer home and winter home twice each year. Many birds fly at night and are not seen as they migrate. Others are so small that no one notices them high in the air. But on some of our coasts flocks of such big birds as ducks, geese, and cranes flying northward or southward are among the common sights of spring and autumn.

In their migrations birds may travel for very long distances. The arctic tern is the champion bird traveller. An arctic tern may make an 11,000-mile journey every spring and every autumn. For the arctic tern nests far to the north in North America and Greenland. Healthy baby terns have been found in nests partly covered with snow. The tern winters far to the south near the southern tip of South America. Other birds travel shorter distances, but even the ruby-throated humming-bird travels hundreds of miles each year. Many humming-birds fly all the way across the Gulf of Mexico without stopping for food or rest.

In some ways bird migration is a puzzle to scientists. How did it come about? Did the great Ice Age start it? Why do some birds migrate while others do not? Why do some birds travel so much farther than others? How do birds find their way

Mallard Ducks Migrating

on their long journeys? No one is yet sure of the answers to these questions. But one thing about migration is certain. It lets the birds that migrate live under better conditions than they could have if they lived all the year round in one place. Swifts, which live almost entirely on insects, are all the year in regions where it is warm and insects are plentiful. Mallard ducks, which feed partly on pickerel weed, wild rice, and other such plants of marshlands, are able to have them both winter and summer. The arctic tern by its long journey gets more hours of daylight in a year than any other living creature. By migrating, birds escape severe cold.

No one should think that birds run no risks in making long journeys. They meet many dangers – storms, enemies, and the chance of killing themselves by flying into obstacles. But the advantages outweigh the dangers.

Although birds are most famous for their migrations, many other animals migrate. The salmon spends part of its life in salt water and part in fresh water. This fish begins its life far from the coast in the branches of rivers that empty into the Atlantic. Then it travels down to the sea. There it lives until it becomes adult and reaches the breeding stage. It then travels back up the stream it travelled down when it was young. It may have to cross dangerous rapids and leap up waterfalls. After it has gone far up the river, eggs are laid and fertilized. Then the salmon dies. It thus begins and ends its life in fresh water.

The eel is another fish that makes a long journey to its breeding grounds. But the eel's story is the salmon's story turned around. The eel spends most of its life in fresh water but goes far out to sea to lay its eggs.

Some animals are able to survive in regions of cold winters because they hibernate. Hibernation is usually thought of as sleeping through the winter. Actually an animal that hibernates may not sleep all the time. But it is not at all active.

Cold-blooded animals have no way of making their bodies any warmer than their surroundings. Many cold-blooded animals die when winter comes on, and leave only their eggs to endure the cold. Those that do live through very cold weather do so by hibernating. No one sees frogs or snakes or newts when ponds are skating rinks and there is snow on the ground. No one sees butterflies or moths or bumblebees.

Frogs bury themselves in mud, often in the mud at the bottom of a pond. Before beginning their winter sleep they store food in their bodies by eating a great deal. While they are hibernating they eat nothing at all. They breathe only through their skins; they need little oxygen since they are so quiet that they are using up very little energy. Even their hearts slow down so that they do not use up much energy in beating.

Snakes and newts hibernate under rocks or old logs. Toads hibernate in the same kinds of places or in the mud at the bottom of a pond. Turtles follow the same plan.

Salmon Migrating

Some butterflies migrate just as birds do. Many die in the autumn. Some hibernate. The red admiral is one that does. This butterfly spends the winter in hollow trees. Some moths live through the winter in the pupa stage. They are wrapped up in cocoons. The queen bumblebee is the only one of a bumblebee colony that lives through the winter. She hides herself in a deep crack in the bark of a tree or inside an old building.

But hibernation is not limited to cold-blooded animals. Many mammals hibernate, too.

Dormice, badgers, hedgehogs and squirrels are among the mammals which hibernate. Dormice eat a great deal of food in the late summer and autumn, so that when they go to sleep enough energy is stored inside them to last until the following spring. Squirrels, on the other hand, do not sleep all through the winter. A mild day in January will bring them out looking for nuts. It is true that they make stores of nuts for themselves. But it is not really likely that they remember where they put them. Badgers, like squirrels, sleep fitfully through the winter.

One very common Canadian superstition has to do with hibernation. If the woodchuck, or groundhog, so the superstition goes, comes out of his winter sleep and sees his shadow on Groundhog Day, February 2, there will be six weeks more of cold weather. The groundhog is supposed to go back into its burrow for six weeks more of sleep. If the groundhog does not see its shadow, spring is just around the corner. Of course, there is no truth in this superstition.

The main secret of survival among animals is being able to eat without being eaten. The colour of an animal may be a great help. It may make the animal match its surroundings so well that it cannot be seen easily. Its colour may be a great protection against its enemies. It may also be a help in getting the food it needs.

The polar bear is an example of an animal that is greatly helped by its colour. The polar bear has no meat-eating enemies. It is one of the chief carnivores in the arctic regions where it lives. But food is not very abundant in those regions. The polar bear lives chiefly on seals and fish. It also catches some birds and foxes. Since it matches its surroundings so well, it can often creep up on an animal it is trying to catch without being seen. It can pounce on a seal, for instance, before the seal knows that one of its enemies is near.

Unfortunately for the polar bear, some of its meat-eating rivals and some of the animals it eats are protected in the same way by their colour. The arctic fox is as white as the polar bear. So is the snowy ptarmigan, a bird of the arctic. It is not strange, therefore, that a polar bear sometimes has to eat dead animals that have been washed up on shore.

Female birds are generally protected by their colour. They cannot be seen easily if they are not moving about. They would be easy prey for bird-eating animals if their colours were so bright that they showed up clearly as they sat quietly on their nests.

Animals that live in forests are often spotted or striped. Sunlight shining down through the trees makes streaks and spots of brightness. The streaks and spots on the animals there keep them from showing up clearly. The tiger, the leopard, the zebra, and the giraffe are among the animals that are protected by their spots and stripes.

The general colour plan of fishes is a good one for protection. A fish, as a rule, is darker above than below. A fish-eating bird, looking down on a fish, may not see it because its back matches the

Weasel in Autumn

Weasel in Winter

bottom of the river or lake or ocean so well. A fish-eating fish, swimming below it, may not see it because its light underside is not very different from the colour of the sky as seen from under water.

Some animals change the colour of their coats with the seasons. In the summer the little weasel is brown. It matches the ground and dry leaves and grasses very well. It can creep up on the animals it eats without being seen easily by bigger animals that would welcome a weasel dinner. But this little animal does not hibernate. It must be able to catch food in the winter. In the autumn in north Britain its brown hair drops out and white hair takes its place. It then matches the snow almost as well as the polar bear.

Some birds change their coats with the seasons. Mallard drakes look very dismal at the end of the breeding period. When they are moulting they are said to be "in eclipse." Cock chaffinches also become dull and moult. But by next spring both birds are resplendent in new feathers.

Some animals actually change colour as their surroundings change. One tiny tree toad is mostly grey or greyish-brown if it is resting on bark. If it is resting on a leaf, it is green. Changing from one colour to another takes this little fellow about an hour.

The squid is another animal that changes colour to match changed surroundings. The flounder is still another. It can make itself almost any shade of grey or brown. It can give itself fine speckles to match sand and big speckles to match gravel, too. The little crab spider may be either yellow or white, depending on the colour of the flower it is resting on.

The chameleon is so famous for colour changes that ability to change colour is the first thing one thinks of when he hears the word "chameleon." But a chameleon's colour-changes do not always make this little lizard match its surroundings better. They seem to have more to do with changes in light and temperature and with excitement.

125

Stick Insect

Tree Toad

When a chameleon is asleep it is usually pale green. When it is excited or in danger it becomes bright green. In the early morning or late evening it is often grey or pale yellow. In bright sunlight it is usually dark brown. But even though a chameleon's rapid changes in colour do not always make it match its environment better, it often happens that they do. At least, a pet chameleon that escapes may be very hard to find because of its colour.

Some animals are made to match their surroundings in the way shown by the picture below of some hermit crabs. Both the rocks and the snail shells the hermit crabs have taken over as homes are covered with tiny pink animals called "hedgehog hydroids."

Hedgehog hydroids look at a glance more like plants than like animals. They have stalks just as many plants have. A colony of hedgehog hydroids is somewhat like a Portuguese man-of-war. Some of the animals in the colony do the eating, some have stingers with which they protect the colony, and some form eggs to produce new animals. The hedgehog hydroids help the crabs by making them match their surroundings. In return they get a free ride on the backs of the crabs and have a better chance to get food than if they stayed always in one place.

The hermit crab has nothing to do with camouflaging itself, but one of its relatives, the spider crab (page 46), does its own camouflaging. It

Hermit Crab

sticks seaweed and small animals on its back and its long legs. It chooses seaweed and animals that match its surroundings. If the spider crab travels to a new home, it may change its plant and animal decorations.

The stick insect shows a way of making itself match its surroundings that is called "mimicry." The stick insect looks like a twig of a tree. Animals that might eat it pass it by without ever seeing it.

The praying mantis is protected by its colour. It matches almost exactly the green of the plants on which it makes its home. It has a relative in the Far East that is one of the very best examples of mimicry. This insect's body looks exactly like two green leaves, one resting on top of the other. They have veins that look like leaf veins. The insect's legs are green and are flattened out so that they look like small leaves. In places they have ragged edges as if other insects had been nibbling at them. When a wind is blowing, this insect moves just as it would if it were a leaf being blown by the wind.

The dead-leaf butterfly is also an excellent mimic. The undersides of its wings look so much like dead leaves that it would deceive almost any passer-by that saw it on a branch.

The viceroy butterfly is another insect that is well known for its mimicry. It does not hide itself by looking like some part of a plant. Instead, it mimics the monarch butterfly, which is very easily seen. The viceroy is good food to many birds, while the monarch has an unpleasant taste because of an acid it produces. By looking like the bad-tasting monarch, the viceroy escapes many an enemy. These are all tropical butterflies.

Some animals are able to hold their own among their neighbours because they have good armour. Others owe their success to good weapons.

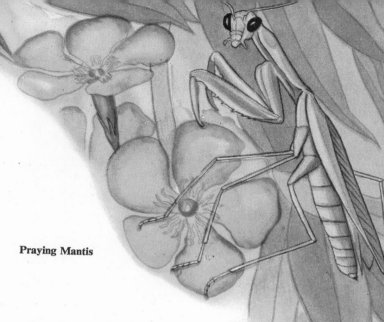

Praying Mantis

The whirligig beetle has two sets of eyes. One set is above, the other below, the surface of the water as the beetle swims about. Some deep-sea animals that live down where no sunlight ever penetrates give off light that attracts prey. The dolphin has very big lungs in which it can store enough air to last for 20 or 30 minutes under water. Some air-breathing snails can stay under water for a long time by sending up a tube to the surface of the water.

The fluids in the body of a deep-sea fish make it possible for the fish to stand terrific pressure. In fact, deep-sea fishes really blow up if they are brought up to the surface. The pressure from inside out is so great that it kills the fish if the pressure on the outside is reduced. Many mammals have developed hoofs that help them in moving about. All these are other ways in which animals have become fitted through the ages for living where they do.

Chameleon

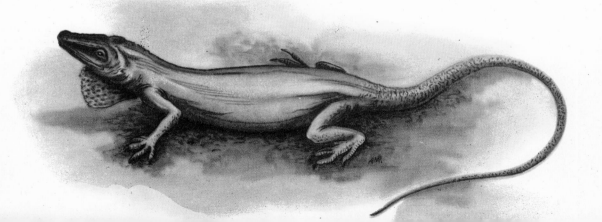

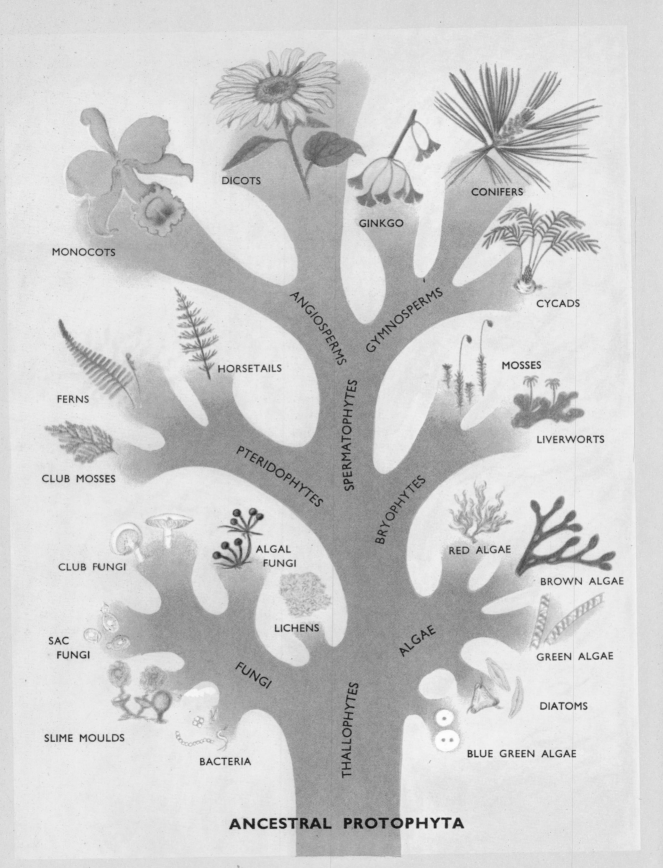

DICOTS

MONOCOTS

CONIFERS

GINKGO

CYCADS

ANGIOSPERMS

GYMNOSPERMS

HORSETAILS

MOSSES

FERNS

SPERMATOPHYTES

LIVERWORTS

CLUB MOSSES

PTERIDOPHYTES

BRYOPHYTES

CLUB FUNGI

ALGAL
FUNGI

RED ALGAE

BROWN ALGAE

LICHENS

SAC
FUNGI

ALGAE

GREEN ALGAE

FUNGI

DIATOMS

THALLOPHYTES

SLIME MOULDS

BACTERIA

BLUE GREEN ALGAE

ANCESTRAL PROTOPHYTA

The Plant Kingdom

THERE are not nearly so many kinds of plants as there are kinds of animals – at least not nearly so many have been discovered thus far. Since some kinds of plants are too small to be seen without a microscope, and since there are still some little-known parts of the world, many more kinds of plants are sure to be discovered in time. But many more animals will surely be discovered, too. It is not likely that the number of kinds of plants will ever catch up with the number of kinds of animals. At present we know of roughly 325,000 kinds of plants as against about 1,000,000 kinds of animals.

Plants are classified very much as animals are. There are phyla, classes, orders, families, genera, and species. There are some subphyla, too. A subphylum, as in the scheme for classifying animals, is between a phylum and a class.

The common primrose is a species of plant. It belongs to the primula genus. The primulas belong to the primulaceæ family. This family, a very large one, includes such well-known flowers as the cowslip, pimpernel and cyclamen – a flower which is not found wild in Britain. The family belongs to the order primulales. The order belongs to the class of dicots. The dicots are a part of a subphylum called the "angiosperms," or flowering plants. The flowering plants belong to the phylum of spermatophytes, or seed plants.

Every plant has a scientific name just as every animal has. The scientific name of the common daisy is *Bellis perennis*.

The chart on the opposite page gives some idea of the whole plant kingdom. All the thousands of plants of today are supposed to have come from very simple one-celled plants that lived on the earth back in the days when it was young. "Protophyta" means "first plants."

There are only four main groups, or phyla, in the plant kingdom. The thallophytes form one of the four great groups, the lowest one.

The thallophytes are plants with no leaves or roots or stems. This group includes the algae, the fungi, and the lichens.

The second group has been given the name "bryophytes." Their name means "moss-like plants." In this group are all the mosses. In it, too, are the liverworts, small plants that many people have never heard of.

Ranking just above the moss-like plants are the ferns and their relatives. They are the pteridophytes. Along with the ferns in this group are the club mosses and the horsetails.

At the top of the plant kingdom are the spermatophytes, or seed plants. As the chart shows, there are two great branches of the seed plants – the angiosperms, or flowering plants, and the gymnosperms, or cone-bearers.

The flowering plants were the last of the great groups of plants to appear on the earth. After they did appear, they almost took the earth over, so far as plants were concerned. Today there are many more kinds of flowering plants than of all other plants put together. If the branches on the chart were made in proportion to the numbers of kinds of plants belonging on them, the "tree" of the plant kingdom would be extremely top-heavy and lopsided.

All the plants pictured below are algae. Most algae are water plants. Our seaweeds are algae. So are our pond scums. The algae that do not actually live in water live in moist places.

Some algae are so tiny that single ones cannot be seen without a microscope. Many of them are made of only a single cell. But by no means all algae are small. A big brown kelp (kelps are algae) may grow to be 150 feet long.

There are blue-green algae, green algae, brown algae, and red algae. In the group of algae there are also the diatoms. These are tiny one-celled plants with glassy shells like little pillboxes. They form an important part of plankton, the "sea soup" on which many animals of the sea live.

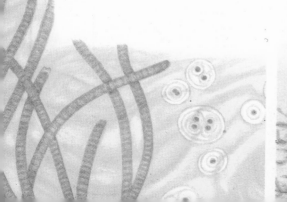
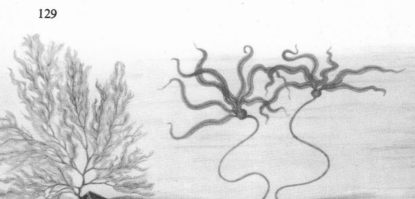

Orchid

Pictured on these two pages are representatives of each of the four great divisions, or phyla, of the plant kingdom. It takes only a glance back at the "tree" to see that the three plants shown at the top are higher in the plant world than those at the bottom.

The mushroom is a fungus. ("Fungus" is the singular of "fungi.") This particular mushroom is poisonous, but, of course, not all mushrooms are. Fungi do not have in them any of the green colouring matter that most other plants have. Many fungi are either colourless or white. Some, on the other hand, are brightly coloured.

Mushroom

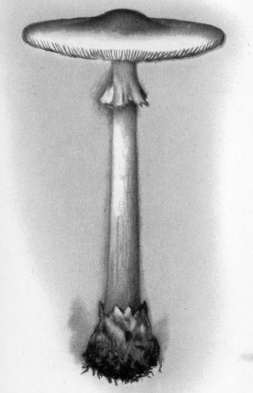

The orchid belongs at the very top of one of the branches of the flowering plants, the monocots. Some orchids grow on the ground, but many, like the one in the picture, perch on the branches of trees in tropical forests. Growing on the tree limb beside the orchid are some lichens. They are much like the lichens on the rock in the picture below.

Lichens are strange plants. They are made up of fungus plants and green algae. If one were to look at a piece of lichen through a microscope, one would see many tiny green dots (the algae) surrounded by white threads (the fungus).

A lichen is one of the best partnerships in the whole world of living things. The algae and the fungi help each other so well that lichens can live on bare rocks where no other plants can grow. The algae furnish the fungi with food. The fungi store up water from rain and dew, and keep the algae from drying out. The fungi also give off an acid that eats down into the rock and helps the lichen anchor itself in place. In time lichens make the rock start crumbling into soil. The places where they grow become fit for other plants. Lichens are plant pioneers.

The pine and the spruce are conifers. The coni-

Lichen

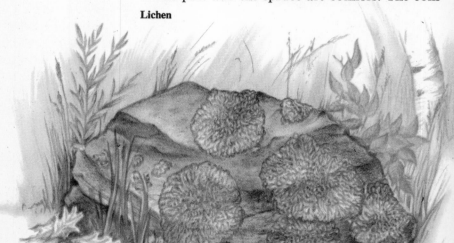

Spruce

Pine

fers rank high on the cone-bearer branch of the seed plants.

Mosses are tiny plants. We often see these little plants growing so close together that they form a velvety green carpet. They grow in many different parts of the world, some even in very cold regions.

Mosses are not quite so common, however, as plant names might make you think. A number of plants are called mosses that do not belong to the group. Among them are Irish moss, long moss, and reindeer moss. Irish moss is one of the brown algae. Long moss is a seed plant, a cousin of the pineapple. Reindeer moss is a lichen.

The slender stems rising from the moss plants pictured have spore cases at the top. Many of the plants that are lower than the seed plants are scattered by spores. Spores are single cells. They are very tiny bits of living material.

The mosses are much better known than their fellow bryophytes, the liverworts. Liverworts are ribbon-like plants that lie close against whatever they are growing on. They are seen most often on shaded walls and damp rocks.

Although most people would consider liverworts unimportant, they are of great interest to scientists. For scientists believe that the first land plants were liverworts. Scientists think, too, that the early liverworts were the ancestors of the mosses and all the higher plants.

The fern pictured, like all ferns, is a pteridophyte. The pteridophytes have fallen far from the place they once held in the plant world. Tree pteridophytes were the first really big land plants. In the great forests from which coal was made, there were tree ferns, tree horsetails, and tree club mosses. Now there are no longer any tree club mosses or tree horsetails. All the club mosses and horsetails of today are little plants. There are still some tree ferns in very warm, moist regions.

Today's horsetails are often called "scouring rushes." They grow only in barren, sandy areas. They may not long be able to keep their foothold even there.

Today's club mosses are found growing close to the ground.

The fern in the picture shows one pattern which every fern leaf follows. When it is young, every leaf is rolled into a "fiddlehead." It then unrolls from the base upward. Two small fiddleheads show in the picture. There is a second way in which all fern leaves are alike. When a vein in a fern leaf divides, it always forks into two equal branches.

There are many kinds of ferns. There are ten times as many species of ferns as there are of horsetails and club mosses together. But, as compared with the seed plants, they make up a very inconspicuous part of the plant world.

Moss

Fern

Grains of Starch

**Grains of Starch
Stained with Iodine**

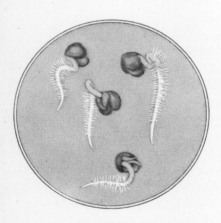

Root Hairs

Sugar Maple

Food Factories

IN parts of the world where sugar maples grow, early spring is "sugaring off" time. Holes are bored in the trunks of the maple trees, little troughs are put in the holes, and buckets are hung at the ends of the troughs. As sap begins to rise in the trees, some of it runs out into the buckets. The sap is mostly water, but it also has sugar in it. It is boiled down to make maple syrup or maple sugar.

The sugar in the sap was stored in the trunks of the trees through the winter. It is gathered up by the water that rises in the trunks in the spring and, if it is not drained out of the tree, is carried to the parts of the tree that need it. New leaves and flowers and branches cannot grow unless there is food to make them do so. Sugar is good food.

The story of how the sap of a maple tree happens to have sugar in it in the springtime is thus a simple one. The story of how the sugar maple gets the sugar it stores in its trunk is much more complicated.

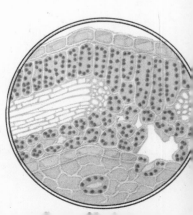

A maple tree has only two places from which it can get materials it needs. One is the soil. The other is the air. It goes without saying that there is no sugar in either soil or air. If it cannot get the sugar from either the soil or the air, it is clear that the maple tree must make it itself. It must make it out of materials it can get from soil or air. A sugar maple tree is a sugar factory.

Sugar maple trees are not unique in this way. All green plants are sugar factories. They do not all make as much sugar as a sugar maple makes. Some of them use it up as fast as they make it. Some of them change it to starch before they store it up. But they all make sugar as food for themselves.

Green plants use two very common materials in making sugar. One is water. The other is carbon dioxide. The leaves are the chief sugar factories of most green plants – of all green plants, in fact, that have leaves.

A leaf is made up of many cells. In the cells of the leaf of a green plant there are many tiny green bodies called "chloroplasts." "Chloroplasts" means "green bodies." They are made green by the wonderful green dye, or pigment, chlorophyll. "Leaf green," its name means.

Green leaves look green because of their chloroplasts. The chloroplasts are the only green part of a leaf, as the magnified bit of leaf shows. The rest of the leaf is, as a rule, colourless. A leaf looks green just as a transparent bag would look red if it were packed full of tiny red balls.

The chloroplasts might well be called the machines of the sugar factory. For these tiny green bodies carry on the manufacture of sugar out of carbon dioxide and water. It is the chlorophyll in them that enables them to do so.

In the leaves of a maple tree and most other green plants there are small openings called "stomata." The word means "little mouths." Air gets to the inside of a leaf through the stomata. The chloroplasts get carbon dioxide from the air that enters the leaf.

Water, even when there is a heavy rain, does not enter a leaf through the stomata. As a rule, the "little mouths" are on the underside of the leaf so that it cannot. The water enters the roots of the plant. Near the end of a root there is a little "brush" of root hairs. The root hairs cling to particles of soil. They soak up water. The water travels from the roots up through the stem and its branches. It goes in special water-carrying tubes.

Oxygen rising from green plant

These tubes make up a part of the wood of tree trunks. The water at last reaches the veins of the leaf. The veins carry it to the cells where the chloroplasts are.

Chloroplasts cannot work without sunlight. Sugar-making, therefore, goes on only during the daytime. When sugar-making is going on, the chloroplasts throw away oxygen. If plants are growing under water, bubbles of oxygen can often be seen rising from them.

After sugar is made, the chloroplasts may make it at once into starch. When a grain of starch is examined under a microscope it is easy to see that the grain has been built up in layers. Iodine, although it is brown, stains grains of starch blue. In grains that have been stained blue the layers show up very clearly.

Green plants, after they have made starch and sugar, can build them into other kinds of food by adding minerals from the soil. Green plants cannot live on sugar and starch alone, just as people are unable to.

Animals cannot make food for themselves. They have to get their food by eating plants or by eating other animals that eat plants. Plants that are not green, except for a very, very few, have to get their food from animals or from green plants. Green plants, it is clear, are the world's food factories.

Stomata

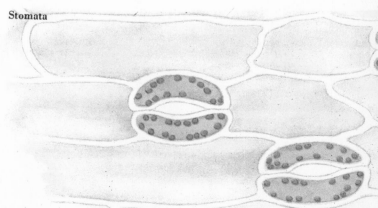

BALSAM FIR

Trees

TREES are our biggest plants. Some people have the idea that trees are too big to be called plants, but this idea is wrong. A tree is built on very much the same plan as a sunflower or a rose-bush; it is simply larger.

In the warm, wet regions of the world there are some tree ferns. All the trees of cooler regions are seed plants. But they are not all flowering plants. Many of them have cones rather than flowers.

The cone-bearing trees are called "conifers." Conifers have narrow leaves, many so narrow that they are called needles. All the trees pictured on these two pages are conifers. Both their needles and their cones are helpful in telling these conifers apart.

The leaves of conifers, although they are narrow, serve the same purpose that the leaves of other green plants serve. They are the trees' food factories.

Most conifers have leaves the year round. They are evergreens. The fact that they are green all the year round does not mean that they never shed any leaves. They do, but they shed them a few at a time all during the year. The trees are, therefore, never bare.

But not all conifers are evergreens. The larch and the bald cypress are among the conifers that shed their leaves in the autumn and send out new ones in the spring.

The conifers include some of our most valuable timber trees. They are often called "softwoods," although that name is not an especially good one. The wood of some conifers is soft, but that of a few is hard. There are, for example, hard pines.

The bald cypress, a valuable timber tree, in one way is a puzzle. Queer growths called "knees" often rise from its roots. This tree grows in swamps. For a long time scientists thought that the knees were a way of getting air for the roots of the tree. The knees, they thought, kept the trees from drowning. But experiments have thrown some doubt on this idea. No one now feels sure how the knees help the cypress.

Many people who do not live near any conifer

LARCH

ENGELMANN SPRUCE

DOUGLAS FIR

forests are familiar with some kinds of conifers. They buy small trees or branches at Christmas time for Christmas-trees and Christmas greens. They learn to tell one tree from another because some of the conifers hold their leaves better than others. The firs, for example, are much better than spruces.

The largest of all trees are conifers. These are the giant sequoias. Another name for them is "big trees." One giant sequoia, so famous that it has been given a name, has a diameter of more than 36 feet at the base and is nearly 280 feet tall. It is as tall as a 20-storey building, and there would be room for a church inside its trunk. This giant is the "General Sherman." There are other big trees that are almost as big.

The oldest giant sequoias are the oldest of all trees. They are the oldest of all plants. They are, scientists think, the oldest of all living things! The

LODGEPOLE PINE

BALD CYPRESS

ELM

OAK

BEECH

"General Sherman" is probably about 4,000 years old. It began growing, scientists say, back in the days when the Egyptians were the most highly civilized people in the world. It was more than 3,000 years old when Columbus first reached the shores of America.

Scientists are not sure exactly how old the "General Sherman" is, but they do know exactly how old some big trees have lived to be. They have been able to tell the age of these trees after they were cut down.

The age of giant sequoias – and of most other trees, too – can be told from rings in the wood. In the trunks of most kinds of trees new wood is formed each year in a layer outside the old wood and beneath the bark. When the trunk of the tree is sawed across, each layer shows as a ring. The rings are called "annual rings." Telling how old the tree is means simply counting the annual rings.

The trees pictured on this page belong to the great group of flowering plants. Their seeds are produced by flowers, not cones. These trees are often called "broad-leafed trees." They are often spoken of as "hardwoods," too, even though some of them have soft wood.

Many broad-leafed trees drop their leaves in the autumn and send out new leaves in the spring. During the winter months their branches are bare. Such trees are called "deciduous." The name comes from the Latin word meaning "to fall."

The oak is a broad-leafed tree that is deciduous. It is a help to broad-leafed trees to drop their leaves in the autumn if they live in a region with cold winters. The living material in the cells of a

SCARLET OAK

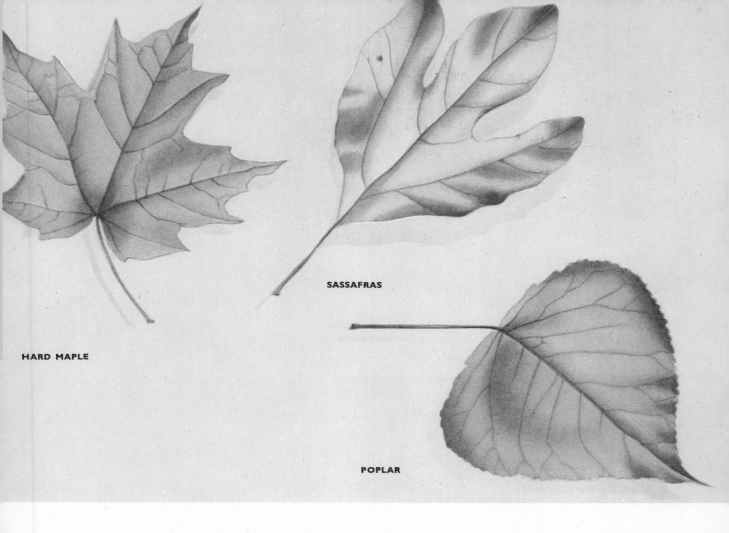

HARD MAPLE

SASSAFRAS

POPLAR

small conifer needle is much better protected from the cold than the living material in the thin leaves of a broad-leafed tree. But in regions where the winters are not cold, broad-leafed trees can be evergreen. The holm oak lives in regions where the winters are never very cold. It is safe for it to have leaves all the year.

Some trees can be told at a distance by their shape. The umbrella shape of the elm, for example, is very different from the broad spread of the oak or the tall, narrow outline of the Lombardy poplar. When a tree is bare in winter, its shape is one of the best ways of identifying it.

Their leaves, of course, are a help in telling broad-leafed trees apart. Every kind of tree has a leaf of a distinctive shape. Some are narrow; some are much broader. Some are very much larger than others. The edges of some are smooth; the edges of others are toothed like a saw. Some leaves have lobes; others are entire – that is, they have no lobes at all. Some leaves are divided into separate leaflets. We say that these divided leaves are "compound."

Some trees play a kind of joke on people trying to identify them from their leaves. They have leaves of different shapes, all on the same tree. The Canadian sassafras is one of the trees with leaves of different shapes. Not all sassafras leaves have lobes on each side as the one pictured above has. Some are lobed on only one side; they are mitten-shaped. Others have no lobes. The mulberry also has leaves that vary in shape.

The veins of leaves differ. In some leaves the veins spread out like the fingers from the palm of the hand. Some branch like a feather. Scientists say, then, that some leaves are palmately and some are pinnately veined. "Pinnate" means "featherlike." The maple leaf is palmately veined. All the other leaves pictured on these two pages have pinnate veining.

The stem of a leaf is called its "petiole." The petioles of most leaves are round. The poplar leaf, on the other hand, has a flat petiole. It lets the leaf move very easily in the wind. The flat petiole explains why poplar trees rustle so in the breeze.

137

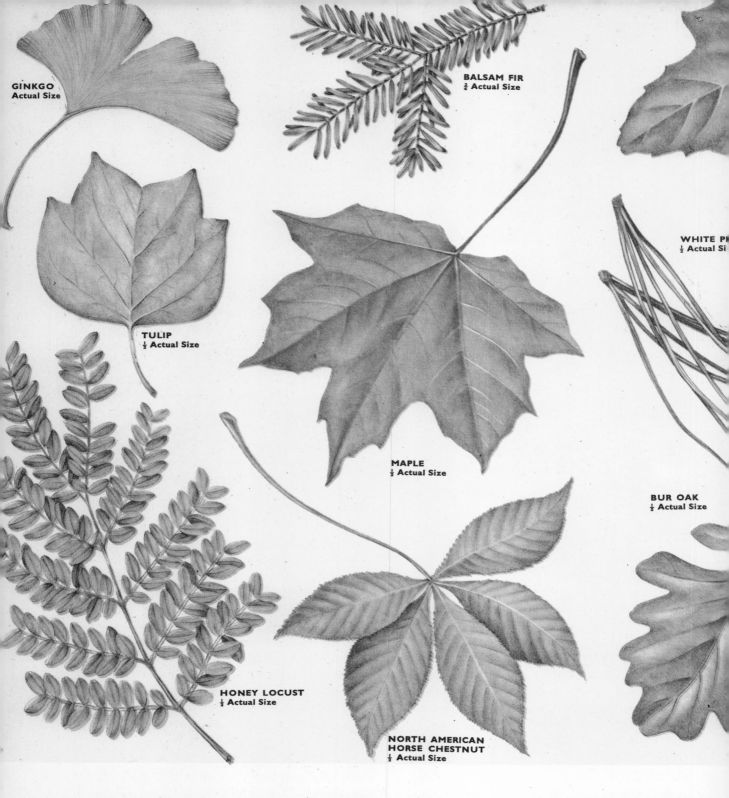

GINKGO
Actual Size

BALSAM FIR
¼ Actual Size

WHITE PI
½ Actual Si

TULIP
½ Actual Size

MAPLE
½ Actual Size

BUR OAK
½ Actual Size

HONEY LOCUST
½ Actual Size

**NORTH AMERICAN
HORSE CHESTNUT**
½ Actual Size

Different trees have their leaves arranged differently on their twigs. Maple and ash trees, for instance, have leaves that are opposite each other. The catalpa tree has three leaves growing in a ring around the twig. But most trees have their leaves coming first from one side of the twig and then from the other. This is called an "alternate" arrangement.

Bark, buds, leaf scars, and thorns are other helps in telling broad-leafed trees apart, especially in winter. In the spring the trees' flowers are a help. Later in the year the seeds are name cards to those who know enough about trees to read them. Acorns, for instance, grow only on oak trees, and every kind of oak has its own special shape and size of acorn.

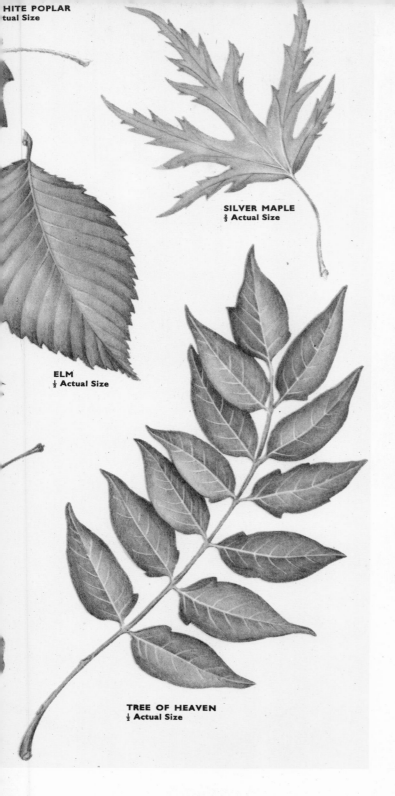

WHITE POPLAR
Actual Size

SILVER MAPLE
⅜ Actual Size

ELM
½ Actual Size

TREE OF HEAVEN
¼ Actual Size

One of the leaves pictured comes from a tree that does not belong to either the flowering plants or the conifers. This is the ginkgo. As the "tree" of the plant kingdom on page 128 shows, the ginkgo belongs to the cone-bearing branch of the seed plants, but it is not a conifer.

A common name of the ginkgo is "maidenhair tree." Its fan-shaped leaves remind people of the leaflets of the maidenhair fern, although they are much larger.

The ginkgo tree has been on the earth longer than any other of the trees whose leaves are pictured here. It is a "living fossil."

Before the days of the flowering plants – back in the early days of the dinosaurs – the ginkgo grew in many parts of the world. It flourished in Europe, North America, and Asia. But now it has been crowded out in most places. It grows wild today only in the mountains of western China. But many people have seen ginkgo trees who have never been in China. They are grown in Kew Gardens, where they look very strange, standing among the different varieties of "modern" tree. Kew is the only place in Britain where you are likely to see ginkgoes. But in some countries they are planted on city streets.

The leaves of two conifers are pictured here: the balsam fir and the white pine. There are leaves from nine broad-leafed trees. Three of them are compound – they are made up of separate leaflets. The three are the tree-of-heaven, the horse chestnut, and the honey locust. In each case only one leaf is shown. The honey locust is doubly compound. Its leaflets are divided into leaflets.

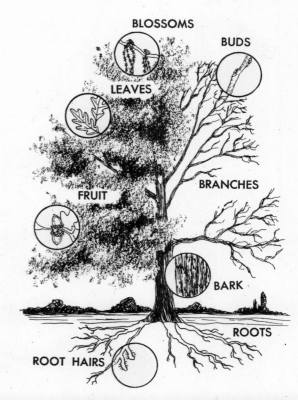

BLOSSOMS

BUDS

LEAVES

BRANCHES

FRUIT

BARK

ROOTS

ROOT HAIRS

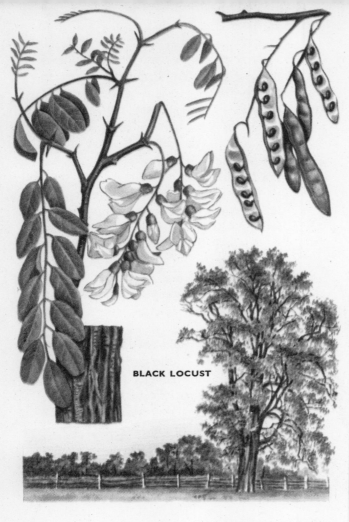

BLACK LOCUST

Our broad-leafed trees belong to the great group of flowering plants, but many of them have flowers that would not be recognized as flowers by most people. Certainly no one would gather the walnut flowers pictured on page 170 for a bouquet. But some trees have large and showy flowers. The trees shown on these two pages are among them. All our cultivated fruit trees belong here, too. No flower garden was ever more beautiful than an apple orchard in full bloom.

The flowers of the North American dogwood, however, are showy only because of big bracts that surround clusters of them. The bracts are sometimes pink, sometimes white. They look like petals, but they are really not parts of the flowers. The flowers themselves are small and greenish.

For some reason which no one understands, one branch of the flowering plants – the dicots – produced many more kinds of trees than the other branch – the monocots. But there is one huge family of trees on the monocot branch – the palms. There are more than twelve hundred kinds of palms. To the people of tropical lands the palms are enormously important. They furnish shelter, food, drink, and fibres.

Palm trees do not have the solid woody trunks that the dicots and the conifers have. Their trunks are more like the stems of sweet corn. Bundles of woody water-carrying tubes are scattered through the trunks. There is soft pith between. No one can tell the age of a palm tree by counting the rings in its wood. There are no rings.

Unfortunately, trees of all kinds have enemies. There are countless kinds of insects that live on the trees of our forests and orchards and the shade trees of our towns and cities. Some of the worst insect enemies of our trees have been brought in

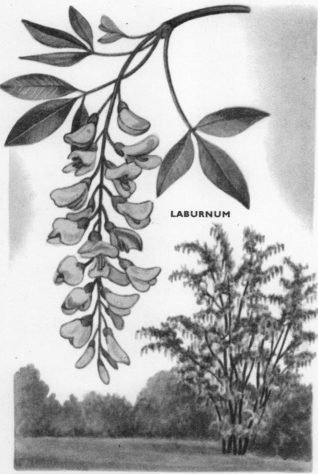

LABURNUM

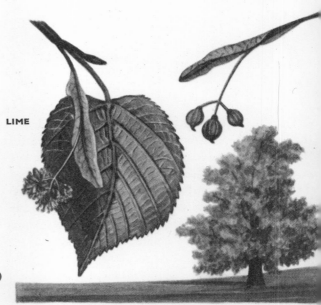

LIME

from other lands. There are many tree diseases, too.

Smoke is an enemy of trees, too. Many kinds of trees cannot stand the soot and smoke of our industrial cities. An exception is the plane tree – one of the few trees which grow really well in the heart of London.

Fire is one of the worst enemies of forest trees. Forest fires, many started by carelessness, have destroyed millions of pounds' worth of good timber in Canada. A field of corn, if it is destroyed by a fire or a storm, can be replaced the next year. Replacing a forest is a matter of many years, perhaps of more than a century. In some cases a forest fire damages the soil so that trees will not grow in it again.

Thinking how many enemies a tree may have helps us choose trees for planting round our homes and on our streets. A tree that is likely to be killed by a disease or that is a prey to so many kinds of insects that a war against them will have to be carried on constantly is not a good choice. Neither is a short-lived tree nor one that has such brittle wood that it is likely to break in every storm. But neither must a tree grow too slowly.

Some trees are unpopular for city streets because they produce so many roots that they clog up sewers beneath the streets. Some are not well liked because their flowers have an unpleasant smell. Some litter up the ground under them too much with their flowers or seeds. But, although there are many questions to be asked about any tree that is being considered for city planting, there are many trees to choose from. Except on our most exposed coasts, there are almost sure to be several kinds of trees that would do well. And no one can overestimate what a help trees are to a city or town.

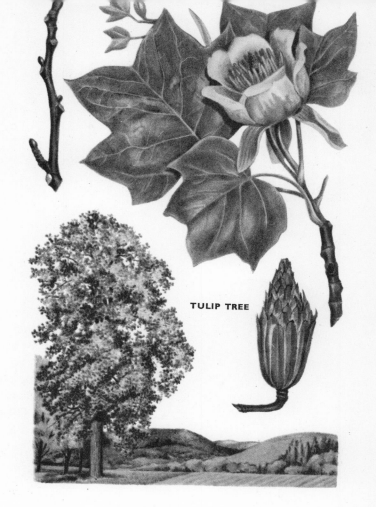

TULIP TREE

HORSE CHESTNUT

HAWTHORN

141

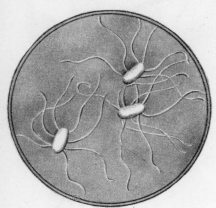

Typhoid Bacilli

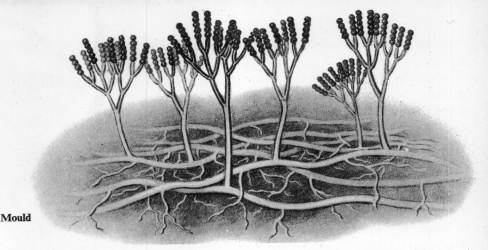

Mould

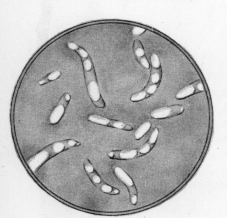

Diphtheria Bacilli

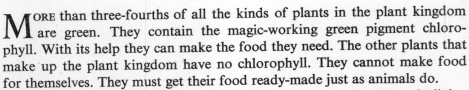

Plants That Are Not Green

MORE than three-fourths of all the kinds of plants in the plant kingdom are green. They contain the magic-working green pigment chlorophyll. With its help they can make the food they need. The other plants that make up the plant kingdom have no chlorophyll. They cannot make food for themselves. They must get their food ready-made just as animals do.

Some plants that are not green get their food by growing on or in living plants or animals. Others get their food from dead plants and animals or from such plant and animal products as flour, milk, and leather.

Plants that must get their food ready-made are often called "dependent plants." About 99 out of every 100 dependent plants are fungi.

Bacteria make up one of the divisions of the fungi. Bacteria are all far too small to be seen without a microscope – and a powerful microscope at that. Some are so tiny that it would take 25,000 of them to make a row an inch long. Each plant is a single cell, although several may be joined to form a chain.

Some bacteria, the cocci, are like tiny balls. Some, the bacilli, are rod-shaped. Some, the spirilla, are twisted. A bacterium may have hairlike cilia which enable the tiny plant to swim about.

Bacteria of one kind or another are found almost everywhere. They are in the air we breathe, the food we eat, and the water we drink. They are in our own bodies and in the bodies of other animals. They are present by the billions in every square foot of soil.

These tiny plants multiply very simply. When a cell reaches a certain size, it simply divides into two cells.

Some bacteria cause disease. Others cause food to decay. Such harmful bacteria have given the whole group a bad name. But there are bacteria that are our very good friends.

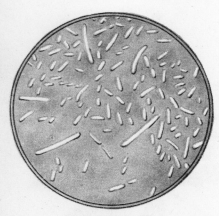

Dysentery Bacilli

Spirilla

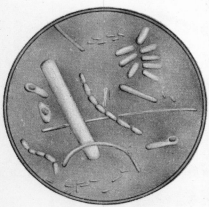

Bacilli

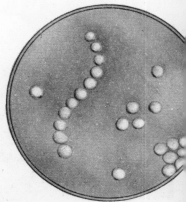

Cocci

Among our important bacteria friends are those that live in small bumps, or nodules, on the roots of such plants as clover. These bacteria are called "nitrogen-fixing bacteria." They help keep soil fertile by taking nitrogen from the air and building it into compounds other plants can use.

Yeasts also are one-celled. Next to the bacteria, they are the smallest fungi. Although larger than bacteria, they are far too small to be seen without a microscope.

Yeast plants depend chiefly on sugar for food. The sugar must be dissolved. As yeast plants use up sugar, they produce carbon dioxide and alcohol. When yeasts are at work in a solution, we say that the solution is souring, or fermenting. These tiny plants, like bacteria, float about in the air. They are likely to drop into any fruit juice or other sugar solution left unprotected.

The yeast plants floating about in the air are wild yeasts. Yeasts are cultivated for use in making bread and in making alcohol and alcoholic drinks. The cakes of yeast used in making bread are made up of millions of yeast plants mixed with flour. In bread making it is the carbon dioxide produced which is important. The bubbles of this gas make the bread rise.

As a rule yeast plants multiply by budding. A small bud grows out of a cell. A wall soon divides it from the parent plant. A whole chain may be formed. But at any time a chain may break apart into separate plants.

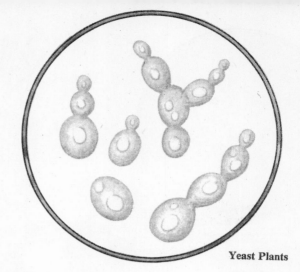

Yeast Plants

Moulds are fungi, too. They are considerably larger than bacteria and yeasts. The main part of a mould plant is made up of colourless threads. The mass of threads formed is called a "mycelium." From the mycelium tiny stalks arise which bear spores. Spores serve mould plants as seeds; new plants grow from them. Their spores give mould plants their colour. Common colours among the moulds are black, blue, and green.

Moulds will grow on almost anything which comes from a plant or an animal. Moulds growing on foods are usually a nuisance. But many kinds of cheese owe their flavour to moulds growing in them. Moulds growing on leather, paper, cloth, or wood spoil its appearance and in time ruin the material. Recently moulds have been a great help in fighting disease. Drugs such as penicillin and aureomycin are produced from them.

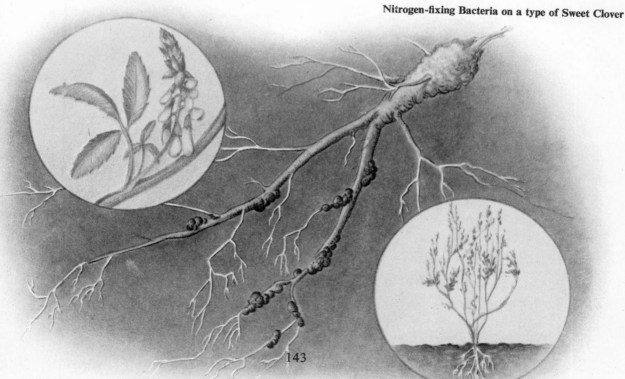

Nitrogen-fixing Bacteria on a type of Sweet Clover

143

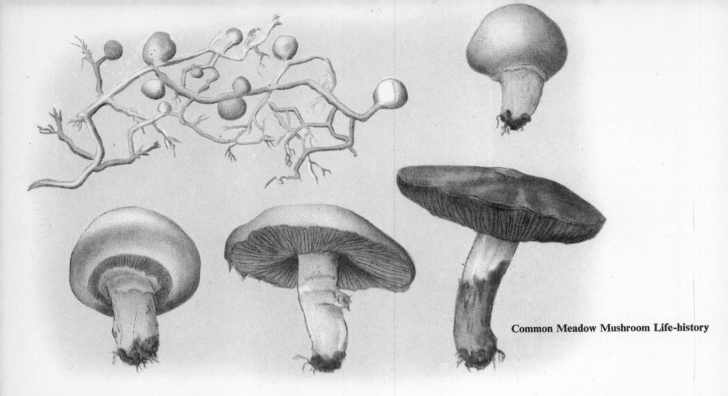

Common Meadow Mushroom Life-history

Mushrooms are the most popular edible fungus in Britain. The general plan of a mushroom is like that of a mould plant. The main body of the plant is a mass of colourless threads, or mycelium. Up from the mycelium grow stalks that bear spores. As a rule the mycelium is well hidden in whatever the mushroom is growing on. The chief difference between moulds and mushrooms is that the spore-bearing stalks of mushrooms are far larger than those of moulds. What we usually call a mushroom is only the spore-bearing part.

The picture at the top of the page tells the story of a common meadow mushroom. A spore starts growing in moist ground. A fine white thread grows from it. It begins getting food from decaying plant materials in the soil. The young mushroom plant grows and branches. It spreads out in the soil. It may grow for many weeks underground.

But at last tiny bumps appear on the mycelium. They are the beginnings of the mushrooms – the spore-bearing stalks. The little mushrooms get bigger. They are finally large enough to push their way up above the ground.

When a meadow mushroom first appears it looks like a round white button. As the button grows, the top opens up into an "umbrella." The umbrella is called the "cap." The "handle" of the

144

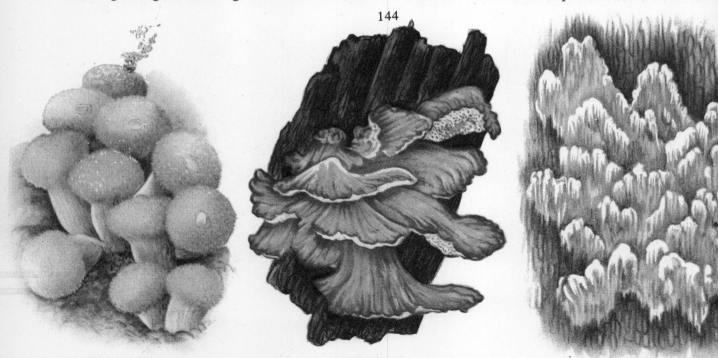

Common Puffball   Sulphur Fungus   Moss Fungus

Ink Cap

umbrella is the "stem." As the umbrella opens up, it leaves a collar around the stem. The cap may grow to be large. Meadow mushrooms have been found that were five inches across the top. Usually they are smaller.

The underside of the cap is made up of many thin folds. These folds are called "gills." They spread out from the centre of the cap like the spokes of a wheel. The gills are pink when the cap first opens up. Later they turn brown and then nearly black. The top of the cap becomes darker, too.

The gills are covered solidly with spores. The spores are brown when they are ripe. There are so many of them on a single mushroom that it would take a person 20 years or more to count them one by one.

When the spores are ripe, some of them fall to the ground. The wind blows some away. Any animal that brushes against the mushroom sends spores travelling.

All mushrooms have histories much like that of the meadow mushroom. But they do not all bear their spores in the same way. The ink cap has gills just as the meadow mushroom has. The gills are white at first. But when the spores are ripe the gills turn to a black, inky liquid.

The common puffball bears its spores in balls. When a ball is broken, a cloud of spores rises from it. The sulphur fungus bears its spores in pores on the underside of the shelves it forms. The delicate moss fungus bears its spores on soft "teeth," the morel in pits on its surface, and the coral fungus on its many branches.

Common Morel

Coral Fungus

Brownie Cap

Gypsy Mushroom

Woolly Milk Cap

Shaggy Ink Cap

Shelf Fungus

Most of the fungi shown on these two pages produce their spores on gills, just as the meadow mushroom does. The shelf fungus is the one exception. It, like the sulphur fungus, bears its spores in pores on the under surface. The underside is nearly white; pictures can be drawn on it, as it is quite hard.

It is easy to see how the shelf fungus got its name. In fact, the names of most of the fungi pictured here are easy to explain. The umbrella of the brownie cap is small and pointed. The woolly milk cap has an orange-coloured milky juice. The shaggy ink-cap umbrella becomes dark and shaggy when it is old. The green-spored

Jack-o'-lantern

Blusher

Green-spored Lepiota

Death Cap

Fly Agaric

lepiota has green spores and green gills. (The green colouring is not chlorophyll.) The brilliant orange jack-o'-lantern shines in the dark. The blusher turns pink or red wherever it is bruised. The fly agaric is sticky on top and attracts insects. The death cap, although a beautiful white, is deadly poison.

The death cap is the most poisonous of the fungi pictured on this page, but none of these should be eaten. In contrast, none of those pictured on the opposite page is poisonous, although they are not all edible. The brownie cap is too small to be worth picking. The shelf fungus is too woody.

FAIRY RING

Of all edible fungi, the common meadow mushroom is probably eaten most often. This species is cultivated. Among the other fungi highly prized as food are the morel and the truffle.

Unfortunately, some poisonous fungi look very much like some that are edible. We should trust no one but an expert to tell us whether mushrooms found growing wild are safe to eat.

Many people think that mushrooms should not be called mushrooms unless they can be eaten. If they are not good to eat, these people say, they should be called toadstools. But "mushroom" to a scientist does not mean a mushroom that can be eaten. Scientists do not use the name "toadstool." "Toadstool" is just a nickname for a poisonous mushroom. No one knows how some mushrooms came to be called toadstools. A toad is no more likely to be sitting on a poisonous mushroom than on an edible one or any other small plant.

Long ago people thought that the rings formed by the fairy-ring mushroom were actually made by fairies. Scientists know now that the mycelium of this plant spreads underground in all directions to form the circle. Another name for this small mushroom is "Scotch bonnet."

Sometimes mushrooms push their way up through very hard soil. They are not woody. It is difficult to see how they can break through a hard crust. They do so by taking in a great deal of water and swelling fast.

Of all the fungi, none cause the farmer more trouble than the grain rusts. They may ruin whole fields of grain. Rusts are much like moulds, but some of them have complicated life-histories. They spend part of their lives on one plant and part on another.

The fungi include also, so most scientists think, the queer slime moulds. One of them is pictured on page 37. Slime moulds are like plants in some ways and like animals in others. They are put among the fungi by most scientists because they are not green and because they bear spores on stalks just as many fungi do.

Compared with the 75,000 kinds of fungi, the other plants that are not green make up a very small part of the plant kingdom. Three of them are pictured on the opposite page. All three of those pictured belong much higher in the plant kingdom than the fungi. They all are flowering plants. But they have no green leaves to serve as food factories.

Some dependent plants, it has been pointed out, take food from living plants or animals by growing on them or inside them. Such plants are called parasites. The bacteria that cause disease are parasites. Some, but only a few, kinds of mould are parasites. Shelf fungi that grow on living trees and a few other kinds of mushrooms are parasites. The rusts are parasites. There are also parasites among the flowering plants that have no chlorophyll. Broomrape is one of them.

Broomrape grows on the roots of other plants. There are several kinds of broomrape. Each kind has a particular kind of plant it grows on.

Suppose a seed of broomrape falls on the ground and begins to grow. The seed has enough food in it to keep the little plant growing for a time. But unless it finds a plant it can grow on before it uses up all the food stored in the seed the little plant dies.

The pine sucker is sometimes called a ghost flower because it is so white. Some pine sucker plants, however, are not so ghostly as others. Some of them are pale pink instead of being pure white.

Once in a while a pine sucker plant grows on the roots of another plant. But as a rule it gets its food from decaying plant material in the soil. It grows most often on piles of dead leaves and branches in thick woods. Almost always there is a mass of fungus threads around the roots of a pine sucker plant. Probably the fungus threads help the pine sucker get the food it needs from the dead wood and leaves.

Dodder twines around other plants. It is always a parasite. It sends suckers into the stem of the plant it is growing on. This vine does not have either roots or leaves. It must get water as well as food from the plant it twines around. Another name for dodder is "love vine." Still another, and a better one, is "strangle weed."

There are about a hundred different kinds of dodder, but they are all much alike. Some kinds must have one special kind of green plant as a "host." One kind, for instance, will not grow on any plant except clover. But many kinds will grow on almost any kind of green plant that is within reach. These kinds of dodder remind one of the old saying that "beggars cannot be choosers."

One of the biggest flowers in the whole plant kingdom is produced by a plant that cannot make its own food. The plant is a rafflesia, a member of a family of parasites that grow only in tropical regions. A rafflesia flower may be a yard across. But it is thick and fleshy, and not at all pretty in colour. It has, moreover, an unpleasant smell. Rafflesias are far from being the most attractive of the plants that are not green.

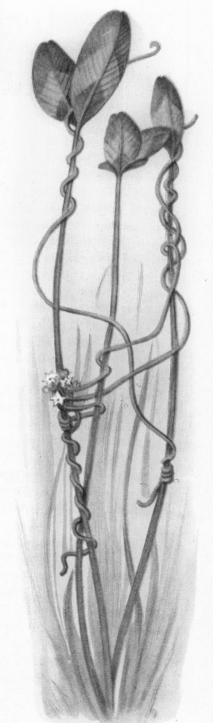

A Tropical Broomrape

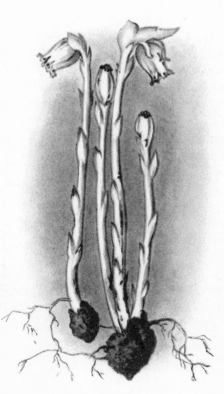

Pine Sucker

Dodder on Clover

Tomato

Turnip

Carrot

Potato

Vegetables

ALL vegetables are parts of plants – of green plants. They are storehouses in which the plants store up food they make and do not need at the time. Different plants use different parts of themselves as storehouses. A vegetable may be any one of several parts of a plant.

Roots are common storehouses. Carrots, turnips, beets, radishes, parsnips, and sweet potatoes are all root vegetables. Fortunately, many root vegetables keep well. They can be stored in vegetable cellars for the winter.

The potato we eat is not a root, although it looks much like one. It is, instead, an underground stem. Such an underground stem is called a "tuber." The story is told that when potatoes were first raised in Germany the Germans did not understand what part of the plant they were to eat. They first ate the green seed balls and found them very unpleasant. They were about to give up the potato as a vegetable when they discovered that they were supposed to eat the tubers instead.

Stalks of asparagus and of celery are stems, too, but they are not tubers. They grow above ground. The fibres that make some celery stringy and some asparagus too tough to be eaten easily are water-carrying tubes.

Many plants store a great deal of food in their seeds. Corn, peas, and beans are seeds. These seeds can all be dried and stored. We can then eat them in the winter months.

In several cases we eat not the seeds themselves but the packages that hold the seeds. Pumpkins and melons are examples.

Scientists call the part of a plant that contains the seeds a "fruit." To a scientist a fruit does not have to be sweet. Pumpkins and the other edible gourds are, therefore, fruits to the scientist's way of thinking. We take the seeds from pumpkins before cooking them. But a number of vegetables are fruits which we eat, seeds and all. Among them are tomatoes, eggplant, cucumbers, and runner beans.

Tomatoes were raised in flower gardens long before anyone thought of eating them. They were called "love apples" and were thought to be poisonous. Now tomatoes have become one of the most popular vegetables.

Lettuce

A head of cauliflower is really a bunch of flowers. We eat both the stems and the flowers of broccoli.

Lettuce, spinach, and cabbage are leafy vegetables. So are parsley, kale, and watercress. Brussels sprouts are tiny bundles of leaves, like little cabbages. Some root vegetables also have leaves that are good to eat. Many people prefer the leaves of beets and turnips to the roots.

The onion is a bulb. A bulb is made chiefly of thick leaves that overlap one another. These leaves are colourless because they are underground, away from the sunlight.

One of the foods stored in many vegetables is starch. Another is sugar. This is not surprising, since sugar and starch are the foods which green plants make from water and carbon dioxide. The potato is a storehouse filled mostly with starch. Some vegetables have enough sugar to taste rather sweet. Sweet corn is one. The sweet potato is another. The beet is still another even though it does not have "sweet" in its name.

Some vegetables have quite large amounts of protein, too. They can be used as substitutes for meat. Peas and beans are the vegetables that are highest in protein.

Perhaps more important than the starch, sugar, and protein stored in vegetables are the vitamins and minerals stored in them. Leafy green vegetables are one of our very best sources of iron and calcium, two minerals that our bodies have to

have. Green vegetables and tomatoes are excellent sources of vitamin C. The yellow vegetables – carrots, parsnips and swedes – furnish us with vitamin A. It is almost impossible to have a good diet without vegetables. The accepted rule is: Servings each day of at least two different kinds of vegetables besides potato. One should be raw. One should be green or yellow.

The vegetables now raised in the gardens of our country came in the beginning from many different parts of the world. Not many of them are natives of these islands. Our vegetable markets would look very queer indeed if they had only vegetables that are natives of Britain. We should have no potatoes, tomatoes or celery, for example.

One wonders whether our wild plants could have been developed into good vegetables. Out in the country many people gather in the spring the leaves of such plants as dandelions and stinging-nettles for greens. We could raise such plants instead of lettuce and endive and spinach. But the list of wild plants that we might have cultivated as vegetables is short. It is lucky that vegetables that are not natives do well in our gardens.

A vegetable's name may give the wrong idea of its history. Indian sweet corn is not a native of India. The Jerusalem artichoke has no connection with Jerusalem. But, as an exception, New Zealand spinach is a native of New Zealand.

Pumpkin

Beet

Egg Plant

Sweet Potato

Edible Gourd

Peas in Pods

As the map shows, South America furnished some of our best-liked vegetables. But far more than half of the kinds of vegetables we raise in our gardens came from the Old World. Many of them came from the lands near the eastern end of the Mediterranean Sea. These lands are sometimes called the "cradle of civilization." Probably plants have been raised for food there longer than in any other part of the world.

The map does not show the origin of broccoli, cauliflower, Brussels sprouts, kale, or kohlrabi. The reason is that these vegetables are all descendants of the wild cabbage of Europe. They do not look much like their wild cabbage ancestor now. But the big heads of cabbage so common today do not look much like their wild ancestor, either. Gardeners through the centuries have improved all vegetables greatly.

The story of the American Burbank potato illustrates one way in which improvement has been brought about.

Many years ago Luther Burbank, who is now famous as a creator of new kinds of plants, saw a seed ball growing on one of the potato plants in his garden. Usually potatoes are not raised from seed. Instead, a potato is cut into pieces with at least one bud, or eye, on each piece. The pieces are then planted. Cultivated potatoes, in fact, do not produce seeds very often. When Burbank saw the seed ball he decided to watch it carefully and to plant the seeds when they were ripe. He was already much interested in ways of getting better plants. Here was a chance to try an experiment. Perhaps by planting these seeds he would be able to get a kind of potato better than any to be had at that time.

When he took the seeds from the seed ball, Burbank found that there were just 23 of them. In the spring he planted them in his garden. They grew. Late in the autumn, when the time came for digging potatoes, he examined the potatoes from each plant carefully. The potatoes from no two were exactly alike. The potatoes from one were small and curiously shaped. Those from another had very deep-set eyes. Those from still another had rough skins. Clearly these potatoes were no improvement over the potatoes he had been raising. But some of the potatoes were good. Two plants produced very large, smooth potatoes different from any then on the market.

Burbank examined these potatoes carefully. The potatoes from one of the two plants, he decided, were slightly better than those from the other. He saved the potatoes from the best one and planted them in the spring. They all produced big, smooth potatoes. He selected the very best of these for raising new plants the next year. They, too, produced big, smooth potatoes. Soon he had enough of this new kind of potato to sell. This experiment was only one of many but Burbank called it his most important experiment because it was his first one.

Careful selection of the plants from which new plants are to be raised is one way in which our

Seedless Tomato

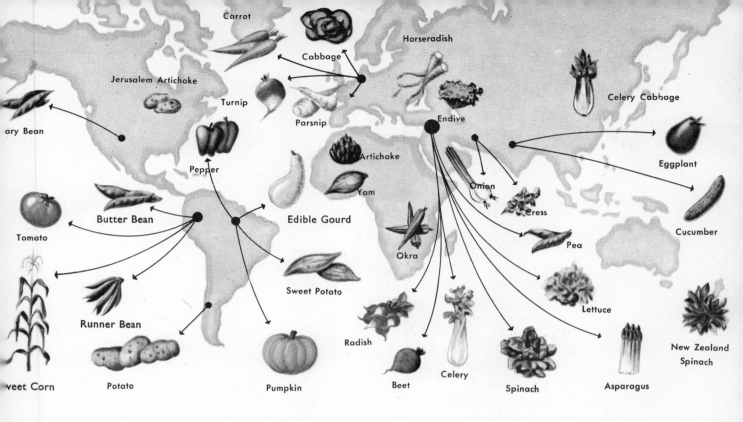

Carrot

Horseradish

Cabbage

Jerusalem Artichoke

Celery Cabbage

Turnip

Parsnip

Endive

ary Bean

Artichoke

Eggplant

Pepper

Yam

Onion

Tomato

Cress

Cucumber

Butter Bean

Pea

Okra

Edible Gourd

Runner Bean

Sweet Potato

Lettuce

New Zealand
Spinach

Radish

veet Corn

Potato

Pumpkin

Beet

Celery

Spinach

Asparagus

ORIGIN OF THE WORLD'S VEGETABLES

vegetables have been improved and new varieties developed. The story of the butter bean illustrates another way in which improvement has been brought about.

One day in the summer of 1850 a man who was walking along a country road in Virginia saw a dwarf butter-bean plant by the roadside. He reported his find. At that time raising butter beans was a great deal of trouble because the plants were long vines and poles had to be stood up in the fields for them to climb on. This plant by the roadside was not a vine but a bushy little plant. So far as anyone knows, it was the first bush butter bean. Seeds of this plant were planted, and the new plants were dwarfs, too. A new kind of butter bean could now be raised.

Close to the spot where the dwarf bean was found there was a whole field of pole-climbing beans. This dwarf evidently grew from the seed of one of those beans. But it was very different from the parent plant. When a new kind of plant thus suddenly appears that is quite different from the parent plant, it is called a "sport" or a "mutant." The word "mutant" comes from the Latin word that means "change." "Mutant" is a good name for a plant that differs greatly from its ancestors.

Many sports appear that are far worse than the parent plants they came from. But watching for desirable mutants and taking care of them when they do occur is another way in which our vegetables have been improved. All the many vegetables that have been developed from cabbage are thought to be mutants.

Still another way of improving our vegetables has been to cross different varieties. A plant produced by crossing two different kinds of plants is called a "hybrid." The story of exactly how plant hybrids are produced must wait for the discussion of flowers.

Another way in which we have produced better vegetables is by fertilizing the soil in which they grow. Scientists have found that tomatoes, let us say, grown in one field may be much richer in vitamins than those grown in another.

Some of the recent improvements in vegetables have been brought about through the use of growth regulators. Growth regulators are chemicals. Seedless tomatoes were produced by the use of a growth regulator. A seedless tomato is not altogether seedless, but it has less pulp and fewer seeds than other tomatoes. Experimentation with growth regulators is being carried on with many different vegetables.

Plant breeders are being encouraged to produce new and better vegetables. Awards are given for especially good ones that are developed.

Fruits

IN a fruit store of today there are sure to be fruits of many kinds. They come to our markets from all over the world. The demand for fruit is so great that it comes to us by the boatload from other lands. Special machines have been invented for unloading fruit from fruit boats. From our own orchards it is carried to our towns and cities by train and lorry.

A balanced diet calls for some fruit every day. But we would eat great quantities of fruit even if it were not an important part of a good diet. No other kind of food looks more attractive or, so most people think, tastes better.

The chief food stored in most fruits is sugar. Sugar is excellent energy-giving food. It is much better for us to get it in fruit, however, than it is to get it in the form of granulated sugar, for in

fruit we get vitamins with it as well, and some minerals, too. For example, the citrus fruits – lemons, oranges, grapefruit, and limes – are one of the best sources of vitamin C, while prunes and dates are good sources of iron.

One vegetable may be one part of a plant while another vegetable is another. Fruits, on the other hand, are always the same part of the plant. They are the packages in which the plants that bear them store their seeds.

Although all fruits are packages of seeds, fruits are built on a number of different plans. Some fruits have only a single seed. Some have several seeds. Some have a great many.

Each type of fruit has a name. The grape is an example of one type. In it several seeds are surrounded by a soft pulp. This pulp, in turn, is surrounded by a skin. The gooseberry, cranberry,

154

bilberry, and currant are built on this same plan. No one commonly calls a grape a berry, but "berry" is the name scientists give to this kind of seed package. Oranges, strangely enough, are berries, too. So are all the other citrus fruits. These fruits are different from other berries in that the pulpy part is divided up into sections.

The apple is a pome. The seeds are in a core in the centre of the fruit. Pears, quinces, and crab apples are pomes, too. The pomegranate is not a pome, even though it has "pome" in its name. It is a berry instead.

The water-melon and honeydew melon are melons, or pepos. The cantaloupe is in this group, too, as its other name, musk melon, suggests. Melons are large fruits with thick rinds. They contain many seeds, often hundreds of them.

The cherry, apricot, peach, and plum are one-seeded fruits. The scientist's name for such fruits is "drupe." Drupes are sometimes called "stone fruits."

We call raspberries, blackberries, and logan-berries "berries," but they are not true berries. Instead, each "berry" is made of many little drupes joined together. Each little round section has a single seed in it, just as does a cherry, an apricot, or a plum.

The strawberry is not a true berry either, but it is not built on the raspberry plan. Its seeds are on the outside. The pulpy part of a strawberry is a cushion on which the seeds rest.

Still other fruits are built on still other plans. The fig and the pineapple are examples of two other types.

If we had to limit our fruits to those that are natives of Britain, we would no fare too well. Several of our berries and so-called berries are American. Many of the fruits we now raise in our orchards are natives of other parts of the world. Our fruits have come from ever so many different countries, just as our vegetables have. The peach, as the map on page 157 shows, came

Golden Delicious Apple

from China, the currant from Europe, and the water-melon from Africa. The grapefruit is a native of the East Indies, the banana of southeast Asia, and the pineapple of South America. Australia is the only continent which has sent no fruit into our orchards and gardens.

A few fruits are shown by the map to be natives of two different regions. The grape is one. Wild grapes grew in both the Old World and the New. They still do. The Concord grape came from one of the wild American grapes. Many of the other grapes we raise in greenhouses came from the wild grapes of the Near East.

Some of the fruits we enjoy we cannot raise in our orchards. The climate is not right for them. We shall have to keep on bringing them in from other lands. The banana, for example, thrives only in very warm, very moist climates.

Fruit probably furnished much of the food of our early ancestors. It is very likely that the cave men ate such fruits as wild grapes and apples and plums. But it is certain that much of the fruit they ate was very different from the fruit for sale in our markets today. And it is certain, too, that there are some kinds of fruit that our early ancestors did *not* eat, for these fruits did not exist then. We have improved all kinds of fruits enormously, and we have produced some entirely new kinds.

We have improved our fruits, just as we have improved our vegetables, partly by raising them under better conditions than they had when they grew wild. More important, we have raised new plants only from the best parent plants. Careful selection, generation after generation, is bound to bring about great improvement. But we have done other things, too.

Occasionally sports, or mutants, appear among fruits, just as they do among vegetables. Fruit-growers have improved our fruits greatly by watching for sports and caring for them when they turned out to be desirable. They have produced many new varieties in this way.

The loganberry is thought by many to be a mutant. It is not on the map, for it never grew wild. In 1881 Judge Logan of Santa Cruz, California, found a new kind of berry growing among his red raspberries. He named it after himself. This new berry is shaped like a blackberry and may well have come from the seed of a wild blackberry.

Sometimes only one branch of a plant will bear fruit of a new and different kind. The Navel orange, which is seedless, began in this way. A seedless fruit, of course, is a freak.

Fruit-growers have improved our fruits, too, by crossing two different varieties. Many of the varieties of fruit listed in today's nursery catalogues are hybrids.

The Golden Delicious apple is probably a

Loganberry

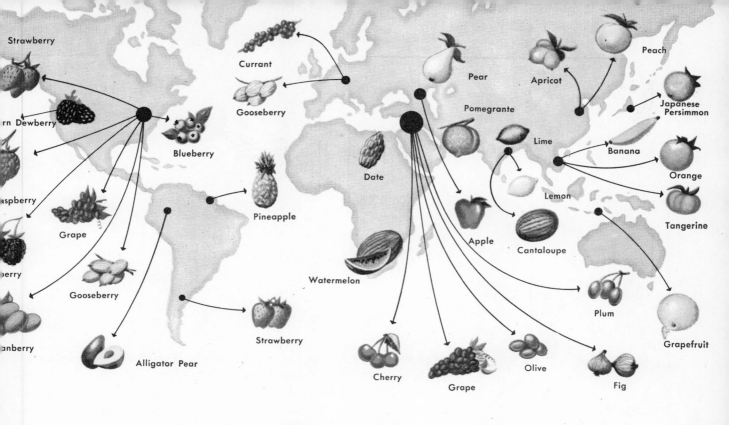

Strawberry

Currant

Gooseberry

rn Dewberry

Blueberry

Pineapple

Date

Pear

Pomegrante

Apricot

Peach

Japanese
Persimmon

Lime

Banana

spberry

Grape

Gooseberry

Apple

Lemon

Cantaloupe

Orange

Tangerine

erry

anberry

Alligator Pear

Watermelon

Strawberry

Cherry

Grape

Olive

Plum

Fig

Grapefruit

ORIGIN OF THE WORLD'S FRUITS

chance hybrid – a hybrid that no person helped bring about. If it is a hybrid, it is doubtless a hybrid between the red Delicious apple and the Grimes Golden. These apples are not commonly grown in Europe, however. But many of our apples, such as the Cox's orange pippin, Worcester pearmain and beauty of Bath, probably came into being as hybrids in the same way. The loganberry, too, may possibly be a chance hybrid rather than a mutant.

Some hybrid fruits are crosses between two quite different kinds of fruit. The plumcot was produced by the "plant wizard," Luther Burbank. It is a cross between the plum and the apricot. The citrange is a cross between the sweet orange and the sour one. The tangelo is a cross between the tangerine and the grapefruit.

Many attempts to cross different kinds of fruit have been unsuccessful. No one, for example, has ever been able to cross the apple and the pear. But doubtless we shall in time have other fruits that our ancestors never knew.

A new kind of fruit is really as much of an invention as a new kind of machine. Some governments, therefore, grant patents on new fruits. In nursery catalogues, patented peaches, apples, cherries, plums, and blackberries are listed.

On the whole, fruits spoil rather easily. Refrigerated vans help fruit-growers get their fruit to

market in good shape. Aeroplanes, because they are so fast, help, too. Another way fruit-growers have solved the problem is to ship their fruit while it is still green. The bananas that reach our country are almost always green. They are ripened after they reach our markets. Chemicals called "growth regulators" are sometimes used to speed up the ripening. Some of the bananas in the bunch pictured below are green while others are ripe. The ripe ones were wiped with a cloth dampened with a growth regulator. Scientists are constantly at work to make it easier for us to get better fruits in better condition.

Bananas

157

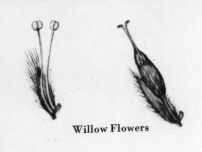

Willow Flowers

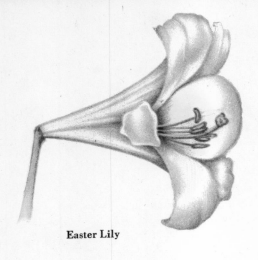

Easter Lily

Tulip

Grass Flowers

Elm Flowers

Maple Flowers

Flowers

LEARNING to call by name all the kinds of flowers in the world would mean learning to know nearly 200,000 kinds, for there are nearly 200,000 different species of plants that bloom. Not all flowers, of course, are showy. It takes careful looking to find the flowers on some plants that are in bloom. Probably, moreover, many people see certain flowers without recognizing them as flowers. Many, for instance, when they find the walks on a spring morning littered with reddish catkins from poplar trees, do not know that these catkins are bunches of flowers.

Many trees besides the poplar have flowers so simple that they are not easily recognized as flowers. The willow, the maple, and the elm are among them. Grass flowers are simple, too.

In contrast, the other flowers pictured on these two pages are showy. Some are favourites in our gardens and flower shops.

Seven of the kinds of flowers pictured here are from plants of the monocot branch of the flowering plants. The seven are the two kinds of grass flowers, the Easter lily, the tulip, the trillium, the narcissus, and the orchid. Grass flowers are among the simplest monocot flowers, orchids among the most complicated.

The remaining flowers, of course, are from dicots. Willows, elms, and maples, although the plants are far larger, rank below daisies, dandelions, asters, and sunflowers.

The thousands of flowering plants are divided up into about 300 families. Flowers are the identification tags that tell to what family a flowering plant belongs. Eight different families are represented by the flowers pictured here.

Both kinds of grass belong to the grass family. This is the most important to us of all the families of flowering plants. It includes maize, wheat, oats, barley, rye, rice, and sugar cane.

The maple tree belongs to the maple family, the willow to the willow family, and the elm to the nettle family.

The Easter lily, tulip, and trillium are in the lily family. The lily family is large. Among the other beautiful flowers belonging to it are the hyacinth, the lily-of-the-valley, and the regal lily. The narcissus belongs to a family closely related to the lilies, the amaryllis family.

Daisy Flowers   Dandelion Flower

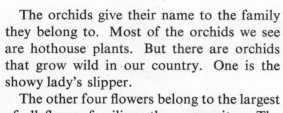

Trillium

The orchids give their name to the family they belong to. Most of the orchids we see are hothouse plants. But there are orchids that grow wild in our country. One is the showy lady's slipper.

The other four flowers belong to the largest of all flower families—the composites. The family is well named, for every so-called flower is composed of many tiny flowers. It is a whole bouquet.

The flowers of composites, however, are not all built on the same plan. The daisy is made of two different kinds of tiny flowers. Those around the edge are quite different from those in the centre. The dandelion, on the other hand, is made up of flowerets all of the same kind. The sunflower and the aster follow the daisy pattern.

Among the other very well-known and important families are the pea family and the rose family. The pea family includes peas, sweet peas, beans, lucerne, and clover. The rose family includes not only all our roses but also most of our fruits. Apples, peaches, pears, strawberries, and raspberries are all cousins of our garden roses.

The chart on page 212 lists a number of flowering plant families and names some of the plants in each. Such a list holds many surprises.

Narcissus, or Daffodil

Orchid

Daisy

Dandelion

Aster

Sunflower

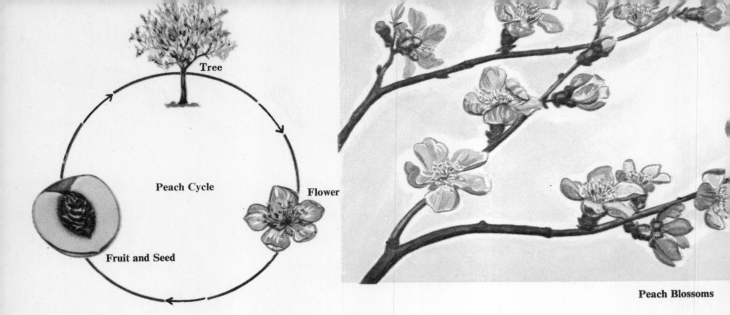

Peach Cycle

Tree

Flower

Fruit and Seed

Peach Blossoms

The role of all flowers, whether they are simple or showy, is to produce seeds. The story of how a peach seed is formed will serve as an example of how seeds are produced by flowers.

A peach blossom has four sets of parts. In the centre of the blossom there is a pistil. It looks like a tiny green vase with a long neck. Surrounding the pistil are many pinkish stems, with sacs full of yellow "dust" at the top. They are stamens. The yellow dust is pollen. Outside the stamens are five bright-pink petals. A ring of five reddish-green sepals surrounds the petals.

Down inside the base of the pistil there are two small bodies shaped like eggs. They are ovules. Ovules are the beginnings of seeds.

Ovules contain female cells, or eggs. Pollen grains contain male, or sperm, cells. Male cells from pollen grains must reach the female cells in the ovules before the ovules can grow into seeds. The male cells and the female cells must join— the eggs must, in other words, be fertilized.

Fertilization in the case of a peach blossom comes about in this way: As soon as a peach blossom opens, bees come to it to get nectar. As a bee gets nectar it brushes against the stamens. Some of the pollen from the pollen sacs sticks to its fuzzy body. When the bee rubs against the stamens it rubs against the pistil, too. At the same time that it is getting pollen on its body it is rubbing pollen from the last peach blossom it visited off on the top of the pistil. The top of the pistil—the

"stigma," it is called—is sticky. It holds fast any pollen grains that reach it.

The picture at the lower left tells the next step in the story. It shows a section down through the pistil of a peach blossom as it would look if it were greatly magnified. One of the ovules in the base of the pistil shows. A grain of pollen is resting on the top of the pistil. Down from it a tube is growing. The tube grows till it reaches an ovule. Then all the living material from the tiny pollen grain enters the ovule. A male cell reaches and joins the female cell. The ovule is now ready to grow into a seed.

As soon as the egg in one ovule is fertilized, the other ovule in the pistil dries up. It does not develop into a seed. A single peach blossom produces only a single seed.

After fertilization has taken place, the petals, stamens, and sepals wither and fall off. So do the neck and top of the pistil. Only the base of the pistil is left, with the young seed inside.

The young seed grows. While it is becoming a large peach seed, the wall of the part of the pistil that holds it is developing into the rest of the peach.

When the peach seed is ripe, it is ready to be planted to grow into a new peach tree. The new tree will bloom, the blossoms will produce seeds, and the seeds will produce new peach trees. The circle of tree—blossom—seed is repeated over and over again.

Pistil   **Stamen**   **Sepal**   **Petal**

Parts of the Peach Blossom

160

Columbine

All complete flowers have the same four kinds of parts peach blossoms have: pistils, stamens, petals, and sepals. But many flowers lack one or more of these sets of parts. A flower must have, however, either stamens or pistils. It cannot play any part in producing seeds if it has neither.

Willow flowers are about as simple as flowers can be. Every kind of willow has two kinds of flowers. The flowers of one kind have no sepals, stamens, or petals. Each flower is made up of just one pistil. A small green leaflike bract protects it. The flowers of the other kind have no pistils, petals, or sepals. Each flower has only two stamens, protected by a small green bract. The "pussies" of pussy willows are little bunches of flowers with stamens.

As a rule the staminate flowers (those with stamens) are on one tree and the pistillate flowers (those with pistils) are on another tree. The trees with only staminate flowers cannot produce any seeds. They can only contribute pollen to make the ovules formed in the pistillate flowers develop into seeds.

Scientists call willow trees "dioecious," because they do not have both pistillate flowers and staminate flowers on the same tree. "Dioecious" means "two households."

The poplars, like the willows, are dioecious. The reddish catkins that fall from some poplar trees are bunches of staminate flowers. The trees that drop these catkins never produce seeds.

Some plants have two kinds of flowers—one with pistils and one with stamens—but bear them both on the same plant. Maize is a good example. These plants are called "monoecious." "Monoecious" means "one household."

Grass flowers have both stamens and pistils but no sepals or petals. Elm flowers have stamens, pistils, and sepals, but no petals. The maple flowers pictured are built on the same plan.

The trillium is a complete flower. In the centre there is one pistil. Surrounding it are six stamens. There are three white petals and three green sepals. The Easter lily, tulip, and narcissus have all four parts, too. But they are somewhat puzzling because their sepals and petals look just alike. The sepals can be told, however, because they form a ring outside the petals.

Orchids, too, have all four parts. Here the sepals and petals differ in shape, but they are all beautifully coloured, and it is hard to tell one from another.

Even the tiny flowers that make up a dandelion are complete. Five petals are joined together to make a yellow "strap." The sepals are white bristles. A pistil rises from the centre of the flower. Joined in a cuff around it are five stamens.

The tiny flowers that make up a daisy have no sepals. Those around the edge— the ray flowers—have no stamens. All the flowers have petals and pistils.

The columbine pictured above has all four parts. The petals and the sepals are all brightly coloured and look much alike. But the petals can be told by their spurs.

In descriptions of flowers the words "calyx" and "corolla" are often used. All the sepals together form the calyx. The petals form the corolla. "Calyx" means "cup." "Corolla" means "crown."

Rose

Carnation

Nasturtium

Pollen Grains, Magnified:

Petunia

Cosmos

Mallow

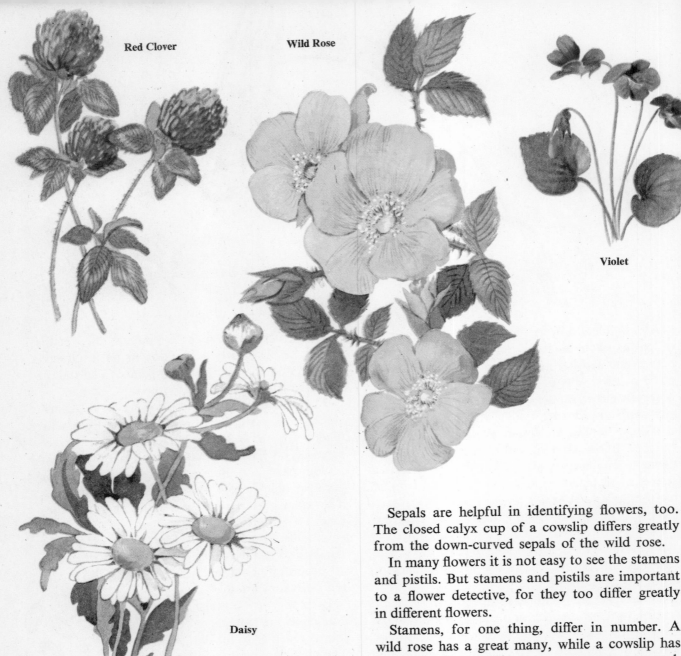

Red Clover

Wild Rose

Violet

Daisy

These flowers are common spring and summer wild flowers. Their petals make it very easy to tell them apart. The petals of both the red clover and the ragged robin are red, but they are not at all the same shape. The petals of the cowslip are joined together, but those of the daisy and wood anemone are separate. Both the clover blossom and the daisy are made up of many tiny flowers, but again the petals are very different. Petals are always a great help in identification.

Sepals are helpful in identifying flowers, too. The closed calyx cup of a cowslip differs greatly from the down-curved sepals of the wild rose.

In many flowers it is not easy to see the stamens and pistils. But stamens and pistils are important to a flower detective, for they too differ greatly in different flowers.

Stamens, for one thing, differ in number. A wild rose has a great many, while a cowslip has only five. The stalks of some stamens are much longer than others. Pollen sacs and even the pollen grains themselves show much variation.

Pistils also differ in number. A wild rose has many, but a violet only possesses one. Pistils differ, too, in shape and size and in the number of ovules they contain. Some flowers produce many seeds apiece. In some cases the base of the pistil is below the ring of sepals and petals.

The yellow star of Bethlehem, a monocot, has six petals, six stamens, and one pistil inside of which there are three rows of ovules. Many monocot flowers have parts in threes or multiples of three. The violet, a dicot, has five sepals, five petals, five stamens, and a pistil. Many dicot flowers have parts in fives or multiples of five.

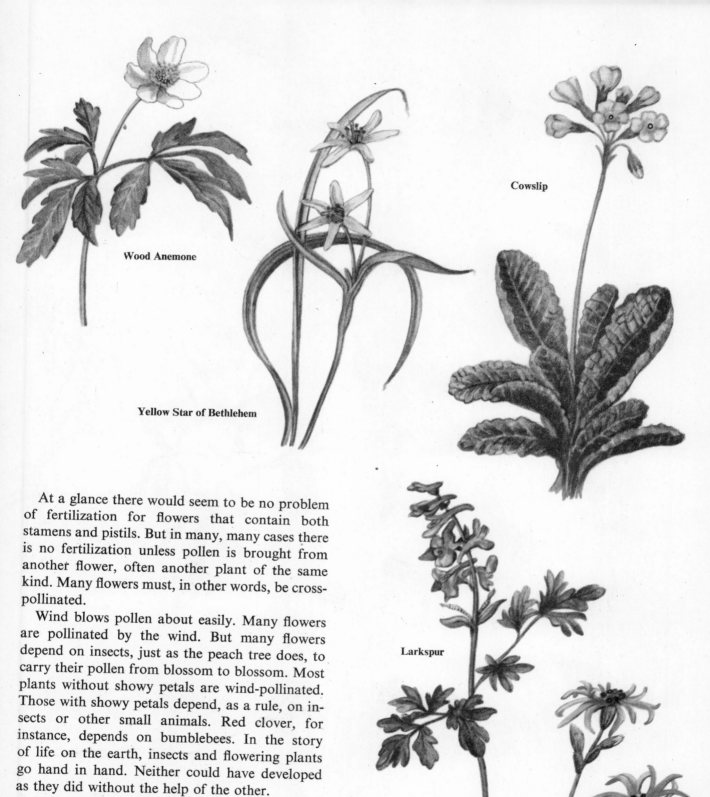

Wood Anemone

Yellow Star of Bethlehem

Cowslip

Larkspur

Ragged Robin

At a glance there would seem to be no problem of fertilization for flowers that contain both stamens and pistils. But in many, many cases there is no fertilization unless pollen is brought from another flower, often another plant of the same kind. Many flowers must, in other words, be cross-pollinated.

Wind blows pollen about easily. Many flowers are pollinated by the wind. But many flowers depend on insects, just as the peach tree does, to carry their pollen from blossom to blossom. Most plants without showy petals are wind-pollinated. Those with showy petals depend, as a rule, on insects or other small animals. Red clover, for instance, depends on bumblebees. In the story of life on the earth, insects and flowering plants go hand in hand. Neither could have developed as they did without the help of the other.

Gay petals are signal flags—SOS calls to insects for help in carrying pollen from flower to flower. It is when the pollen sacs open up that the petals are freshest and brightest. The perfume of a flower helps call insects, too.

Of course, the insects that carry pollen do not know that they are helping the plants. To them the petals and perfume are simply a dinner bell.

163

Wild Sunflower

Goldenrod

Cardinal Flower

Wild Aster

Toadflax

Black-eyed Susan

Hemp Agrimo

Many of our spring wild flowers are found in our woodlands. They come into bloom before the trees are fully in leaf. Before there are leaves on the trees, sunshine can reach the floor of the woods. The spring woodland flowers take advantage of this sunshine. Spring wild flowers, as a rule, are perennials. They live, that is, for several or many years. In bulbs or roots or underground stems they store up food which they use to come into bloom quickly. In the spring sunshine, moreover, their leaves make food which they store for the next year's blooming.

Although many spring flowers are perennials, as a rule nothing remains above ground during the winter to show that the plant is living on. Instead of merely losing their leaves for the winter as elm trees and rose-bushes do, the whole upper part withers and dies.

The garden flowers and wild flowers on these two pages are flowers of the late summer and autumn. Most of them are perennials. The sunflower is an annual instead—it grows, that is, from seed, blooms, and dies in one season. And the black-eyed Susan is a biennial. It lives for two years.

Some wild flowers have the word "weed" in their names. They are weeds in the sense that they can take care of themselves; they do not have to be planted and cultivated as our garden flowers do. But a better definition of the word "weed" is "a plant that grows where it is not wanted." Any plant can be a weed. Grass, for example, although wanted very much in lawns, can be a real nuisance in a vegetable garden.

To the North Americans who work to keep their roadsides clear, many of the flowers pictured here are weeds. To us, the wild sunflower and wild aster are cultivated garden flowers because they do not grow wild in Europe.

The dandelion, everyone agrees, is a weed. But if it did not bother us so much by getting into our lawns we would surely think of it as a gay wild flower.

Some of our most beautiful wild flowers are in danger of disappearing. People have been too careless about picking them. If all the flowers are picked from a plant, it cannot make seeds to start new plants. To get its flowers, people sometimes pull up a whole plant. Sometimes, too, they dig up plants to take home to their gardens. Many wild flowers die in the transplanting.

We are killing off our wild flowers, moreover, by taking away their homes. We have cut down woodlands and have ploughed up downland. We are mowing or burning over our roadsides and our railway embankments. We are keeping our fields very clean. Sooner or later many of our wild flowers are bound to disappear unless everyone does his share in protecting them.

Therefore you should not collect wild flowers which are becoming rare. If you do you will make them die out faster, just as the thoughtless collectors of birds' eggs kill off rare birds by stopping them from breeding.

Some foreign wild flowers fortunately have an amazing ability to live even under unfavourable conditions. After a good rain many hot desert lands "come into bloom" in an astoundingly short space of time. The plants produce their flowers with amazing speed when the conditions are good. Then they produce their seeds and wait patiently until conditions are good once more.

Some wild flowers, as well as some cultivated flowers, have to be several years old before they bloom. The century plant, a native of Mexico and a relative of the yuccas that grow in the Californian desert, got its name because people thought that it had to live for a hundred years before it bloomed. Now we know that many century plants bloom in less time—in only 25 years or so. As soon as a century plant blooms, it dies.

Day Lily

Butterfly Weed

Hybrid Roses

Many plants—hundreds of kinds—are raised just for the beauty of their flowers. Flower catalogues list many varieties of some of them.

It goes without saying that the ancestors of all our cultivated flowers once grew wild. Plant growers have changed many of them so much, however, that even if we could see their wild ancestors we would not recognize them. The picture below shows a wild tulip. Wild tulips of this kind can still be found in western Asia. It does not look much like the gorgeous tulips we have now.

Plant breeders have gone about improving our flowers just as they have improved our fruits and vegetables. Careful selection, watching for sports and taking care of desirable ones, and producing hybrids are the chief ways.

The three roses pictured at the top of the page are hybrids. Knowing about the parts of flowers helps us understand exactly how hybrids can be produced.

Crossing two flowering plants means taking the pollen from the flower of one plant and putting it on the pistils of a flower of a different variety. Often a plant breeder has in mind some new characteristic he would like the new flower to have. He may have in mind some special colour, or some special shape, or some certain number of petals. He may be thinking more of the plant itself and want an especially hardy one, or one that climbs well, or one that will grow well in poor soil, or one that can stand the attacks of insect pests, or one that can withstand disease.

The plant breeder may, let us say, be trying to get a very hardy climbing rose that has bright-yellow flowers. He has a yellow rose of the colour he wishes, but it is a small bush. He has a very vigorous climbing rose that stands cold weather well, but its flowers are white. The two roses are in bloom at the same time. He cuts away the petals and sepals and stamens of several of the roses of one plant. Let us suppose it is the plant with yellow flowers. With a soft brush he takes some of the pollen from the white flowers of the other plant and brushes it on the pistils of the yellow flowers. Then he ties paper bags carefully over these pistils so that no other pollen can reach them.

Perhaps no seeds will develop. The pollen of the white rose may not be of any use in fertilizing the eggs in the ovules of the yellow rose. If seeds do develop, some of the plants that grow from them may have the worst traits of their two parents. But perhaps one will have the characteristics the breeder is working for.

Obviously the plant breeder might cross the

Wild Tulip

two plants the other way round. He might put the pollen of the yellow rose on the pistils of the white one. The results might be either better or worse.

The Peace rose is a recently evolved, very popular hybrid. Roses are one of the most favoured plants for experiments in hybridization. Every year new strains are produced and special awards are given for them in the important horticultural shows.

Organizations have been formed that rate the new varieties of some kinds of flowers. They give each variety a grade. A certain kind of peony, let us suppose, is rated 9.8. This means that it is rated on a scale of 10. It would be the same as giving a plant a grade of 98 if the highest possible score was 100. A peony rated 9.8 is much better in at least some ways than one rated 7.2. Daffodils, irises, and tulips are among the other flowers that are sometimes given a grade in flower catalogues.

Garden clubs and flower shows have done a great deal to interest people in producing lovelier flowers. Many cities take great pride in their gardens. In some countries one city may have a tulip festival, another a lilac festival, and still another may specialize in azaleas. No one could have a better hobby than raising lovely flowers.

Cultivated Tulips:

Breeder

Cottage

Parrot

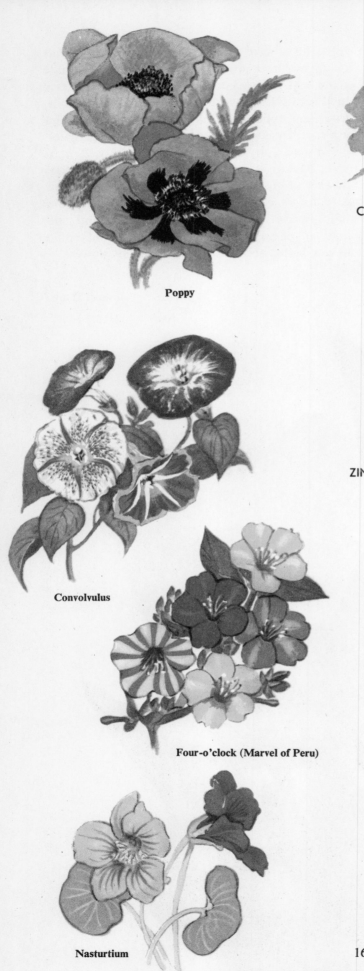

Poppy

Convolvulus

Four-o'clock (Marvel of Peru)

Nasturtium

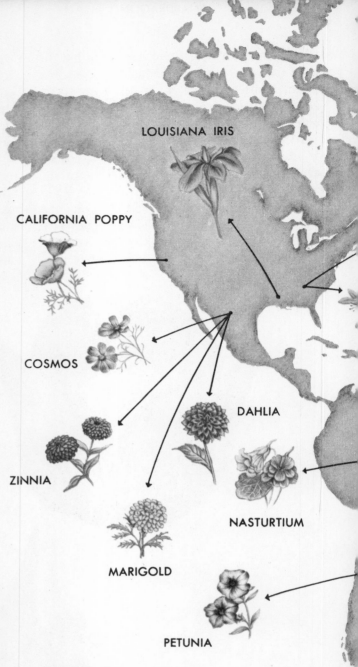

LOUISIANA IRIS

CALIFORNIA POPPY

COSMOS

ZINNIA

DAHLIA

NASTURTIUM

MARIGOLD

PETUNIA

Origin of Some Garden Flowers

Our flower gardens are full of immigrants, just as our vegetable gardens and our orchards are. Some of our own wild flowers have made their way into our gardens, too. There they "rub shoulders" with strawflowers from Australia, hollyhocks from Asia, Californian poppies, nasturtiums from South America, and gladioli from Africa. The Michaelmas daisy is a form of the wild North American aster. The many splendid varieties of tulip which are grown today are derived from Russia. But the snapdragon is one of our garden plants which has taken a shorter journey to reach us—its home is in Europe.

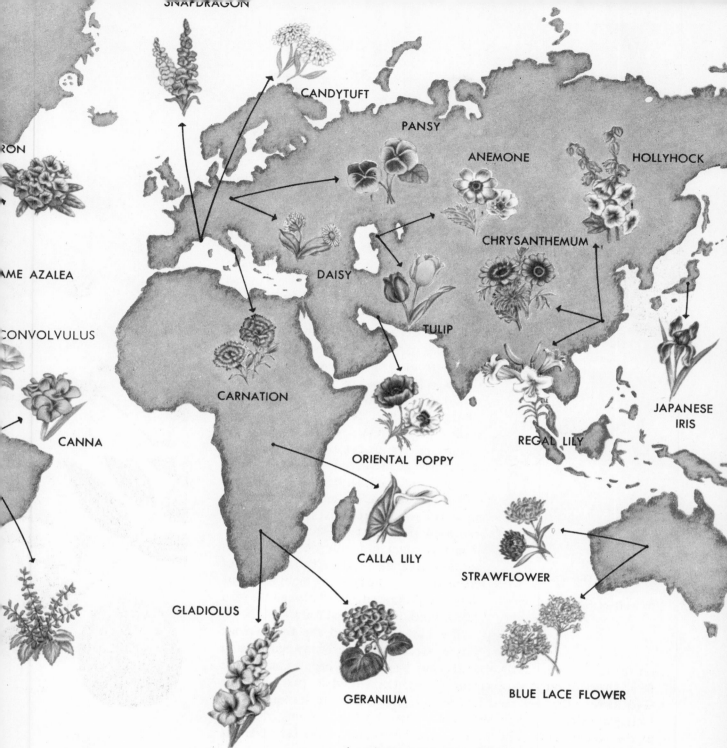

SNAPDRAGON

CANDYTUFT

PANSY

ANEMONE

HOLLYHOCK

RON

AME AZALEA

CHRYSANTHEMUM

CONVOLVULUS

DAISY

CANNA

CARNATION

TULIP

JAPANESE
IRIS

REGAL LILY

ORIENTAL POPPY

CALLA LILY

STRAWFLOWER

GLADIOLUS

GERANIUM

BLUE LACE FLOWER

Comparing the map above with the one on page 153 shows that the petunia and the potato came to us from the same region of South America. It is not surprising that they did, for they are cousins. Both of them belong to the nightshade family.

The convolvulus and the sweet potato both come from another region in South America. They, too, are cousins; they belong to the convolvulus family. Asparagus, onions, and tulips are immigrants from south-western Asia; all three are members of the lily family. But candytuft and cabbage, which belong to the mustard family, are natives of Europe.

Some of our garden flowers have been cultivated for many centuries. A trip through a flower garden of today may well take one back in imagination to the gardens of the ancient emperors of China or the monastery gardens of medieval Europe or the flower-bordered highways leading to Aztec temples.

Seeds

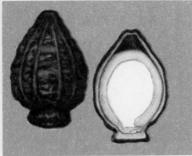

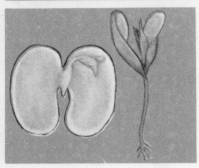

Maize Seed

Four-o'clock Flower Seed

Butter Bean and Seedling

A SEED is made up of a tiny plant, food for the plant, and a seed coat for protection. The tiny plant inside the seed is sometimes spoken of as the "embryo." No other part of the seed can grow. A seed may look perfect from the outside, but if the embryo plant has died, the seed will never sprout.

Garden seeds left over from one year's planting will not be likely to do well the next year. Too many of the embryo plants will have died. Amazingly, however, seeds more than a century old have sprouted.

The chart on page 128 shows that the flowering plants are divided into two great groups—the monocots and the dicots. "Monocot" is short for "monocotyledon." It means "one seed leaf." "Dicot" is short for "dicotyledon." It means "two seed leaves." These two great groups of plants get their names from differences in their seeds.

A grain of maize shows the general plan of a monocot seed. The embryo plant takes up only a small part of the seed. It rests on the food that has been stored up for it. The tiny plant has only one leaf, which never leaves the seed. When a grain of maize sprouts, the growing plant forces its way out of the seed coat. Through the seed leaf it takes in the stored food.

The butter bean and the four-o'clock flower are dicots. The bean seed is built on the more common dicot seed plan. The embryo bean plant has no food stored around it. Instead, the food is stored in two big thick seed leaves—the two seed leaves that give the group its name. The little plant thus fills the whole seed. When this bean sprouts, the stem of the young plant pulls the two seed leaves out of the seed coat. It pulls them up out of the ground. Soon, after most of the food stored in them has been used up, they drop off the plant.

In the four-o'clock flower's seed the two seed leaves are thin. But they are wrapped around a ball of stored food which is mostly starch.

Some seeds are far, far larger than others. They range all the way from orchid seeds, which are so tiny and light that they are blown about like dust, to coconuts, which may weigh more than a pound. The flowering plants form by far the biggest group of seed plants. Most seeds, therefore, are produced by flowers. Some flowers are very much bigger than others. But big flowers and big seeds by no means always go together.

Petu

Walnut

Sweet Pea

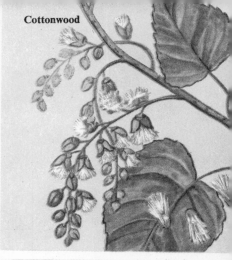

Cottonwood

Plane

Petunias are larger than sweet peas, but sweet pea seeds are far larger than petunia seeds. Walnut flowers are not nearly so large as sweet peas, but their seeds are far larger. The seeds of even the biggest, most beautiful orchids are like dust.

If all the seeds of a sycamore tree were to fall under the tree that bore them, they would not have a good chance to grow. Many of them might start growing, but one tiny tree after another would die because it was so crowded that it could not get all the water, minerals, and sunshine it needed. It is important for every seed plant, if it is to hold its own, to have some way of getting its seed scattered.

Many kinds of seeds travel by air. All those pictured on this page are airborne. They are all helped in their travels through the air by having parachutes of down. As one would expect, only light seeds are equipped with parachutes.

The parachutes of the plane and dandelion, are made up of short, silky hairs. The parachutes of the clematis are quite different. They are like slender, curled feathers.

The seeds of a cotton plant often have so much down in their parachutes that it completely hides the seeds. The plant looks as if it were covered with fluffy snowballs. The down, or lint, on cotton seeds is very useful to us. Cotton growers have, in fact, improved cotton so that we could get more lint from it. In some cases there is so much that it is tangled and interferes with the scattering of the seeds.

Seeds that travel by parachute are sometimes called "fly aways." Of course, they really float rather than fly.

For the most part parachutes are very effective in helping seeds get scattered. Some plants whose seeds have parachutes have been spread for thousands of miles. Each head of a reed-mace is made up of thousands of tiny seeds with parachutes. These plants now grow on the edges of swamps and ponds all over the world. The constant fight people have to make to keep their lawns free from dandelions is another sign that parachutes are a big help in getting seeds scattered.

Milkweed

Dandelion

Clematis

Cotton

Witch Hazel

Violet

Touch-me-not

Pansy

Monkeys' Dinner Bell

Maple

Elm

Box Elder

Ash

Lime

Wafer Ash

The seeds of the maple tree travel by air, but they do not have parachutes. They travel by means of wings instead. As the picture above shows, wings help scatter ash, elm, and other tree seeds, too.

Wings not only help seeds travel by air; they also help them travel by water. Seeds cannot stand being in water long, but with wings to help them, they may float on the surface of a pond or stream until they reach a bank.

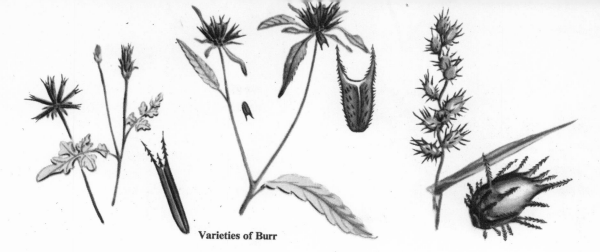

Varieties of Burr

Some seeds make long air journeys without the help of either wings or parachutes. They travel "by bird." Wading birds carry many seeds in mud on their feet. Birds may carry sticky seeds for a long way on their bills. When they clean their bills they scrape the seeds off. Mistletoe is one of the plants that have been scattered in this way. Birds may also carry small seeds in their feathers.

Riding on the feet or in the feathers or on the bill of a bird is like riding on the outside of an aeroplane. There is always danger of falling off. Sometimes seeds ride on the inside of their bird aeroplanes. Birds eat fruits. If the seeds are small, as they are in such fruits as the blackberry and the wild grape, they swallow the fruit, seeds and all. The bird digests the soft part of the fruit, but it may not digest the seeds. The seeds may go through the bird's body and still be able to grow when they are dropped to the ground.

Birds carry most seeds quite by accident. But sometimes they carry seeds to store them away as food. They may even plant them! Jays, for instance, dig holes in the ground and put acorns in them. They may never come back to get the acorns they have buried; the acorns have a chance to grow. Squirrels plant nuts of different kinds in the same way.

The seed pods of some plants shoot out their seeds. Witch hazel pods pop open like tiny fire-crackers and shoot out their seeds. The ripe pod of a touch-me-not plant shoots out its seeds if it is touched. Violet and pansy seed pods also shoot out their seeds.

Another plant that has pods that explode is the sandbox tree that grows in the hot, wet lands of South America. Travellers have given this tree another name. They call it the "monkey's dinner bell." Its seed pods shoot out their seeds with so much force that the noise is like a pistol shot. There are monkeys in the forests where this tree grows. The pods make so much noise that people say the tree is calling the monkeys to dinner.

The seeds that are carried by birds might be called hitch-hikers. The seeds pictured at the top of the page might be called hitch-hikers, too. They are carried in the fur of animals and in the clothing of people. The sharp prickles on the hard cases that hold the seeds can catch in fur or clothing easily. They often cling so securely that the seeds are hard to pull off. Anyone who has ever walked through a patch of burrs knows how easy it is for burr seeds to catch a ride.

Wings help seeds float for short distances. The American lotus has a much better way of sending its seeds on journeys by water. The seed holder it produces is a regular boat. It can float for a long way. The seeds are held firmly inside it until the "boat" breaks or rots away.

Big seeds like walnuts may roll quite a distance. Whole plants may spread in a form of chain; they are blown along the ground, dropping their seeds as they go. Seeds in pods may skid over a snowy surface. A flat pod like that of the locust, or false acacia, makes a good sledge for this purpose. A few kinds of seeds can actually crawl along the ground a little way. Some grass seeds, for instance, have stiff hairs that move when they get wet. Seed plants certainly have many different and very good ways of getting their seeds scattered. Is it any wonder that, after seed plants once appeared, they spread over most of the earth, crowding out many simpler plants?

House Plants

Wandering Jew

African Violet

Cacti and Hen-and-Chickens

Sedum, Aloe, and Peperomia

EVEN in cold winter weather, when the trees are bare and our gardens show nothing but dead stalks, we can have growing plants around us. For many different kinds of plants can be raised indoors. Florist shops are full of plants for indoor gardens. Some of these plants are liked for their flowers, others for their leaves. The pictures at the left show a few of the plants that can be grown indoors successfully.

Wandering Jew is a trailing plant. It was a favourite with our grandmothers because of its pretty leaves. For a time this and other such plants lost their popularity, but now they are again much in demand in the florists' shops. Philodendron is another trailing plant which makes a window-sill look decorative. Philodendron can be grown without soil. It will do quite well if it is simply planted in water.

African violets are worth growing because they bloom so well. They have, however, tender leaves. Water that touches them makes ugly spots.

Cactus plants make an interesting indoor garden. Different kinds have different shapes, some of them rather grotesque. Cactus plants have no leaves. But they have beautiful flowers when they bloom.

Some cactus plants are tiny. Several can be grown in a bowl only a few inches across. In the bowl with the two cacti in the picture there is a hen-and-chickens plant.

For many years the aspidistra was a very popular—perhaps the most popular—plant for indoors if one was not interested in having flowers. But in time people came to think of it as dull and no longer fashionable, so that aspidistras are not nearly so common in houses today as they were at the beginning of this century. These plants are often rather large, and that may be another reason why they lost their popularity—they took up too much room.

The plant with the small, thick leaves is a sedum. Some people call it "Chinese jade." It grows into interesting shapes and throws pretty shadows when the sun shines on it. The plant beside it is an aloe. The one with the heart-shaped leaves is peperomia.

The secret of being a successful indoor gardener is knowing that not all plants that will grow indoors should be treated the same way. They do not all thrive in the same amount of light. Some like a sunny south window best, others a north

Terrarium, a glassed-in garden

window. They do not all need the same amount of water. Some must be protected from draughts. Some can stand higher or lower temperatures than others. Some need well-drained soil, while others will grow in pots with no drainage.

A good rule is to try to give plants as nearly as possible the conditions they would have outdoors. A cactus, for instance, is a desert plant. It lives in regions where there is little rain for long periods but where there are occasional heavy showers. A cactus plant, therefore, should be watered thoroughly. Then it should not be given any more water until the soil is quite dry. If the soil around it is kept wet all the time, a cactus is likely to rot.

At Christmas time and other special times potted plants by the thousands are sent as gifts. Some of them do not last any longer than a bouquet of cut flowers would last. A poinsettia that has lost all its leaves is, for instance, a common sight a day or two after Christmas. Some florists now send a card with every potted plant telling how the plant should be cared for. The directions should be followed carefully.

A little glassed-in garden, or terrarium, is fun to plan and plant. The one in the picture above has four kinds of plants in it; twinberry, the plant with the red berries; moss; a small fern; and a lichen called the "British soldier" because of its red cap. (British soldiers used to wear red uniforms.)

An aquarium is too often thought of only as a home for fish. But if it is planted carefully it can be made into an attractive underwater garden. Some of the plants that will grow well in an aquarium are very pretty.

Of course, to have an attractive garden indoors it is not necessary to buy plants at a florist's. Some of our common vegetables, like the beans, will do quite well in a jam-jar containing cotton-wool and water. If they are placed in such a glass "flower-pot" you can watch both roots and shoots growing.

Grapefruit seeds planted in a pot of earth grow into plants with dark-green, shiny leaves. Slips taken from such plants as begonias and geraniums may be planted with every hope of their growing well. Interesting plants for a terrarium can be gathered in almost any woods.

The convolvulus and some other garden flowers can be raised indoors from seed. With proper care they will bloom in the winter.

Among the most successful of the blooming plants that can be raised indoors are some that can be raised by planting bulbs in water. Some narcissus bulbs, for instance, can be planted in water and pebbles, and need little care. On a cold, dark morning in winter a bowl of blooming narcissi does a great deal to make one forget the weather.

Aquarium, an under-water garden

New Plants from Old

Almost all the plants we raise are seed plants. The commonest way of raising new plants is to plant seeds of the kinds of plants we want.

Planting a seed means putting it in a situation that will allow the small plant inside the seed to break its way out through the seed coat and keep on growing. Warmth and moisture and air must be provided. Many people who plant seeds do not understand that seeds need air. It is possible to drown the tiny plants in seeds just as it is possible to drown animals by having so much water that it shuts out air.

Unless there is enough warmth, a seed is likely to rot instead of sprout. But too much heat is as dangerous as not enough.

The depth at which a seed is planted is also important. In every seed some food is stored for the baby plant. If the seedling is to keep on growing, this food must last until the plant is above the surface of the ground and can begin to make food for itself.

A bean seed has enough food stored in it to let a young bean plant grow to be several inches high. A bean seed, therefore, can be planted several inches deep without any danger that the young plant will run out of food. There is an advantage in planting such a large seed as a bean seed rather deep. If it is planted close to the surface, a heavy rain is likely to wash away the soil from around it.

A petunia seed, in contrast with a bean seed, is very tiny. There is room in it for only a little food. If, therefore, a petunia seed is planted deep in the ground, the seedling will run out of food before it reaches the sunshine. Fortunately, there is not much danger that the soil will be washed away from around such a small seed.

In some cases there are other ways of raising new plants that are better than planting seeds. Many kinds of flowers are commonly raised from bulbs. Almost no one, for instance, plants tulip seeds except flower growers who are trying to produce new varieties of tulips. Bulbs furnish an easy way of growing sturdy plants. A bulb is made up mostly of thick leaves that overlap one another. A great deal of food is stored in them. There is very much more food in a tulip bulb than in a tulip seed. A strong, vigorous plant can grow from a bulb and come into bloom much more quickly than from a seed.

A corm is very much like a bulb. Anemones are commonly raised from corms rather than from seeds.

Some plants can be raised from roots. The dahlia has fleshy roots in which a large amount of food is stored.

A potato is a thick underground stem of the kind called a "tuber." The eyes of a potato are buds. A gardener, to plant potatoes, cuts potatoes into pieces, each piece with an eye. There is enough food in the piece of potato to let the bud grow.

A rhizome is another kind of thick underground stem. Iris plants are usually raised from rhizomes. Tubers, rhizomes, corms, and fleshy roots have the same advantage over seeds that bulbs have.

Geraniums are usually raised from slips, or cuttings. A slip is a branch of the plant. Plants can be raised from slips only if the slips will send out roots when put in a moist place.

The branches of some plants send out roots wherever they touch the ground. New plants can be started by bending a branch down to the ground, fastening it in place until it sends roots down and a shoot up, and then cutting the branch so that it is no longer joined to the parent plant. This plan of starting new plants is called "layering." Many blackberry and raspberry bushes are started by layering.

Stages in the development of a bean plant

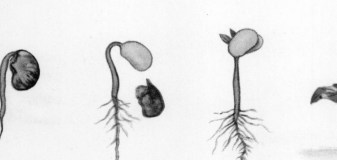

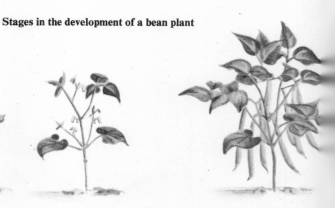

Bulb

Corm

Fleshy Root

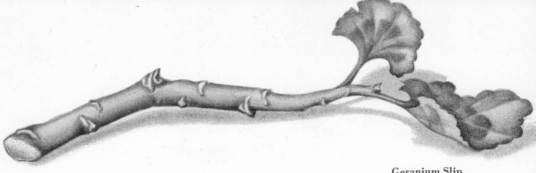

Geranium Slip

Rhizome

In some cases it is not possible to raise a seed plant from its seeds. The idea is rather startling, but true. Suppose a new kind of apple has been produced by crossing two kinds of apples. Let us call the new kind of apple "Apple X." The apples on the Apple X tree have seeds in them. If planted, these seeds would probably grow. But they would not produce more Apple X trees.

The reason the seeds would not produce Apple X trees is that the tiny plants in them have two parents. One is the Apple X tree. The other is the apple tree that furnished the pollen that made the seeds develop. In the case of apples, the tree that furnishes the pollen must be a different apple tree from the one the seeds are formed on. The apple trees that grew from the seeds on the Apple X tree would not, therefore, be Apple X trees. They would be crosses between Apple X and some other variety of apple. They might bear rather poor apples.

A good way has been found of raising new plants of such kinds as apple trees. A woody cutting is made. This cutting is then grafted on to another plant. A cutting of Apple X, for instance, could be grafted onto a young hardy crab apple tree. The branches of the young crab apple tree could then be cut off and only the cutting of Apple X be allowed to grow. Soon the tree would look like the parent Apple X tree. No one would know by looking at it that it had crab apple roots. It would bear apples just like those on the tree the cutting came from.

When an apple tree "sport" is made an established strain, it can still be said that there is only one tree of that strain in the world—the original "sport." All its descendants came from cuttings of the first tree, which had been grafted on to some other kind of apple tree. The same thing could be said of many other varieties of woody plants. For many of the fruit trees, rose-bushes, grape-vines, and ornamental shrubs and trees nurseries sell are grafted. Grafting is an important help in multiplying plants of new varieties that are developed.

Cuttings for Grafting

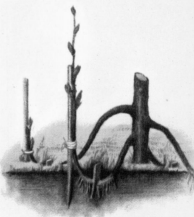

Layering

177

Hen and Chickens

Cactus

Plant Adaptations

MANY plants, like many animals, are specially fitted for living where they do. They are so well fitted for living in certain kinds of places that they cannot live anywhere else. A seaweed and a hyacinth could not change habitats any more successfully than could a swallow and a cod.

A desert is one of the kinds of places that present many problems to plants. The sub-tropical deserts, for instance, are often very hot in the daytime and cool at night. The air as well as the soil is usually dry. When rain does fall, it frequently comes down in torrents. Much of the water runs off instead of sinking into the ground.

Cacti are among the plants that have solved the problems of living in such a desert. They are beautifully fitted for growing where the rainfall is low but where there are occasional heavy showers.

Most cactus plants have no leaves at all. Some have tiny leaves for a time but soon lose them. The stems of cacti do the work which leaves do for such plants as elm trees and sunflowers and cabbages. Cactus stems are thick. They are pulpy inside and serve as excellent storage tanks for water. It would do a cactus plant no good to have a storage tank if it had no way of filling the tank. Its roots spread out near the surface of the ground. They are ready to soak up fast any water that reaches them.

Having no leaves helps a cactus plant save the water it has stored. Many gallons of water may evaporate from a lime tree on a hot summer day, because there is an enormous amount of surface from which evaporation can take place. In the case of a cactus there is little surface from which the water in it can evaporate. Besides, the cactus stems are covered with wax. The wax helps reduce evaporation.

Many desert animals get a great deal of the water they need from the plants they eat. Juicy cactus plants would not have much of a chance to escape being eaten if they were not covered with thorns. Thorns, then, are another of the adaptations of a cactus plant for living in the desert.

The little hen-and-chickens plant is also fitted for living in dry regions. It has thick leaves that make good water reservoirs. The leaves, moreover, form a rosette close to the ground. There is not much exposed surface.

A bog is very different as a habitat from a desert. Here there is a great deal of water, but there may be a shortage of another important material—nitrogen. Plants as a rule get all their nitrogen from the soil or water in which they are growing. But some bog plants get nitrogen just as we and many other animals do— by eating meat.

Sundew

Venus's-flytrap

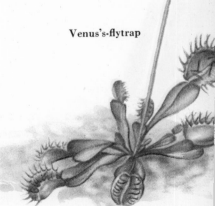

Water Lily

The tiny sundew is one of the meat-eating bog plants. Its leaves are insect traps. Most of the leaves lie flat on the ground. They are covered with hairs, and there is a drop of liquid at the end of each hair. The plant gets its name from these drops of liquid, which look like dew but which do not go away when the sun shines. The dew is sticky. A little insect that crawls up on a leaf is caught in the dew on one of the hairs. This hair bends over to the centre of the leaf. All the other hairs bend down, too. They hold the insect tight against the leaf. The dew helps turn the soft part of the insect into a liquid, which is absorbed by the leaf. When the sundew has finished "digesting" the insect, the hairs open out again. The hard parts of the insect blow away. The leaf is then ready for another meal.

The Venus's-flytrap is another plant that is fitted for living in a bog because it can eat insects. The ends of the leaves of this plant are good traps. They catch insects by folding together. On each half of the trap at the end of a leaf there are some stiff hairs that stand up. These are the triggers that make the trap work. As soon as an insect touches one of the hairs, the trap closes. Stiff hairs around the edges keep the insect from escaping. The trap stays closed until the insect is digested. Then it opens out again.

Pitcher plants are insect-eating plants, too. They trap the insects in pitcher-shaped leaves that often are partly full of water.

Water lilies are well fitted for living in fresh-water lakes and ponds. Their broad leaves float on the surface. They are different in an important way from the broad leaves of such plants as lime trees and sunflowers. Water lilies, like all green plants, are able to make sugar and starch for themselves when they have sunlight. For this food-making they must get carbon dioxide from the air.

When they are not making food, they have to have oxygen, just as animals do. As a rule, the tiny openings, or stomata, through which most plants with leaves take in air are on the undersurface of the leaves. The stomata do not become clogged with rain and dirt so easily when they are in this position. But the stomata of water lilies are on the upper surfaces of the leaves. The leaves can therefore float right on the surface of the water and still get plenty of oxygen and carbon dioxide.

In warm, rainy forests plants have to struggle to get the light they need. Some put themselves in the sunshine by perching on the branches of trees. Such perching plants are called "epiphytes." Perching high on a plant makes it possible for an epiphyte to get light, but it makes it hard for the epiphyte to get water. Different epiphytes solve the problem in different ways. The epiphyte pictured has stiff leaves that form a rain barrel. These leaves have a special way of taking in the water that is caught in the rain barrel.

The trunk of the silk-cotton tree of Africa flares out at the base into giant folds that are like the flying buttresses of Gothic cathedrals. They keep the tree from being uprooted easily in windstorms.

The tendrils that enable ivy to cling to a wall, the hooks that anchor brown kelps to rocks along our shores, the hairy covering of mullein leaves, and the air bladders of the water hyacinth are among the many other adaptations of plants to the places where they live.

An Epiphyte

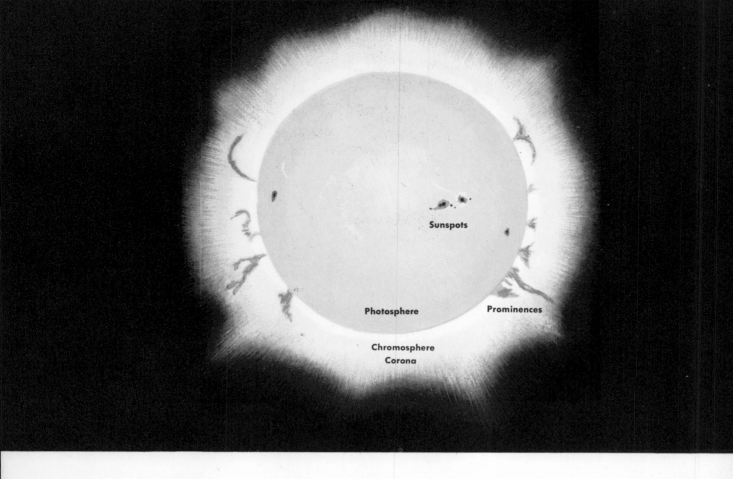

Sunspots

Photosphere

Prominences

Chromosphere
Corona

The Sun and Its Family

For centuries people believed that the earth was the centre of the universe. They thought that the earth stood still while the sun and the stars did all the travelling. It was hard to convince them that the earth, with many more heavenly bodies, travels around the sun. The sun is not the centre of the universe, but it *is* the centre of what we call the solar system. "Solar system" means "sun's system." The solar system is made up of the sun and of planets, moons, comets, meteors, and planetoids that travel around it. The earth is one of the sun's planets.

The sun is a star. It is only a medium-sized star—there are stars that are hundreds of thousands of times as large—but even so it is tremendously big. If there were a hollow ball the size of the sun, it would take more than a million earths to fill it.

As we see it in the sky, the sun looks to be about the size of a dinner plate. It does not look as big as the house next door or even the letter-box at the corner. It appears to be small because it is so far away from us. On the average it is about 93,000,000 miles away.

The sun is not one of the hottest stars. But it is tremendously hot. The temperature at its centre is believed to be about 20 million degrees on the Fahrenheit scale—the scale we use on our ordinary thermometers. The temperature at the surface is about 11,000°F.

By using an instrument called a "spectroscope," scientists can tell from the light that comes from the sun what its outer layers are made of. They have found in these outer layers a large number of substances which are found on the earth. Among them are iron, silver, copper, aluminium, and lead. On the earth these materials are solids. In the sun they are gases instead. The sun is far too hot for any material there to be a solid. It is far too hot for any material there to be a liquid either. All the materials the sun is made of are gases.

Sometimes the sun is called a "ball of fire." This name is not a good one. The gases of the sun are so hot that they glow just as the white-hot filament in an electric lamp glows. They are not burning up as the gas in a gas stove burns. The word that means "so hot that it gives off light without burning" is "incandescent." The sun, then, is a huge ball of incandescent gases.

One gas was found on the sun before it was found on the earth. This gas is helium. Its name comes from the Greek word for sun. Helium is now used in many balloons because it is very light and will not burn. Hydrogen, once generally used, is lighter, but it does burn.

Shooting up from the sun there are great rose-coloured streamers of glowing gas. They may shoot up for more than 100,000 miles. These great streamers of gas are called "solar prominences." Beside one of them the earth would be a mere dot, as the picture shows.

Long before people knew that the earth travels around the sun, they realized that the sun is very important. They saw that without its heat and light life on the earth would be impossible. Many early peoples worshipped the sun. Even many of those who did not worship the sun thought of it as something perfect. When the telescope was invented and astronomers turned their telescopes toward the sun, they saw that there are darker

Relative size of earth

Umbra

Penumbra

Sunspot

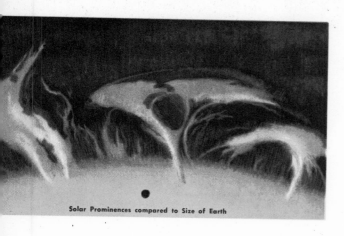

Solar Prominences compared to Size of Earth

spots on its disc. The idea of blemishes on the sun was not popular. Some scientists almost lost their lives because they told of them. But there are certainly sunspots.

A sunspot is a great tornado in the white-hot gases on the surface of the sun. Sunspots last much longer than tornadoes last on the earth. Sometimes they can be seen for weeks or even months. Sunspots cover much more space than do the earth's tornadoes, too. Some are much larger than others. The whole earth could easily be swallowed up in one of the larger whirlwinds on the sun.

Sunspots are not really dark. They are merely dark when compared with the rest of the sun's

surface. They are brighter than the white-hot iron that pours from the blast furnaces of our steel mills here on earth. The gases in a sunspot, however, are cooler by several thousand degrees than the gases in the rest of the sun's surface.

By watching sunspots, scientists have found that the sun rotates; it spins round, that is, like a top. It takes the sun about 25 days to make a complete turn. This, it would seem, is not spinning very fast. It means, however, that a spot on the sun's equator is moving a million miles a day.

The picture below shows an eclipse of the sun— a solar eclipse. The moon is blotting out the main disc of the sun. The solar prominences show. So does the mysterious corona. The corona forms a beautiful pearly halo. Probably it is made up of very, very small gas particles lighted up by the main body of the sun. Seeing the corona is one of the rewards for making a long trip to see a solar eclipse.

No one should look directly at the sun without protecting his eyes. It is even more dangerous to look at the sun through a telescope. Sunlight is altogether too bright.

Corona

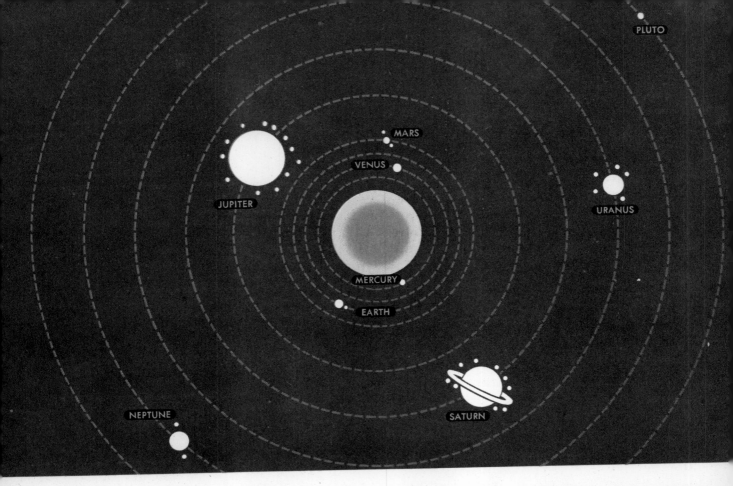

There are eight planets besides the earth in the sun's family. The word "planet" means "wanderer." When the people of ancient times studied the sky, they gave names to the groups of stars they saw. They learned to know the stars that made up each group. They saw some "stars," however, that did not stay in any one group. These "stars" came to be called "wanderers" or "planets." Finally it was found that they are not stars at all but are bodies which, like the earth, keep travelling around the sun. They seem to wander from star group to star group because of their journeys round the sun.

Planets look to us like stars, but they are really very different. Stars are very, very hot. They shine with their own light. The planets do not shine with their own light. They shine only because the sun is shining on them. Moonlight, as most people know, is secondhand sunlight: the moon merely reflects the light that shines on it from the sun. The light from the planets is secondhand sunlight, too.

Of our eight fellow planets, only five can be seen with the naked eye. The people of ancient times knew of only five "wandering stars." The planets that are visible without a telescope are Mercury, Venus, Mars, Jupiter, and Saturn. The other planets were not discovered until after telescopes were invented.

The days of the week are named after the sun, moon, and these five planets. Sunday is, of course, the sun's day. Monday is the moon's day. Saturday is Saturn's day. Tuesday is named after Mars, Wednesday after Mercury, Thursday after Jupiter, and Friday after Venus. The names of these five planets are also names of Roman gods. In coming down to us as names of days of the week the names of Norse gods were substituted – Tiu for Mars, Woden for Mercury, Thor for Jupiter, and Freya for Venus. If the people of long ago had been able to see Uranus, Neptune, and Pluto, we might have ten days in a week instead of seven.

The path of a planet is called its "orbit." The chart at the top of the page shows the order of the orbits of the planets from the sun. The orbits are all slightly flattened circles. They are flattened too little to show in so small a chart. Flattened .circles are called "ellipses."

It takes the earth a year to make its journey around the sun. It is, in fact, the journey of the earth round the sun that gives us the year as a measure of time. The earth cannot go sauntering along to make this journey in a year. It has to travel at the rate of 1,100 miles a minute. In the time it takes to read this page the earth travels at least 1,000 miles.

Mercury, the planet closest to the sun, has a much shorter path. It also travels much faster. Mercury's year is only about three months long. Pluto, the most distant planet in our solar system, has a path that is 40 times as long as the earth's. Moreover, Pluto travels more slowly. A year on Pluto is about 248 of our years long. The two planets that are nearer the sun than we are have shorter years than ours. All those that are farther away have longer years.

The chart makes it look as if the space around the sun were somewhat crowded with planets. Actually it is not at all. An artist cannot use the same scale in drawing the orbits of the planets that he uses in drawing the planets themselves. If the earth were kept the size it is in the diagram and its orbit were drawn on the same scale, the orbit would be 250 feet across. Pluto's orbit would be nearly two miles across!

Every one of the nine planets is small compared with the sun. (To be in proportion, the sun in the chart below would have to be a 15-inch circle.) But compared with the earth some of them are giants. Some, on the other hand, are smaller than the earth. The four planets nearest the sun are all rather small. The earth is the largest of the four. Venus is almost as large, Mars is considerably smaller, and Mercury is smaller still.

The next four planets in order from the sun are all much larger than the earth. Jupiter, as the chart shows, is the largest. Saturn is next largest. Uranus and Neptune come very close to being twins, just as do the earth and Venus.

Pluto, farthest planet from the sun, is small. Only Mercury is smaller.

Many of the planets have moons that travel round them as they travel round the sun. The earth is poor in moons: it has only one. Mercury, Venus, and Pluto, so far as we know, are poorer. They have none. Jupiter, in contrast, has twelve. Mars and Neptune have two; Uranus has five; and Saturn has nine.

Relative Sizes of the Planets

Mercury
Venus
Earth
Mars
Jupiter
Saturn
Uranus
Neptune
Pluto

The planets keep travelling their same orbits century after century. They do not run away from the sun because the sun is pulling them with so much force that they cannot. Scientists call the kind of pull with which the sun is pulling the planets the force of gravitation. Often it is called gravity for short.

It would seem, if the sun is pulling them with so much force, that the planets should fall into the sun. They do not because they are moving too fast. Each planet moves with a speed that just balances the pull of the sun. The outer planets are so far away that the pull on them is less than on the planets closer to the sun. They can travel more slowly and still not be pulled in.

Saturn is set apart from all the other planets by its rings. They make it the most beautiful of all heavenly bodies when viewed through a telescope. Unfortunately, Saturn's rings cannot be seen without a telescope.

These rings are a puzzle to scientists. They must be made up of millions or trillions of tiny particles, perhaps as fine as dust. Some scientists believe that some of the particles may be ice crystals.

The outermost ring is rather dull. Next there is a dark space. Then comes the widest, brightest ring. Inside that there is a dusky, almost transparent, "crepe" ring.

The nine moons of Saturn are outside the rings. There may once have been another moon. For it is quite possible that the rings of Saturn were made from a tenth moon which came very close to Saturn in its travels—so close that it was pulled to pieces.

Saturn's year is nearly 30 times as long as the earth's year. A person 60 years old on the earth would be only two of Saturn's years old.

The earth rotates as it travels round the sun. The spinning of the earth makes the sun rise and set and seem to move across the sky. It gives us our day and night, for the sun can shine at one time on only the side of the earth turned toward it. Half of the earth is having night while the other half is having day.

It takes the earth a 24-hour day to spin round once. In fact, the spinning of the earth has given us the day as a measure of time. At the equator each 24 hours is divided into 12 hours of light and 12 hours of darkness. The day is not divided this way all over the earth, because the earth's axis— the imaginary line around which it spins—is tilted.

Saturn spins round just as the earth does, except that it spins much faster. It spins round once in 10 hours and 14 minutes. Every place on the equator of Saturn has only 5 hours and 7 minutes of light and then 5 hours and 7 minutes of darkness. Sunset, that is, would be only a little more than five hours after sunrise. Its rings and moons would keep night on Saturn from being very dark.

The earth's gravity keeps the objects on the surface of the earth from flying off into space as the earth whirls round. It keeps the water in the oceans. It holds an ocean of air around the earth. Everything on the earth has weight because of the earth's pull.

Although Saturn is very much larger than the earth, gravity at its surface is not much greater

SATURN

than the earth's surface gravity. A person on Saturn would not weigh much more than he weighs on the earth. The low surface gravity is accounted for chiefly by the fact that Saturn is made in large part of very light materials.

Ever since people have known there were other planets travelling round the sun, they have wondered whether these other planets were inhabited. Scientists are certain that there are no people living on Saturn. It is far too cold. Its atmosphere, moreover, is made of gases that would suffocate people like us.

When we see Jupiter in the sky, it looks like a very bright star, considerably brighter than

JUPITER

Jupiter's year is 12 times as long as ours. But its day is even shorter than Saturn's. Jupiter spins round once in only 9 hours and 50 minutes. One would not need three meals in one of Jupiter's days.

There are certainly no people on Jupiter. Although closer to the sun than Saturn, it also is too cold. Its atmosphere, moreover, like Saturn's, would suffocate us. It is probably made of ammonia and marsh gas. There may be some ice on Jupiter's surface; some scientists think there is a great deal. Any water there would certainly be frozen.

Scientists do not know much about the three planets that cannot be seen without a telescope. The charts on pages 205 and 206 tell much of what they have found out.

Uranus was discovered by the famous astronomer Herschel in 1781. Before that time everyone who had seen it had thought that it was a faint star. When this planet was first discovered it was called Herschel by some astronomers.

Neptune was discovered in 1846. The discovery was made by two different astronomers in two different countries at almost the same time. They were both looking for something that was pulling Uranus out of the path scientists had expected it to follow. They found a new planet. Of course, it was not really new, but no one had ever seen it before. The two astronomers were Leverrier, a Frenchman, and Adams, an Englishman.

Since its discovery, Neptune has not had enough time to make one complete journey round the sun. For Neptune's year is 165 times as long as ours.

Pluto was discovered by astronomers of the Lowell Observatory at Flagstaff, Arizona. Its discovery was first announced on March 13, 1930. Pluto, since it was first seen, has had time to cover only a small part of its orbit. It will not be back in the place where it was on its path in 1930 until the year 2178.

Pluto is so far from the sun that from it the sun would look only like a bright star. The sunlight that reaches it is less than a thousandth as bright as sunlight here on the earth. There is not much difference between day and night on this distant planet.

Obviously no one could live on Uranus, Neptune, or Pluto. They are far too cold. The temperature on Uranus is probably lower than 300 degrees below zero, Fahrenheit. Neptune is even more of a refrigerator. And Pluto is so cold that even air would freeze there.

Saturn. It is not surprising that it does, for Jupiter comes closer to us than Saturn and is much bigger. Some of Jupiter's moons are giants, too. Two of them are larger than Mercury.

Jupiter as seen through a telescope has streaks across it. They are caused by currents in Jupiter's atmosphere. One marking on this planet scientists do not understand. It is called the "great red spot." It has disappeared and reappeared, and it is still a mystery.

The surface gravity of Jupiter is much greater than the earth's surface gravity. A person who weighs 100 pounds on the earth would weigh 260 pounds on this giant planet.

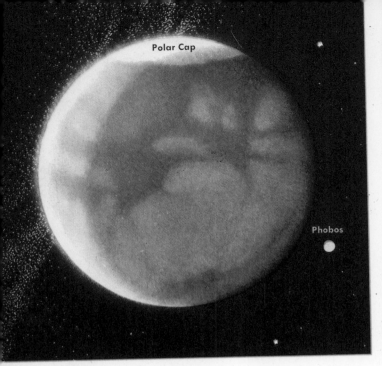

Polar Cap

Phobos

Mars

Scientists know more about Mars than they know about any other planet except, of course, the earth. But they would like to know much more. Mars comes closer to us than any other planet

SEASONS ON MARS

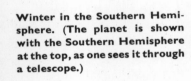

Winter in the Southern Hemisphere. (The planet is shown with the Southern Hemisphere at the top, as one sees it through a telescope.)

Early Spring or Late Autumn

Late Spring or Early Autumn

Summer

except Venus. It looks like a reddish star. Perhaps its colour led the Romans to name it after their god of war.

Through a telescope many markings are seen on the surface of Mars. Much of the surface is dull red. But there are also areas that are sometimes green and sometimes brown, and there are white caps at times at the poles. The markings on Mars have caused many debates among scientists.

Mars, scientists are sure, has an atmosphere. This planet is smaller than the earth, and its surface gravity is much less than the earth's. A person weighing 100 pounds on the earth would weigh only 40 pounds on Mars. But even with less gravity Mars is able to hold a thin atmosphere. Probably there is a little oxygen in it. Probably there is some water vapour in it, too. Without any question it contains carbon dioxide.

Mars has seasons just as the earth has and for the same reason. The earth has seasons because of the tilt of the earth's axis. It spins around like a top leaning over to one side, and leaning always in the same direction. The southern half of the earth gets more heat and light from the sun when the tilt of the axis from South Pole to North Pole is away from the sun. The southern half of the earth then has summer and the northern half winter. The northern half of the earth gets more heat and light from the sun when the tilt from South Pole to North Pole is toward the sun. The northern half of the earth then has summer and the southern half winter. The axis of Mars is tilted, too. Since Mars has a longer year than ours, its seasons also are longer.

When the northern half of Mars is having winter, the white cap at its north pole is large. It gets smaller and smaller as spring advances, and disappears entirely in the summer. But when the southern half of Mars has winter, a white cap appears at the south pole. Many scientists believe that the polar caps on Mars are fields of snow with banks of fog over them.

At one time scientists thought that the reddish areas on Mars were land and that the darker regions were water. They now believe that both the red and the dark areas are land. The red areas, they believe, are desert. Perhaps the darker areas are wetter regions in which plants are growing.

Mars has so much less water and so much less oxygen than the earth has that people like ourselves could not possibly live there. Even if there are plants growing there, moreover, it is not probable that they are plants of a kind that would make good food for people. There are many stories of the inhabitants of Mars. Of course, they are all imaginary, but the idea is widespread that there are intelligent beings on this planet.

The idea of inhabitants on Mars came chiefly from the straight markings which some astronomers have seen on its surface. These straight markings, many people think, are bands of vegetation growing along artificial canals. No rivers, they argue, would be so straight. If there are canals, the argument goes, there must be intelligent beings to dig them.

But there is much disagreement about the straight bands. The pictures of Mars on page 186 were drawn from Mars as seen through a telescope. Photographs do not show the lines, and many astronomers have not been able to see them. If there are no canals, the chief reason for believing in intelligent beings there is gone.

Mars has two moons, but they are both tiny ones. Moonlight on Mars would not be bright.

A day on Mars is almost the same length as ours. Its year is 687 of our days long.

Circling round the sun between the orbits of Mars and Jupiter there are hundreds of tiny planets, or planetoids. The largest planetoid we know about is Ceres. It is 480 miles in diameter, much smaller than our moon. Many planetoids are only a few miles in diameter. Amor, discovered in 1932, is only a mile across.

The surface gravity on a planetoid is not great enough to hold an atmosphere. A person or even a huge locomotive would weigh almost nothing on the smaller planetoids. Anyone who can imagine himself on Amor can imagine lifting a loco-

Location of Asteroids (Planetoids)

motive or taking a jump and sailing off into space.

There are some planetoids whose paths are out beyond Jupiter and others whose paths come closer to us than Mars. In 1932 the tiny planetoid Apollo was only 6½ million miles away from the earth. For a time there was some fear that it would collide with the earth.

Some scientists believe that the planetoids are the wreckage of a planet that once had an orbit between Mars and Jupiter. This planet, they think, may have come too close to Jupiter and have been pulled to pieces.

Venus, when it is closest to us, is closer than any other planet. Unfortunately, we cannot then see Venus at all. It is between the earth and the sun and its dark side is turned toward us.

When Venus can be seen it is brighter than any star except, of course, the sun, and brighter than any other planet. Of all the heavenly bodies only the sun and the moon are brighter.

The orbit of Venus is between the earth's orbit and the sun. Venus is seen, therefore, either in the western sky after sunset or in the eastern sky before sunrise. But it is far enough away from the sun not to be lost in the glow of sunrise and sunset. It can sometimes be seen for three hours after sunset or before sunrise. When it shines in the western sky after sunset it is often called the "evening star." When it shines in the eastern sky before sunrise it is often called the "morning star."

The people of ancient times had two names for Venus. When the Romans saw it as an evening star they called it Hesperus. When they saw it

187

Venus in the Crescent Phase

as a morning star they called it Phosphorus. They did not know that they were simply seeing the same heavenly body in two different positions.

Through a telescope Venus seems to change shape. Sometimes it looks like a little full moon. At other times it looks like a half-moon, and at still other times it is a crescent. When it is on the opposite side of the sun from us, its lighted side is turned toward us. Then it looks like a tiny full moon. In its other positions we cannot see its whole lighted side. When it is between us and the sun, the side toward us is entirely dark. The picture on page 187 shows it as a crescent. We are seeing only a small part of the side that is lighted up.

Although Venus is our nearest neighbour among the planets, scientists know very little about conditions on it. The surface is covered with dense clouds in which there is never a break. Perhaps these clouds are made of dust. It does not seem probable that they are clouds like ours. No one has yet found any trace of water on Venus. No one has found any trace of oxygen either. One thing we do know about the atmosphere of our twin planet is that there is a great deal of carbon dioxide in it.

Since scientists cannot see through the clouds on Venus, they cannot see any markings to help them tell how fast Venus turns on its axis as it travels round the sun. Probably its day is about a month long. Without knowing more about conditions on Venus, scientists cannot tell whether it is a fit place for living things of the kinds we have on the earth.

Mercury, the smallest planet, is visible to the naked eye. But not many people see it. It is so close to the sun that, if it is in a position in its orbit so that it can be seen, it sets soon after sunset or rises just before sunrise. It is often lost in the glow of sunset or sunrise.

In ancient times this planet had two names, just as Venus had. The Romans called it Mercury when they saw it low in the west after sunset. They called it Apollo when they saw it low in the east before sunrise.

Mercury appears to change shape when seen through a telescope, just as Venus does and for the same reason. When it is closest to us, the side toward us is totally dark. Occasionally Mercury shows as a small black spot against the sun.

No one is sure how long Mercury's day is—how long, that is, it takes Mercury to turn on its axis. Most scientists believe that its day and its year are the same length—88 days. They think that it

The Moon, Its Phases: New, First Quarter, Full, Third Quarter, Old Crescent

PYRENEES MTS.

Picc

MARE NECTARIS

Vendelinus

Theo

Langrenus

MARE FOECUNDITATIS

MARE TRANQUI

MARE CRISIUM

MAR

Posi
L
SOM

turns on its axis just fast enough to keep the same side always toward the sun. If these scientists are right, one side of Mercury always has day and one side always has night.

Mercury is so much closer to the sun than we are that the part on which the sun shines is terrifically hot. It is so hot that lead would melt in the sunshine. If one side always has night, however, that side is terrifically cold. For there are no winds on Mercury to carry warmth from one place to another. So far as scientists have been able to find out, Mercury has no atmosphere at all. Neither does it have any water. It goes without saying that it could support no living things of the kinds we know.

Scientists once thought that there was a planet closer to the sun than Mercury. They even gave it a name—Vulcan. Now it seems certain that there is no such planet. Scientists are not nearly so sure that there are no planets out beyond Pluto. Perhaps there are still new worlds to find.

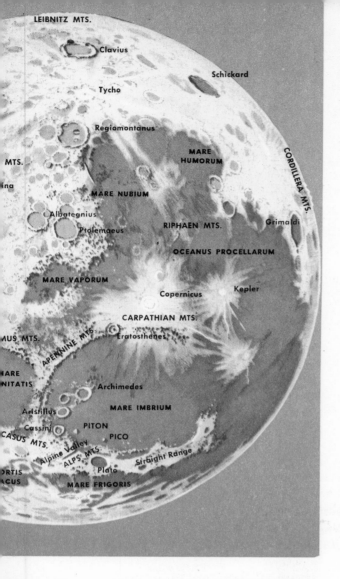

The moon is the earth's nearest neighbour in space. It is only about a quarter of a million miles away.

No other planet has a moon that is so big in proportion to the planet itself. Fifty moons would be enough to make a ball as big as the earth.

The moon as it travels around the earth seems to change its shape. The different shapes are called the "phases" of the moon.

Moons, like planets, shine only because the sun shines on them. Our moon is no exception. The sun, of course, can shine on only half of it at one time. Only half is lighted up.

As the moon travels round the earth, it keeps the same side toward us. It turns on its axis just fast enough to keep the same face in our direction. At times it is possible to see a little farther than usual in one direction round the moon, at times a little farther in another, but 41 per cent of the moon has never been seen.

When the moon is in this position, E M S , the

face of the moon—the side toward us—gets no light. We cannot see the moon at all. This phase of the moon is often called the "dark of the moon." Scientists call it the "new moon" instead.

A day or so later the moon has moved so that the sun shines on a small part of the face. The part we see makes a slender crescent. This is the phase most people call the new moon. Thus "new moon" does not mean the same to everyone.

A few days later the moon has travelled so that half of the face is lighted up. This phase is called the " first quarter."

More and more of the face is lighted up until at last, when the sun, earth, and moon are in this position, M E S , the entire face shines brightly. This phase is the full moon.

When the moon seems to be growing larger each night we say that it is "waxing." The moment it has become a full moon it begins to wane.

A week after the time of the full moon, only half of the face is again lighted up. This phase is the third quarter.

In a few days the moon again appears to be a narrow crescent. Within a night or two it disappears from view, only to start the round of its phases once again.

It takes the moon about $27\frac{1}{2}$ days to make its journey round the earth. But all the while the moon is travelling around the earth, the earth is travelling round the sun. The moon, therefore, cannot make the trip from its full-moon position to its full-moon position again in $27\frac{1}{2}$ days. It needs about $29\frac{1}{2}$ days instead.

The time from full moon to full moon served many ancient peoples as a measure of time. Our word "month" comes from "moon." But our months now differ in length. We no longer measure time by true moon-months.

The moon can often be seen in the sky in the daytime. Because of the brightness of the sun, the moon when seen in the daytime looks very pale.

The moon rises and sets because the earth turns on its axis. But since the moon travels round the earth, its times of rising and setting change greatly from day to day. The young crescent moon always rises soon after sunrise and sets soon after sunset. At the first quarter the moon rises about noon and sets about midnight. The full moon rises at about sunset and sets at about sunrise. At the last quarter moonrise is at midnight and moonset is at noon.

Sometimes at the time of the crescent moon it is possible to see the rest of the face of the moon faintly. We see it by "earthshine." Part of the sunshine that reaches the earth is reflected to the moon. It is then reflected back to the earth, as the diagram below shows.

The full moon is not evenly bright all over. The darker areas make the eyes, nose, and mouth of the "man in the moon." They also help form all the other pictures different people see in the moon—an old man with a bundle of sticks, a girl reading a book, a jumping hare, a man with a load of cabbages, or a child with a bucket of water.

Scientists used to think that the darker areas on the moon were seas. As the map of the moon on page 189 shows, they are still called seas; *mare* is the Latin word for sea. Mare Serenitatis means "Sea of Serenity"; Mare Imbrium means "Sea of Clouds"; and so on. But scientists now know that the darker areas are not seas. They could not be, for there is no water on the moon. Instead they are great flat plains. They look less bright than the rest of the moon because they do not reflect the sunlight so well.

The rest of the moon's surface is very rough. There are many ranges of mountains and many great craters with high rims. The scientists who named the mountains on the moon did not use much imagination. They gave them the names of mountains on the earth. The craters were named after famous scientists.

The artist's drawing shows a moon landscape. The earth is shining down upon the moon from a black sky. The shadows are very black.

Earthshine on the Moon

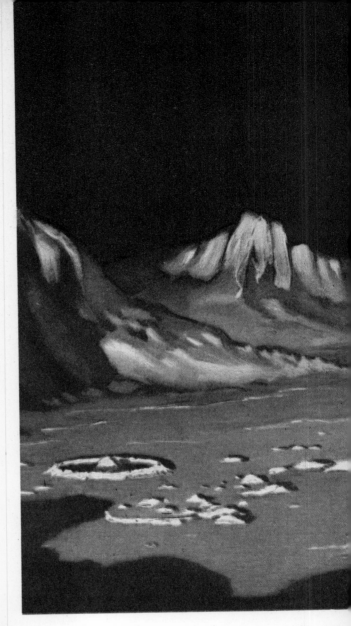

The sky on the moon would be black because there is little or no atmosphere—probably none—to scatter the sunlight and make the sky look blue. The shadows would be very black for the same reason. The earth would light the moon by earthshine, if it were in the right position, just as the moon lights the earth by moonlight.

The craters on the moon are a puzzle. Possibly they are the craters of dead volcanoes. But if so, they are larger by far than the craters of any volcanoes on the earth. One crater, Copernicus, is larger than several English counties.

If the craters are not the craters of volcanoes, they may have been made when huge meteors or groups of meteors hit the moon. Meteors are pieces of rock and iron, most of them smaller than peas but some weighing tons, which travel round the

190

Landscape on the Moon

sun. We know that they can make craters, for there are meteor-made craters on the earth. But the earth has very few in comparison with the moon.

There is much talk now of rocket trips to the moon. To escape from the earth, a rocket would have to start away from the surface of the earth at a speed of nearly seven miles a second. This speed is far greater than that of a rifle bullet.

A visit to the moon would certainly be full of danger. A person unless protected would blow up, just as a deep-sea fish does when it is brought up from deep water. Since there is little or no atmosphere, there is no outer pressure to balance the pressure from the inside out. There are no living things there to furnish food. A visitor marooned on the moon would not die of starva-

tion, however, because he would have already died of thirst. Another danger in making the trip is that the rocket might miss its mark. It is not easy to reach a target moving more than a thousand miles a minute.

Still other risks would be the danger of being hit by a meteor, the danger of getting too hot or too cold, and the danger of being killed by ultra-violet rays from the sun. The earth's ocean of air protects us from these dangers.

But there would be pleasant features about a visit to the moon. Gravity is so much less there that a person would feel very light and buoyant. The moon, moreover, is a quiet place: there is little or no atmosphere to carry sound waves. To most people these pleasant features would not be worth the risk of the trip.

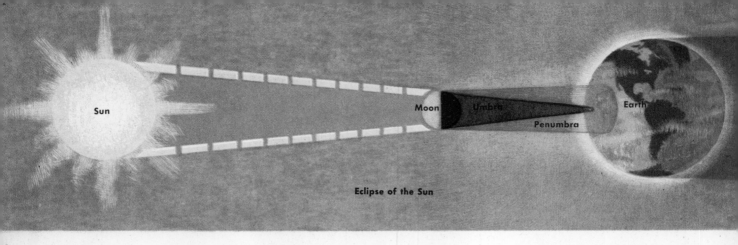

Eclipse of the Sun

An eclipse of the sun occurs when the moon, on its trip round the earth, comes between the earth and the sun. The shadow of the moon falls on the earth. To anyone in the deep shadow—the "umbra" it is called in the diagram above—the sun looks as it does in the lower right-hand picture on page 181. The eclipse is a total eclipse. To anyone in the penumbra the view of only a part of the sun is cut off. The eclipse is only a partial eclipse.

The sun and the earth are both so much larger than the moon that the moon's shadow never covers a very large part of the earth. In fact, the deep shadow is never more than 168 miles across. Since both the earth and the moon are moving,

Moon During an Eclipse

the shadow of the moon moves, too. The path of the moon's shadow is called the path of the eclipse. The moon and the earth move so fast that a total eclipse of the sun never lasts at any one place for more than eight minutes.

Eclipses of the sun cannot occur except when the moon is new. The moon cannot come between the earth and the sun at any other time. There is not always, however, an eclipse of the sun at the

time of a new moon. Usually the moon is a little too high in the sky or a little too low. There are always at least two solar eclipses in a year, but never more than five.

Astronomers look forward to total eclipses of the sun. There are many problems about the sun and the stars that they can study best at the time of a total eclipse.

An eclipse of the moon—a lunar eclipse—occurs when the moon on its travels round the earth gets into the earth's shadow. Sometimes the moon passes through only the edge of the earth's deep shadow. Then there is a partial eclipse of the moon. Sometimes it plunges wholly into the earth's shadow and there is a total eclipse.

Even when the moon is wholly in the earth's shadow, it does not entirely disappear. The earth's air bends some of the rays of light from the sun so that they strike the moon. The moon looks dull red.

The earth's shadow is so wide at the place where the moon crosses it that the moon may be totally eclipsed for nearly two hours. If the sky is clear, a lunar eclipse can be seen from any part of the earth that is having night.

There cannot be an eclipse of the moon unless the moon is full. The moon cannot possibly be in the earth's shadow at any other time. Even when the moon is full it does not often get into the

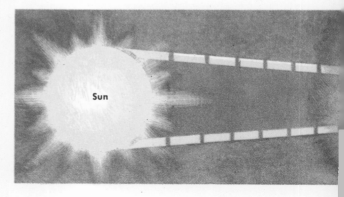

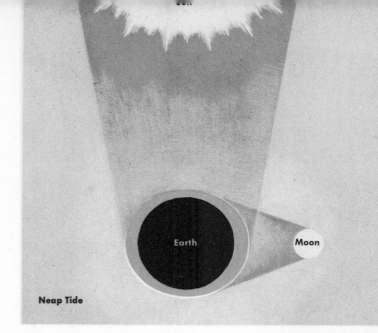

Neap Tide

earth's shadow. It usually passes a little above the earth's shadow or a little below it. There are never more than three lunar eclipses in one year, and in some years there are none.

Astronomers can predict eclipses very accurately. They can tell us when eclipses will occur for thousands of years to come. They can also tell us when they occurred in the past. One astronomer has listed all the eclipses between 1207 B.C. and A.D. 2162.

Anyone who has visited or lived on a seacoast knows that at certain times of the day the water is higher than at other times—that there are high tides and low tides. The changes from high tide to low tide and from low tide to high tide are not sudden. After the water reaches its highest point it begins to go out; that is, the water gets lower and lower. It gets lower for several hours until low tide is reached. Then for several hours the water slowly rises until the tide is high once more.

We have the moon to thank for the tides. The earth pulls the moon and keeps it from travelling off into space. At the same time, the moon is pulling the earth. It pulls hardest on the part of the earth nearest it. It lifts the water on that part of the earth and makes it bulge out. When the moon is pulling up the water in the seas at any place, there is high tide at that place.

When the spinning of the earth has brought another part of the earth beneath the moon, the water is lowered at the first place and pulled up at the second. Thus the bulge toward the moon moves round the earth.

At the same time that the moon lifts the water up on the part of the earth that is nearest it, the moon pulls least on the opposite side of the earth and the water there bulges away from the moon. About half a day after a place has had high tide it has high tide again.

High tides at any place would come at almost the same times day after day if the moon were not travelling round the earth. As it is, high tides come about an hour later each day than they came the day before. Almanacs are published to tell exactly when high tides and low tides will be.

The sun causes tides just as the moon does. The sun, however, is so much farther away that the tides it causes are not nearly so noticeable as the tides the moon causes. But it makes a difference whether the sun and the moon are pulling to-

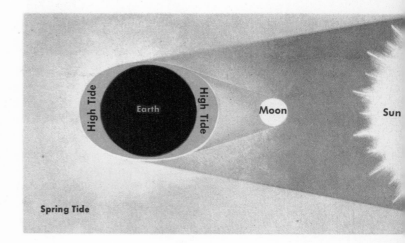

Spring Tide

gether. In the top diagram the sun keeps the high tides from being as high as they would otherwise be. Such tides are called "neap tides." In the second diagram the tides are higher than usual because the sun is helping the moon. These extra-high tides are called "spring tides."

Tides are important not only to seamen but to all people who live near the ocean shores. They scour the sea-coasts as nothing else could.

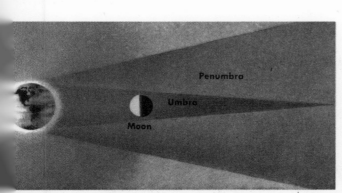

Eclipse of the Moon

Comet

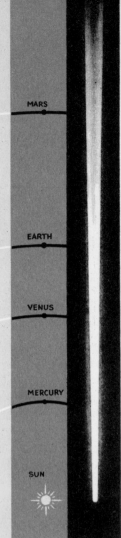

MARS

EARTH

VENUS

MERCURY

SUN

In the sun's family there are many hundreds of those strange heavenly visitors we call "comets." The word "comet" comes from an old Latin word that means "hair." Many comets have tails that stream out behind them.

A comet may be so bright that it can be seen even in the middle of the day. Most comets, however, are seen only through telescopes.

Comets are huge. A comet's head may be bigger than Uranus or Neptune. Its tail may be long enough to reach out from the sun to beyond the orbit of Mars—some 150,000,000 miles.

In earlier times comets terrified people. They considered them a warning of some great disaster. Now scientists know that they follow regular paths round the sun just as planets do.

A comet does not have a tail until it comes fairly close to the sun. A comet without a tail looks, through a telescope, like a fuzzy ball of light. The head is made up partly of a great swarm of tiny pieces of rock and iron. It is made up partly of gases of different kinds. The gases form a bright cloud around the swarm of solid particles. When a comet comes near the sun, the sunlight drives out some of the gas from the head to form the tail. The tail of a comet always streams out *away* from the sun.

Comets have paths round the sun, but they are not the same shape as the paths of the planets. Their paths are very much flattened ellipses. At one part of its journey a comet is close to the sun. At the opposite end of its orbit it may be out beyond the orbit of Pluto.

The orbits of comets cross the orbits of the planets. At a crossing there is always a chance that a planet and a comet will collide. In 1910 the earth went through the tail of Halley's comet. (Halley's comet was named after the English astronomer who discovered that comets have paths round the sun.) The earth was not damaged.

The path of Halley's comet extends out to beyond the orbit of Neptune. This comet visits the earth rather frequently for a comet—every 76 years!

Sometimes comets are expected and do not arrive. As a comet passes near a planet it may be pulled to pieces. Probably in time most comets will be destroyed.

194

Trail of a Shooting Star

Meteorite

Shooting stars are badly named. They are not at all like true stars. The smallest star scientists know anything about is almost as large as the earth. Most stars are far larger. Shooting stars, on the other hand, are little bits of stone or iron so small that you could hold hundreds of them in your hand at once.

But no one ever has held hundreds of shooting stars in his hand at once, because they never reach the earth's surface. Friction makes them so hot as they fall through the air that they are destroyed. Only a little fine dust from them ever lands.

The bits of rock and iron that become shooting stars are meteors. Meteors are far too small to be seen as they follow their orbits. They glow only when they happen to come close enough to the earth to be pulled into our ocean of air.

A shooting star we see is never very far away from us as sky distances go. Most of them are less than a hundred miles above our heads.

Some meteors which the earth pulls toward it are much bigger and brighter than shooting stars. These meteors are called "fireballs." A fireball may explode into small pieces in its rush through the air. It may instead reach the ground as a large chunk of stone or iron. Remains of meteors which reach the earth's surface are known as "meteorites." The first iron ever used by man probably came from a meteorite.

Peary, the explorer who discovered the North Pole, found a very large meteorite lying on top of the snow in Greenland. This meteorite is now in a museum in New York. It weighs 36½ tons.

The great crater pictured above is supposed to have been made by a group of meteors which fell in what is now Arizona many thousands of years ago. Scientists think that the main meteor must have weighed over 50,000 tons. If meteors made the craters on the moon, some of them must have weighed hundreds of thousands of tons.

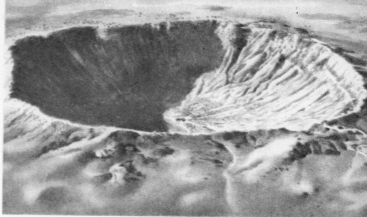

Meteor Crater

Meteorites are not very common. Probably several hundred meteors reach the earth's surface every year, but, since the oceans cover a large part of the earth, many meteors are lost in the sea.

Shooting stars, on the other hand, are very common. Millions of them fall through the air every day. It is fortunate for us that they are destroyed before they reach the earth's surface, for, although they are small, they are falling so fast that they could do great damage to anything they hit. They would be like rifle bullets.

At times during the year there are "showers" of shooting stars. As far back as the days of ancient Egypt people noticed that on some nights "the stars jumped about like grasshoppers." The showers of shooting stars occur when the earth runs into a swarm of meteors. There are many such swarms. Scientists believe that they are the remains of comets. Their paths are like the paths of comets.

Not all meteors belong to these swarms. Where the others come from no one is sure. They may be pieces of old planets. They may be bits left over when the planets and moons were formed from, as many scientists believe, a great disc-shaped cloud of gas that once surrounded the sun. They may even have wandered into the solar system from outer space.

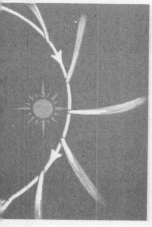

Comet Near the Sun

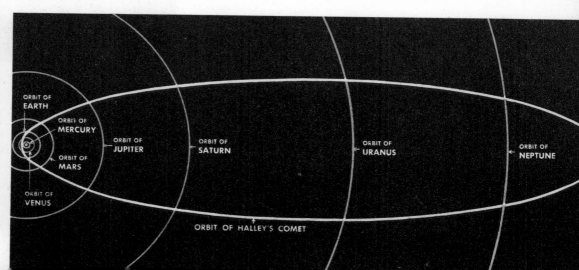

ORBIT OF EARTH

ORBIT OF MERCURY

ORBIT OF JUPITER

ORBIT OF SATURN

ORBIT OF URANUS

ORBIT OF NEPTUNE

ORBIT OF MARS

ORBIT OF VENUS

ORBIT OF HALLEY'S COMET

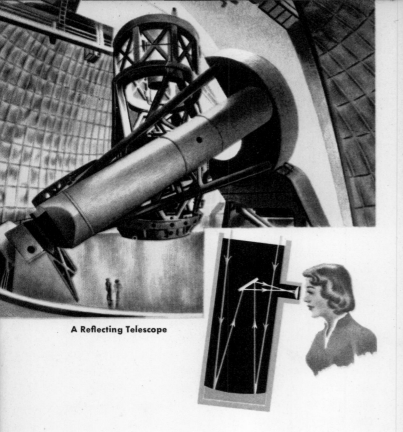

A Reflecting Telescope

The Stars

THE solar system, big as it is, is only a speck in the whole universe. The universe is so vast that it is almost impossible to imagine its size. Out beyond the farthest planet in the sun's family there are millions of millions of millions of stars. Probably there are as many stars as there are grains of sand on all the seashores of the world.

Scientists have used telescopes to learn about the sun and its family. They have used them, too, to discover the secrets of the stars. Telescopes of two kinds are used in studying the stars: reflecting telescopes and refracting telescopes.

In a reflecting telescope the light is gathered by a large curved mirror. It is reflected to a small mirror and then through a lens to the eye of the observer. The reflecting telescope pictured is the largest one in the world. It is on Mount Palomar in California. Its big mirror is 200 inches—almost 17 feet—across.

In a refracting telescope a large lens gathers the light and sends it through smaller lenses to the observer's eye. The largest refracting telescope is in Yerkes Observatory at Williams Bay, Wiscon-

A Refracting Telescope

sin. Its big lens is 40 inches in diameter, probably the limit in size for a telescope lens.

Much of what we know about the stars has been discovered from photographs taken through telescopes. Among the group of stars called Andromeda there is a faint patch of light that looks like a

196

Right: Great Spiral Nebula

large, fuzzy star. The picture at the right is a photograph of the "fuzzy star" taken through a refracting telescope. The "star" is really a great star city, or galaxy, made up of many millions of stars. Astronomers call it the Great Spiral Nebula in Andromeda.

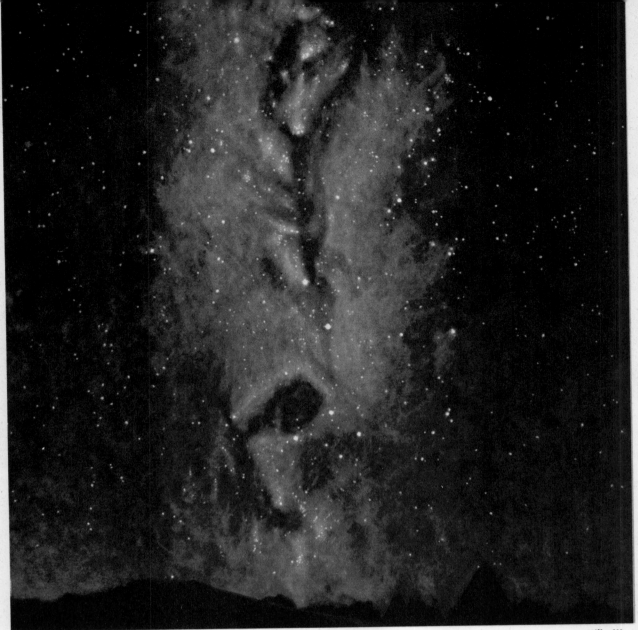

The Great Spiral Nebula in Andromeda is about 900,000 light-years away from us. A light-year is roughly 6 million million miles. It is the distance which light, travelling at its amazing speed of 186,000 miles a second, can travel in a year. This great star city is, then, 900,000 times 6,000,000,000,000 miles away.

There are millions of galaxies like the Great Spiral Nebula in Andromeda. Most of them are even farther away. But we ourselves live inside a galaxy. Our sun is one of a vast number of stars—about 100,000 million—that makes up the Milky Way galaxy.

Almost everyone on a clear summer evening has seen the Milky Way stretch across the sky. The Milky Way is the light from millions of stars too distant to be seen as separate stars. They are the stars that make up the rim of the Milky Way galaxy. The galaxy is something like the shape of a bun. The sun and its planets are about halfway between the centre and the edge. There are stars of the galaxy round us in all directions, but there are more in the direction of the rim. There is therefore a Milky Way instead of an even glow of starlight over the whole sky.

All the stars we can see with our eyes alone as separate stars are in the Milky Way galaxy. There are not so many of these stars as one might think. They are not, as people are in the habit of saying, countless. Of course, not all people see the same number of stars. Some people have better eyes than others. A person with good eyes can see about 3,000 stars on a cloudless night. Of course, not all the stars bright enough to be seen without a telescope can be seen at one time.

What stars a person can see when he looks up at the sky on a clear night depends chiefly on three things: where he is on the earth, where the earth is on its path around the sun, and what time of night it is.

Some stars can never be seen from some parts of the earth. Others can never be seen from other parts of the earth. The North Star, for example, which is almost exactly above the North Pole, can never be seen from the South Pole. The earth itself is in the way. In fact, the earth itself shuts off the view of the North Star from the whole southern hemisphere.

To see stars one has to look away from the sun. The light of the sun is so blinding that it hides the stars in the daytime. Looking away from the sun in winter means looking in exactly the opposite direction from looking away from the sun in summer. Different stars, therefore, are visible. The same thing is true of spring and autumn.

Because of the turning of the earth on its axis, the night sky is never the same for any two minutes in succession. The turning of the earth makes the stars appear to move in the sky. A star which is directly above us at midnight is low in the western sky five hours later, and stars that could not be seen at midnight have come into view in the eastern sky.

It is easy to see why people need star maps like those on pages 206 and 207 to help them locate the stars. It is easy to see, too, why different star maps must be made for different places and for different times of the night and the year.

Because of the turning of the earth on its axis, many stars rise and set. But the North Star, since it is almost exactly above the earth's North Pole, stays at almost exactly the same place in the sky. For this reason it has served for centuries to guide travellers on their journeys. The stars that are near the North Star do not rise or set, either. Instead, they appear to travel counterclockwise in a circle around the North Star.

The distance from the sun to Pluto is more than $3\frac{1}{2}$ thousand million miles. But this distance is only a step as compared with the distance to our solar system's nearest star neighbour. This nearest star neighbour is Proxima Centauri. It is about $4\frac{1}{4}$ light-years away—$4\frac{1}{4}$ times 6,000,000,000,000 miles. It is a faint star which, in spite of the fact that it is our nearest neighbour, can never be seen without a telescope. Sirius, the Dog Star, which is the brightest star in the sky, is nearly 9 light-years away. Antares, another very bright star, is much, much farther away—400 light-years. If Antares were to explode tonight, it would be 400 years before we here on earth could see the explosion. Of course, the distance to Antares is short compared to the distance to the Great Spiral Nebula in Andromeda, but it is still so great as to be hard to imagine.

The brightness of a star depends on how far away the star is and how much light it is giving off. Although Antares is very far away, it shines brightly in our sky because it is a very, very large and brilliant sun. Sirius is not nearly so large and gives off less light, but it is much closer to us.

An Observatory

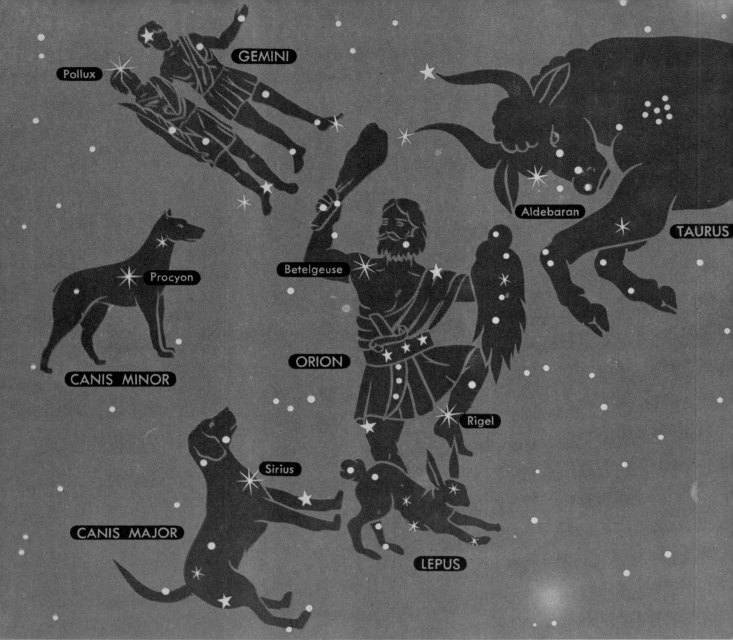

Familiar Constellations

The brightest twenty stars, as we see them from the earth, are called "first-magnitude stars." They are listed on page 207. Other stars are classified into other magnitudes.

Not all stars are single suns. About one out of every three is a double star—two suns travelling round and round each other. Each of the stars in a double star may be a double star. A single twinkling point of light in the sky may even be six suns travelling round one another.

Antares is a giant among the stars. It is 70 million times as big as the sun. It consists of glowing gas, so thin that the earth's air is 2,000 times as thick. Betelgeuse, another first-magnitude star, is a giant, too. If put in place of our sun, it would reach out beyond the earth's orbit. Both these stars are reddish. Most giants are. In contrast to the giants are the stars called "white dwarfs." Some are not much larger than the earth. But each one has thousands of times as much material in it as the earth contains. The material is packed together so closely that if a ball of it the size of a golf ball could be brought to the earth it would weigh many tons. These dwarf stars are called white dwarfs because their light is white. Most stars are neither giants nor dwarfs. About eight-tenths of the stars are medium-sized stars. Our sun is one of these.

In addition to white stars and reddish stars, there are blue-white, yellowish-white, yellow, and orange stars. There are stars of all these different colours among the first-magnitude stars. Spica, for example, is blue-white. Sirius is white; Canopus, yellowish-white; Capella, yellow; and Aldebaran, orange. Although we talk about the white light of the sun, the sun is a yellow star.

It is possible to tell something about the temperature of a star from its colour. Hottest of all the stars are the bluish-white ones. Then in order come the white, the yellowish-white, the yellow, the orange, and the red stars.

The stars which are bright enough to be seen without a telescope are not scattered evenly across the sky. Instead, they are arranged in groups called "constellations." The word "constellation" means "stars together." The people of olden times imagined that each group of stars they saw in the sky was a picture of something or somebody. To them the sky was a great picture book. Many of the people of early days were shepherds, and, as they watched their flocks by night, they learned to know the constellations far better than most of us do now.

The charts on these two pages show some of the well-known groups of stars, or constellations. The chart on page 200 shows constellations that are in the southern sky in our part of the world.

They can best be seen in winter. The chart below shows some of the constellations that circle round the North Star. They can be seen all the year round.

Orion (The Hunter) is the brightest constellation in the sky. It can be told easily from the three bright stars that make the hunter's belt. This constellation has two of the twenty first-magnitude stars in it. Betelgeuse, one of the red giants, marks the hunter's right shoulder. Rigel, a blue-white star that is even farther away than Antares, marks the left foot.

Not far from Orion are the two constellations of Canis Major (The Great Dog) and Canis Minor (The Little Dog). Sirius, the brightest star in the whole sky, is in Canis Major. It is almost in line with the three stars of Orion's belt. Canis Minor has in it the yellowish-white first-magnitude star Procyon.

Lepus (The Hare) at Orion's feet is not easy to find in the sky. It has no bright stars in it.

Taurus (The Bull) faces Orion. It has in it the first-magnitude star Aldebaran, a red star. In Taurus there are two small groups of stars that were well known to ancient peoples—the Pleiades and the Hyades.

Pictures in the Sky

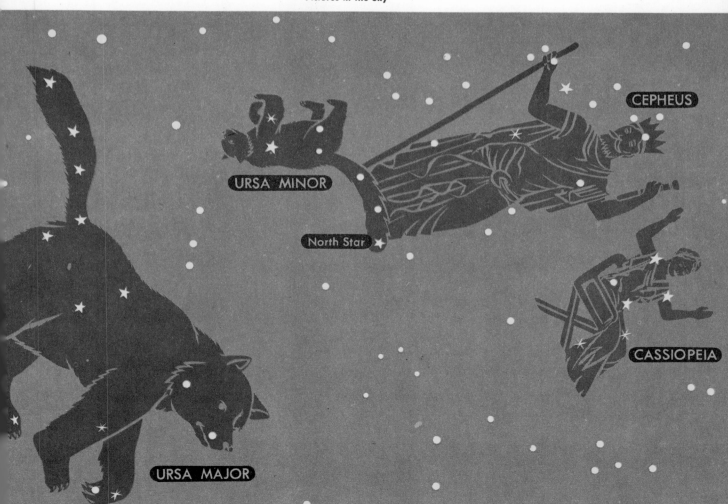

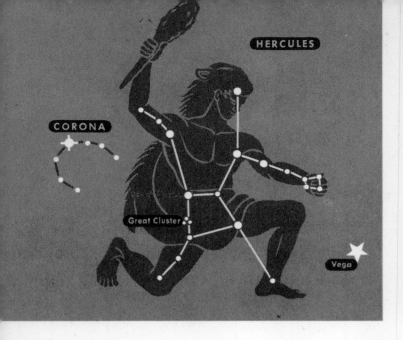

Gemini (The Twins) contains one first-magnitude star, Pollux, and another star that just misses being in the group of the brightest twenty. It is Castor. Long ago Castor is thought to have been brighter than, or at least as bright as, Pollux. But now it is less bright than its twin. Castor is a multiple star. Instead of being a single sun, it is a system of six suns.

Ursa Minor (The Little Bear) is one of the northern constellations. In fact, the North Star itself is in this constellation. It is the star that marks the end of the bear's tail.

Ursa Major (The Great Bear) is probably the best known of all the constellations. It has had many different names among different peoples. To many British people the Great Bear is "The Plough." The Scandinavians call it "Thor's

Chariot." To the Italians it is "The Car of Boötes." The Pawnee Indians see in it a sick man on a stretcher. But, strangely enough, many people far away from one another have seen in this constellation the picture of a bear.

There are no first-magnitude stars in Ursa Major, but there are several second-magnitude stars. Six of the second-magnitude stars together with a fainter star or two make the outline of a dipper—"The Big Dipper" it is often called. Two of the stars of the Dipper are on a line with the North Star. They are often called "The Pointers."

Cassiopeia (The Woman in the Chair) is on the opposite side of the North Star from the Big Dipper. Five of the stars of this constellation make a W. Cepheus (The King) is not an easy constel-

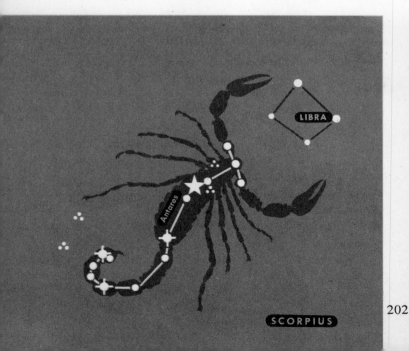

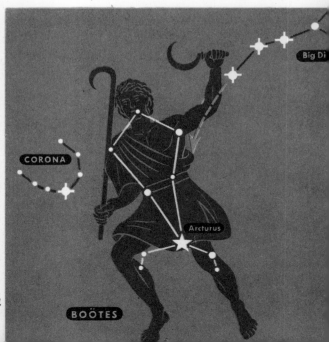

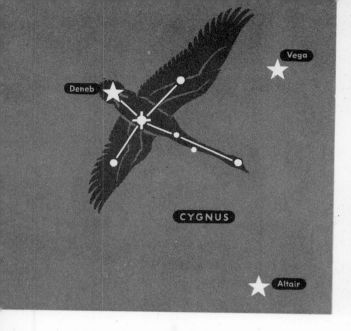

Deneb · Vega · CYGNUS · Altair

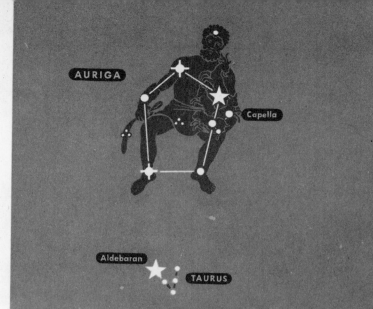

AURIGA · Capella · Aldebaran · TAURUS

lation to pick out in the sky. Its stars do not make a clear pattern. Cepheus and Cassiopeia belong to a group of constellations that is sometimes called "The Royal Family."

The constellations on these two pages are other well-known groups of stars. Leo (The Lion) and Virgo (The Virgin) are spring constellations. Hercules, Scorpius (The Scorpion), Boötes (The Herdsman), and Cygnus (The Swan) are best seen in the summer. Pegasus (The Winged Horse) is high in the sky on autumn nights and Auriga (The Charioteer) in the winter.

Each of these constellations with the exceptions of Hercules and Pegasus has one first-magnitude star which is a help in locating the constellation. Four stars in Pegasus form the Great Square, which makes identifying Pegasus easy.

Hercules has no very bright stars in it, but it is interesting for two reasons. One patch of light which looks like a faint star is shown by a telescope to be a great ball of stars, or star cluster. There are more than 50,000 stars in the cluster. Inside our Milky Way galaxy there are over a hundred such clusters of stars, but the one in Hercules is the best known.

The sun, moreover, is moving toward Hercules and is carrying all its planets and moons and comets and planetoids along with it. At the same time, then, that the earth is whirling round on its axis and is travelling at an amazing speed on its yearly journey round the sun, it is moving through space along with the rest of the solar system toward Hercules. It is moving at about 12 miles a second.

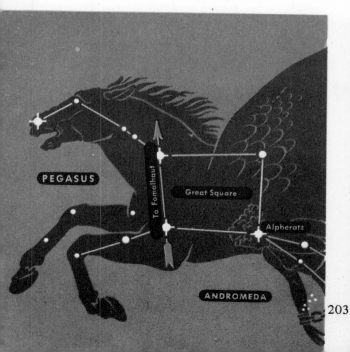

PEGASUS · To Fomalhaut · Great Square · Alpheratz · ANDROMEDA

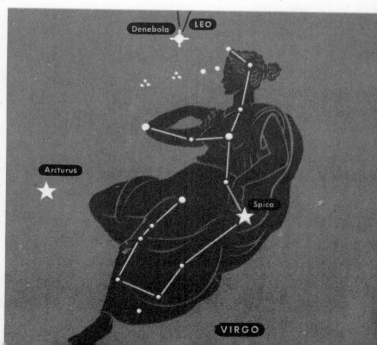

Denebola · LEO · Arcturus · Spica · VIRGO

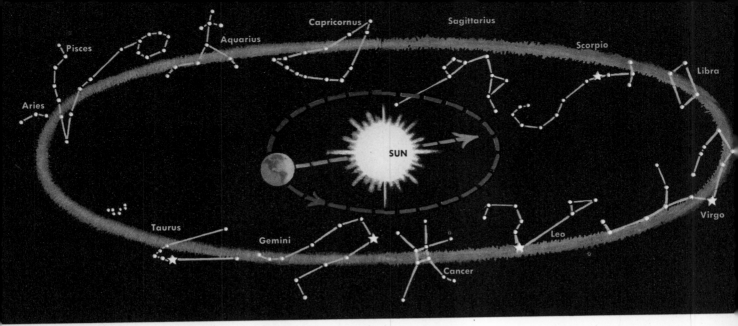

The Zodiac

If we could see stars during the daytime, the sun would appear to be in first one group of stars and then another. It would appear to be in each one for about a month at a time. It would seem to move from one group of stars to the other, because of the travelling of the earth round the sun. When, as in the diagram above, the earth is exactly opposite the sun from the constellation Libra, the sun would look to be in Libra. The stars of Libra would rise and set with the sun. A month later the sun would be in Scorpius; and a month after that in Sagittarius.

The "street" along which the sun seems to move is called the "zodiac." The word "zodiac" means "animal circle." All 12 constellations of the zodiac were first named after animals.

For centuries people have tried to tell their fortunes from the stars. Astrologers, who thought they could foretell the future from the stars, were important people in olden times. Often an astrologer was called in to read the stars as soon as a child was born. During the Middle Ages many astronomers had to make their living as astrologers. A person's future, according to the astrologers, depended largely on where the planets were among the constellations of the zodiac when he was born. In spite of all that scientists have found out about the stars, some people still believe that their fortunes can be told from them.

Scattered far out in space among the stars of our Milky Way galaxy there are some vast clouds of gas called "gaseous nebulae." One of the best known is shaped like a ring. It is in the constellation Lyra (The Lyre). Many nebulae are bright just as the Ring Nebula is. But some are dark.

They show only because they shut off our view of stars farther away. The Horsehead Nebula in Orion is a well-known dark nebula.

Occasionally a star suddenly becomes very much brighter than before. It may be 100,000 times as bright as it was before. Later—in a few months or years—it fades. The increase in brightness is due to a great explosion; the star throws out glowing gas in all directions. Exploding stars are called "novae." The name means "new stars." Since they are not new, "novae" is not a very happy name for these stars that explode.

Novae are not uncommon. Usually at least one is found every year. But as a rule they are not bright enough to attract much attention. The brightest nova on record was seen in 1572. It came to be brighter than Venus and could be seen even in the daytime. This star started a young Dane, Tycho Brahe, on his way to becoming one of the world's most famous astronomers.

Some of the distant suns that we call stars probably have planets circling round them just as our sun has. There may even be inhabited planets circling round distant stars. No one can tell. We certainly do not yet know all the secrets of the universe.

There are many star myths. They are stories made up by primitive peoples to explain the pictures these peoples see in the sky. The Greek myths are the best known to most of us, but some of the Indian myths are well known, too. These myths should be thought of as real attempts of primitive peoples to explain what they saw in the world about them. They were the forerunners of the science of today.

THE PLANETS AND THE MOON:
THEIR SURFACE GRAVITY AND SPEED

WHAT A BOY WHO WEIGHS 100 POUNDS ON THE EARTH WOULD WEIGH ON OUR MOON AND ON THE OTHER PLANETS

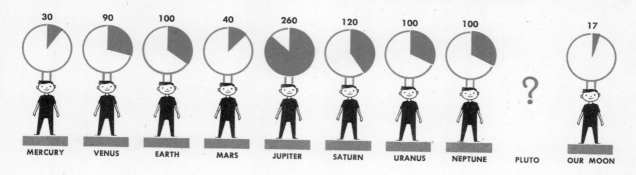

MERCURY 30 · VENUS 90 · EARTH 100 · MARS 40 · JUPITER 260 · SATURN 120 · URANUS 100 · NEPTUNE 100 · PLUTO ? · OUR MOON 17

HOW HIGH A BOY WHO CAN JUMP 3 FEET ON THE EARTH COULD JUMP ON OUR MOON AND ON THE OTHER PLANETS

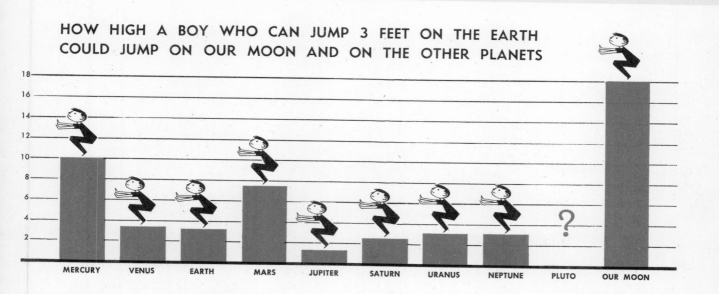

MERCURY · VENUS · EARTH · MARS · JUPITER · SATURN · URANUS · NEPTUNE · PLUTO · OUR MOON

MILES COVERED BY THE PLANETS IN ONE SECOND IN THEIR ORBITS AROUND THE SUN

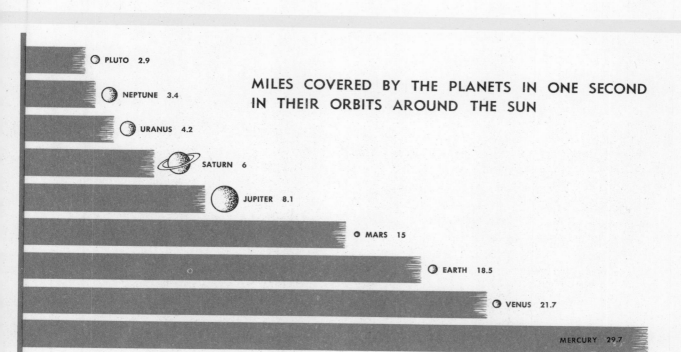

PLUTO 2.9
NEPTUNE 3.4
URANUS 4.2
SATURN 6
JUPITER 8.1
MARS 15
EARTH 18.5
VENUS 21.7
MERCURY 29.7

SOLAR SYSTEM FACTS—SUMMER CONSTELLATIONS

Planet	Average Distance from the Sun in Millions of Miles	Diameter in Miles	Length of Time Taken for Revolution around Sun	Length of Time Taken for Rotation on axis	Number of Known Moons
Mercury	36	3,000	88 days	88 days (?)	0
Venus	67	7,600	225 days	(?)	0
Earth	93	7,900	365¼ days	23 hr. 56 min.	1
Mars	141	4,200	687 days	24 hr. 37 min.	2
Jupiter	489	87,000	12 years	9 hr. 50 min.	12
Saturn	886	72,000	29½ years	10 hr. 14 min.	9
Uranus	1,782	31,000	84 years	10 hr. 40 min.	5
Neptune	2,793	33,000	165 years	15 hr. (?)	2
Pluto	3,670	3,600	248 years	(?)	0
Sun		864,000		25 days	

CONSTELLATIONS OF SUMMER

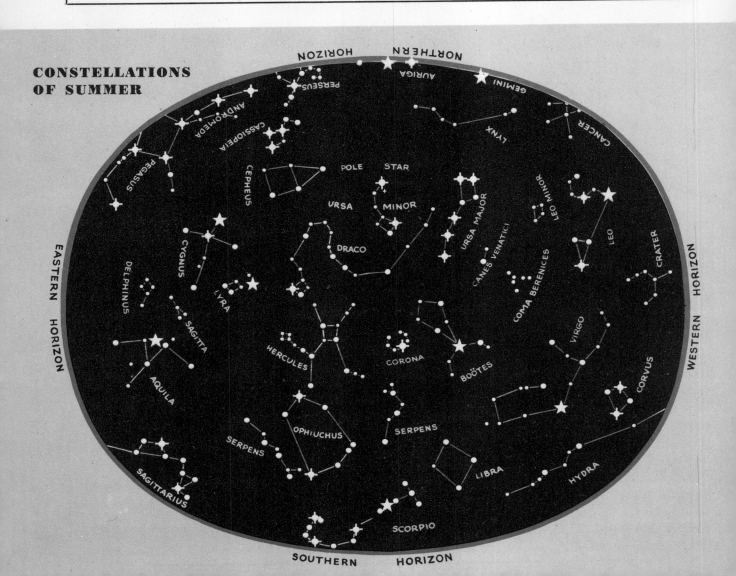

WINTER CONSTELLATIONS—FIRST-MAGNITUDE STARS

CONSTELLATIONS OF WINTER

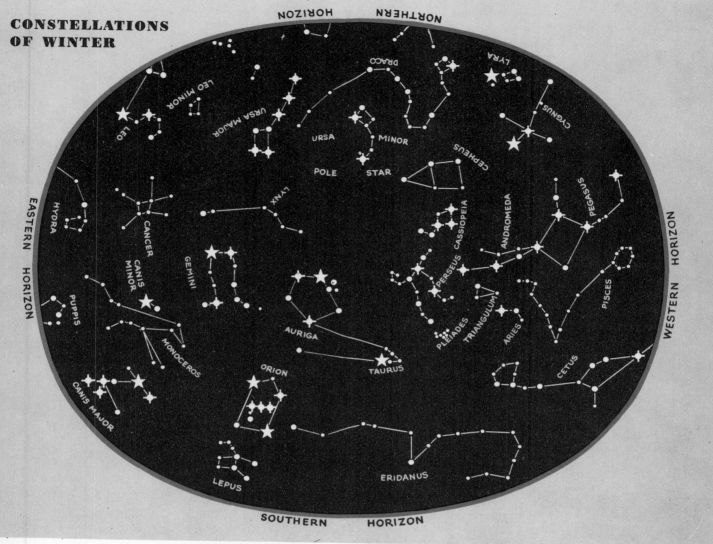

THE TWENTY BRIGHTEST STARS

Star	Distance in Light-Years	Constellation
Sirius	8.8	Canis Major ("The Great Dog")
Canopus	200	Argo ("The Ship")
Alpha Centauri	4.3	Centaurus ("The Centaur")
Vega	26	Lyra ("The Lyre")
Capella	50	Auriga ("The Charioteer")
Arcturus	40	Boötes ("The Herdsman")
Rigel	600 (?)	Orion ("The Hunter")
Procyon	10.4	Canis Minor ("The Little Dog")
Achernar	70	Eridanus ("The River")
Beta Centauri	90	Centaurus ("The Centaur")
Altair	16	Aquila ("The Eagle")
Betelgeuse	300	Orion ("The Hunter")
Alpha Crucis	100	Crux ("The Cross")
Aldebaran	60	Taurus ("The Bull")
Pollux	32	Gemini ("The Twins")
Spica	200	Virgo ("The Virgin")
Antares	400	Scorpio ("The Scorpion")
Fomalhaut	24	Piscis Australis ("The Southern Fish")
Deneb	400	Cygnus ("The Swan")
Regulus	60	Leo ("The Lion")

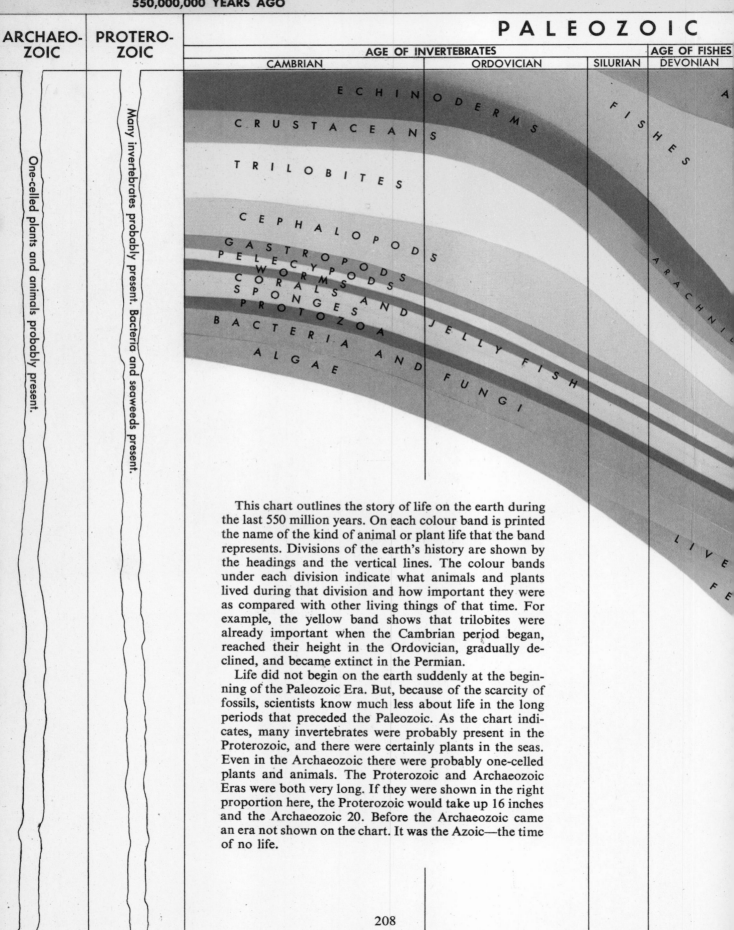

PALEOZOIC

AGE OF INVERTEBRATES

CAMBRIAN | ORDOVICIAN

AGE OF FISHES

SILURIAN | DEVONIAN

ARCHAEO-ZOIC

One-celled plants and animals probably present.

PROTERO-ZOIC

Many invertebrates probably present. Bacteria and seaweeds present.

ECHINODERMS

CRUSTACEANS

TRILOBITES

CEPHALOPODS

GASTROPODS

PELECYPODS

WORMS

CORALS AND JELLY FISH

SPONGES

PROTOZOA AND FUNGI

BACTERIA

ALGAE

FISHES

ARACHNI

This chart outlines the story of life on the earth during the last 550 million years. On each colour band is printed the name of the kind of animal or plant life that the band represents. Divisions of the earth's history are shown by the headings and the vertical lines. The colour bands under each division indicate what animals and plants lived during that division and how important they were as compared with other living things of that time. For example, the yellow band shows that trilobites were already important when the Cambrian period began, reached their height in the Ordovician, gradually declined, and became extinct in the Permian.

Life did not begin on the earth suddenly at the beginning of the Paleozoic Era. But, because of the scarcity of fossils, scientists know much less about life in the long periods that preceded the Paleozoic. As the chart indicates, many invertebrates were probably present in the Proterozoic, and there were certainly plants in the seas. Even in the Archaeozoic there were probably one-celled plants and animals. The Proterozoic and Archaeozoic Eras were both very long. If they were shown in the right proportion here, the Proterozoic would take up 16 inches and the Archaeozoic 20. Before the Archaeozoic came an era not shown on the chart. It was the Azoic—the time of no life.

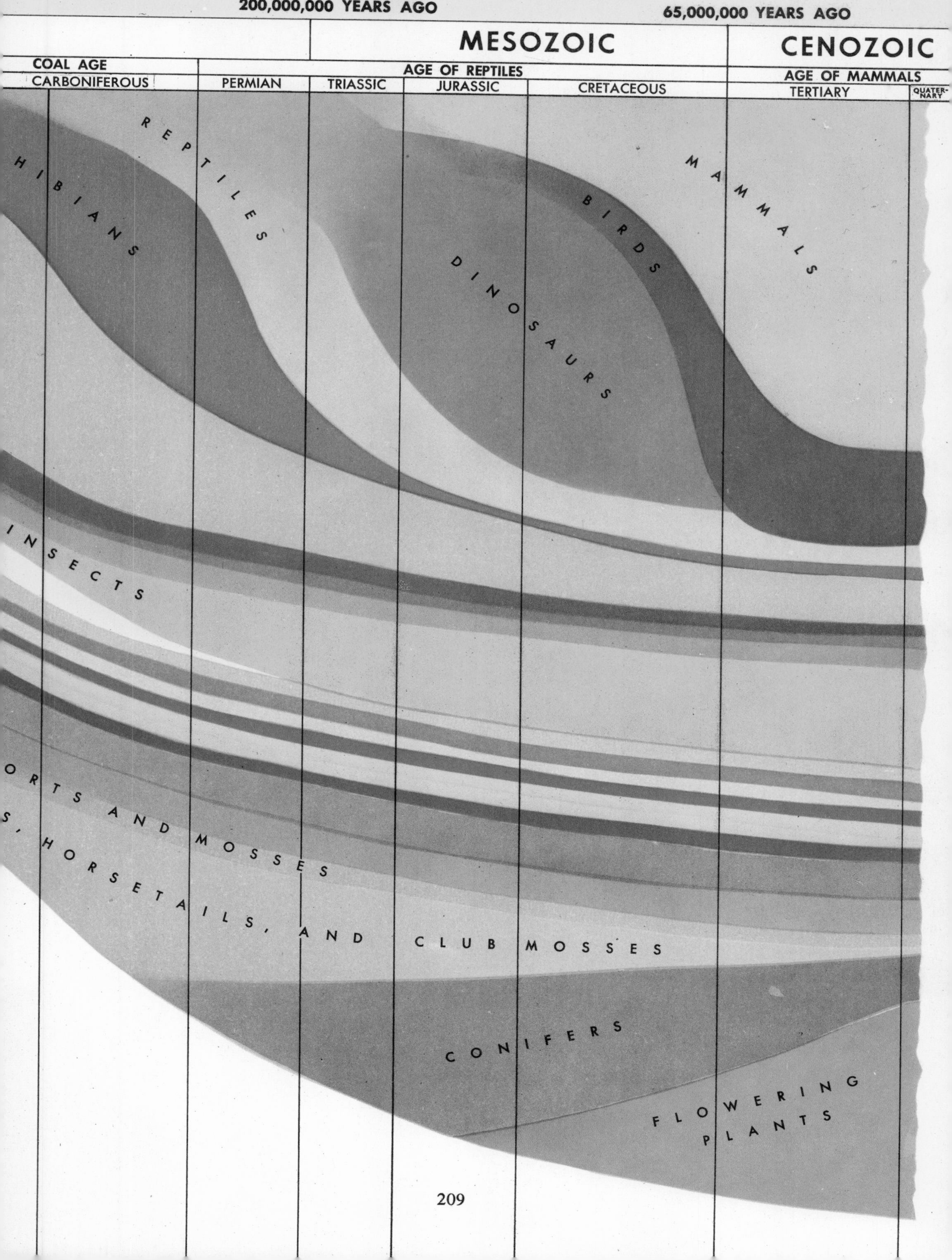

200,000,000 YEARS AGO

65,000,000 YEARS AGO

MESOZOIC

CENOZOIC

COAL AGE		AGE OF REPTILES				AGE OF MAMMALS	
CARBONIFEROUS	PERMIAN	TRIASSIC	JURASSIC	CRETACEOUS		TERTIARY	QUATER-NARY

REPTILES

HIBIANS

REPTILES

MAMMALS

BIRDS

DINOSAURS

INSECTS

ORTS AND MOSSES

S, HORSETAILS, AND

CLUB MOSSES

CONIFERS

FLOWERING PLANTS

SOME GIANT ANIMALS COMPARED IN SIZE

MAMMOTH

STEGOSAURUS

DIPLODOCUS

PTERODACTYL

SAIL-BACKED REPTILE

ICHTHYOSAURUS

TYRANNOSAURUS

MAN - 6 FEET TALL

PLESIOSAURUS

BLUE WHALE

ORDERS OF INSECTS, BIRDS, AND MAMMALS

INSECTS

THYSANURA
Silverfish, Firebrat

PLECTOPTERA
Mayflies

ODONATA
Dragon-flies, Damsel-flies

ORTHOPTERA
Grasshoppers, Locusts,
Katydids, Crickets

PHASMATODEA
Stick Insects

MANTODEA
Praying Mantids

BLATTARIAE
Roaches

ISOPTERA
Termites

MALLOPHAGA
Bird Lice

ANOPLURA
True Lice

HOMOPTERA
Aphids, Tree Hoppers,
Scale Insects, Cicadas

HETEROPTERA
True Bugs

NEUROPTERA
Snake-flies, Lacewing Flies

SIPHONAPTERA
Fleas

DIPTERA
Flies, Gnats, Mosquitoes

COLEOPTERA
Beetles

HYMENOPTERA
Ants, Bees, Wasps

LEPIDOPTERA
Moths, Butterflies

BIRDS

FLIGHTLESS BIRDS
Ostriches, Cassowaries,
Emus, Rheas, Kiwis

DIVERS

GREBES

**PETRELS AND
ALBATROSSES**

PENGUINS

**PELICANS AND
CORMORANTS**

**HERONS, STORKS,
FLAMINGOS, AND
BITTERNS**

**RAILS, WATERHENS,
AND CRANES**

**GULLS, TERNS,
SANDPIPERS, AUKS,
AND PLOVERS**

**DUCKS, GEESE, AND
SWANS**

**GROUSE, QUAIL,
PHEASANTS, TURKEYS
AND CHICKENS**

**VULTURES, HAWKS,
AND EAGLES**

OWLS

PIGEONS AND DOVES

PARROTS

**CUCKOOS AND
ROAD-RUNNERS**

NIGHTJARS

**SWIFTS AND
HUMMING-BIRDS**

**KINGFISHERS AND
HORNBILLS**

**WOODPECKERS AND
TOUCANS**

PERCHING BIRDS

MAMMALS

MONOTREMES
Duckbill, Spiny Anteater

MARSUPIALS
Opossums, Kangaroos,
Wombats, Bandicoots, Koala,
Tasmanian Devil

INSECTIVORES
Moles, Shrews, Hedgehogs

CARNIVORES
Cats, Lions, Tigers, Dogs,
Wolves, Foxes, Bears,
Raccoons, Otters, Skunks,
Weasels, Seals, Walruses,
Hyenas, Sea Lions

**ODD-TOED
UNGULATES**
Horses, Asses, Zebras, Tapirs,
Rhinoceroses

**EVEN-TOED
UNGULATES**
Pigs, Hippopotamuses, Deer,
Cattle, Sheep, Goats, Giraffe
Camels, Llamas, Alpacas,
Antelopes

CETACEANS
Whales, Dolphins, Porpoises

ELEPHANTS

SEA COWS
Manatee, Dugong

HYRAX

RODENTS
Rats, Mice, Squirrels,
Rabbits, Beavers, Porcupines,
Guinea Pigs, Hamsters

EDENTATES
Sloths, Armadillos, Anteaters

**PANGOLINS or SCALY
ANTEATERS**

AARDVARKS

BATS

FLYING-LEMURS

PRIMATES
Lemurs, Monkeys, Apes, Man

SOME FAMILIES OF FLOWERING PLANTS

MONOCOTS

REED-MACE FAMILY (*Typhaceae*)—Reed-mace

WATER-PLANTAIN FAMILY (*Alismaceae*)—Arrowhead, Water Plantain

GRASS FAMILY (*Gramineae*)—Corn, Wheat, Rye, Oats, Bamboo, Sugar Cane, Timothy, Ryegrass

SEDGE FAMILY (*Cyperaceae*)—Sedge, Bulrush, Umbrella Plant, Spike Rush

PALM FAMILY (*Palmaceae*)—Coconut Palm, Date Palm, Raffia Palm, Rattan Palm

PINEAPPLE FAMILY (*Bromeliaceae*)—Pineapple, Long Moss

LILY FAMILY (*Liliaceae*)—Onion, Day Lily, Easter Lily, Dog's Tooth Violet, Star of Bethlehem, Hyacinth, Asparagus, Lily-of-the-valley, Trillium, Tulip, Tiger Lily, Garlic, Yucca

AMARYLLIS FAMILY (*Amaryllidaceae*)—Daffodil, Poet's Narcissus, Century Plant, Amaryllis

IRIS FAMILY (*Iridaceae*)—Iris, Blackberry Lily, Blue-eyed Grass

ORCHID FAMILY (*Orchidaceae*)—Lady's Slipper, Orchid, Vanilla, Bird's Nest Orchis

DICOTS

WILLOW FAMILY (*Salicaceae*)—Willow, Poplar

BEECH FAMILY (*Fagaceae*)—Beech, Chestnut, Oak

NETTLE FAMILY (*Urticaceae*)—Elm, Mulberry, Nettle, Hemp, Hop

GOOSE-FOOT FAMILY (*Chenopodiaceae*)—Goose-foot, Beet, Spinach, Lamb's Quarters, Russian Thistle

PINK FAMILY (*Caryophyllaceae*)—Pink, Carnation, Chickweed

WATER LILY FAMILY (*Nymphaeaceae*)—Water Lily, Pond Lily, Sacred Bean, Lotus

BUTTERCUP FAMILY (*Ranunculaceae*)—Buttercup, Meadow Rue, Hepatica, Anemone, Monkshood, Marsh Marigold, Baneberry, Columbine, Larkspur

POPPY FAMILY (*Papaveraceae*)—Poppy, Prickly Poppy

MUSTARD FAMILY (*Cruciferae*)—Mustard, Sweet Alyssum, Peppergrass, Radish, Turnip, Cabbage, Watercress, Cauliflower, Shepherd's Purse, Toothwort

ROSE FAMILY (*Rosaceae*)—Rose, Spiraea, Hawthorn, Strawberry, Plum, Apple, Peach, Pear, Cherry, Blackberry, Raspberry

PEA FAMILY (*Leguminosae*)—Pea, Sweet Pea, Bean, Lucerne, Clover, Lupine, Peanut, Locust, Honey Locust, Vetch

VIOLET FAMILY (*Violaceae*)—Violet, Pansy, Viola

PARSLEY FAMILY (*Umbelliferae*)—Parsley, Carrot, Parsnip, Celery, Queen Anne's Lace, Caraway, Dill, Poison Hemlock

HEATH FAMILY (*Ericaceae*)—Heather, Rhododendron, Cranberry, Trailing Arbutus, Azalea, Mountain Laurel

PRIMROSE FAMILY (*Primulaceae*)—Primrose, Pimpernel, Loosestrife, Moneywort

MILKWEED FAMILY (*Asclepiadaceae*)—Milkweed, Butterfly Weed, Anglepod

CONVOLVULUS FAMILY (*Convolvulaceae*)—Bindweed, Dodder, Sweet Potato, Convolvulus

MINT FAMILY (*Labiatae*)—Peppermint, Sage, Horse Mint, Thyme, Horehound, Wild Marjoram, Catmint

NIGHTSHADE FAMILY (*Solanaceae*)—Nightshade, Bittersweet, Eggplant, Potato, Petunia, Tomato, Tobacco

HONEYSUCKLE FAMILY (*Caprifoliaceae*)—Honeysuckle, Twinflower, Cranberry, Elder

GOURD FAMILY (*Cucurbitaceae*)—Gourd, Pumpkin, Cucumber, Watermelon

COMPOSITE FAMILY (*Compositae*)—Daisy, Sunflower, Aster, Goldenrod, Ragweed, Dandelion, Marigold, Cosmos, Zinnia, Scotch Thistle, Lettuce

INDEX

Heavy type indicates those pages on which illustrations of the subjects appear. Where illustrations concerning a subject are numerous, only those pages containing the more important illustrations are indicated in heavy type.